LAW & GRACE

Journey to Calvary

BOOK ONE

LAW & GRACE

Journey to Calvary

BOOK ONE

A need has been revealed and a journey begun.
There is no turning back!

JUDSON McCAWL

Copyright

Law and Grace: Journey to Calvary
Book One

For information please visit www.thehumblesaint.com

Book Cover design by GERMANCREATIVE
(germancreative on Fiverr)

ISBN 978-1-990977-24-4

Duke of Valmary Publishing House

Dedication

To the LORD. May He be honoured and His name praised
forever.

Acknowledgement

I firstly have to acknowledge the help, encouragement and
inspiration that the LORD Most High afforded me. He kept me
going and provided the support that I needed.

To my parents, for their help and support where required.

Contents

Preface

THE books in the *Law & Grace* series are for the non-Christian and Christian reader alike, and they will challenge each in different ways. The first book clearly tackles the specific issue of Law and Grace, with all the books incorporating its concept in detail.

The books in the series challenge the status quo, challenge complacency, challenge current world views and challenge the heart of man towards God. They make plain the way of Salvation and in vivid illustration present the saving grace of God, biblical principles and explain God's working.

Added at the back of each book is a reference section where works referred to and verses quoted or alluded to are recorded.

The world is moving forward at an alarming rate, and historical events and milestones are being reached ever faster. Biblical prophecy too has come to the fore, with many of the foretold events taking place right before our eyes. We too often follow the path fashioned before us and get stuck in the rut created, without stopping to check where we are, where we are headed, what it ultimately means to us or what the final outcome may be.

Whether Christian or non-Christian, the reader will themselves be challenged and inevitably have to ask and answer some pertinent questions for and of themselves.

Enough said, it is now time for the first book in the series, *Law and Grace: Journey to Calvary*.

Judson McCawl

Chapter 1

The dawning of a new season

'I WONDER where Andrew is?' mused Kelly Renshaw as she stood in the kitchen preparing a hearty breakfast of Andrew's favourite – fried tomato and French toast. 'He should have been down here by now!'

Kelly Renshaw was a tallish lady of medium build, with honey-brown hair and bright blue eyes. Although she was nearing her mid-forties, she could easily have been mistaken as a mid-thirties lady. She was sweet in nature, thoughtful and bubbly at times, and always game for a friendly jest with her son, Andrew and nephew, Timothy.

'Andrew!' called Kelly frustratingly, having leaned out the kitchen entrance and shouted in the direction of the upstairs. 'Are you actually out of bed yet? It's seven o'clock already and your breakfast is almost ready to be served. Tim will be here in 45 minutes' time and you know how he hates to wait! Besides, there will be others waiting eagerly to get going on the hike!

'Oh dear,' mumbled Kelly to herself as she returned to her kitchen duties, 'I suppose cold French toast is almost as enjoyable as hot French toast!'

By now, the kitchen was filled with the fresh aroma of cooked tomato and sizzling bread, coupled with a percolating pot of freshly brewed coffee that Kelly usually kept as a speciality for Saturday and Sunday mornings.

Andrew, who had just stirred as a result of Kelly's last call, turned in his bed and looked at his alarm clock; it read 07:01.

'It's Thursday morning and start of the long weekend,' grumbled Andrew as he pulled his eiderdown back over his head, his multi-coloured stripped pyjamas disappearing from the view of the early morning sun rays that penetrated the otherwise quiet realm of his bedroom.

Andrew Renshaw was a young man of twenty years of age, relatively tall, slim but well-built, quite athletic looking and had the same honey-brown hair as his mother. He was always one for the outdoors and whenever the opportunity afforded it, he would not be found anywhere else. He was enrolled at the local university, Ailensbury, where he was studying Biology, following in the footsteps of his father who was a microbiologist.

Suddenly, from beneath the depths of slumberland, Andrew's eyelids shot open as if being awakened by a revelation.

'Oh, no!' blurted out Andrew in a panic, as if it had not been mentioned to him before. 'Smoking Gorge hike! Why didn't someone remind me! It's the start of the new hiking season, we cannot be late!' His eiderdown shot back as though tied to a spring, and his pyjamas fought back the sun's rays in defiance. Nothing would now stand in his way as the revelation of the current reality rang like church bells in his ears.

Andrew's athleticism was matched with eager efforts in an attempt to get dressed, clean his teeth and brush his hair, which at this stage looked like it had been in an endless fight the whole night, pack his fishing tackle and still have time for breakfast before Tim arrived. He was thankful that he had at least got his hiking backpack ready the night before and placed it at the front door.

'Where *is* Andrew?' muttered Kelly between her teeth as she strode towards the stairs.

Kelly, who was patience personified, was becoming fidgety. Just as she was about to call a second time, Andrew appeared from around the corner at the top of the staircase. Kelly caught her words just in time as Andrew sped down the stairs, the old mahogany handrail and ornately turned balustrade spindles vibrating while the wooden stairs groaned in objection to being treated with disrespect and abuse by a young man on a mission.

Kelly, with nimbleness and prior knowledge as to what was about to happen, moved out of the way of being taken out like a National Football League quarterback.

'Morning, Mom,' greeted Andrew as he bolted past her and off to the garage.

'Good morning, Andrew,' said Kelly as she took it in her stride, calmly and slowly answering him. 'Are you officially up?' She did not receive a response as Andrew had long since disappeared into the garage to sort out his fishing tackle.

Kelly, knowing the process of events, returned to the kitchen to put the final touches on what was a scrumptious breakfast for any hungry young man who loved French toast, fried tomato and coffee. After a few minutes, she heard the interleading door to the garage close.

'What are you cooking, Mom?' asked Andrew from just outside the kitchen door, which Kelly could mime almost perfectly every time. 'It smells really good!'

Kelly chuckled to herself as Andrew strutted into the kitchen, a sense of achievement written all over his face.

'Fried tomato, French toast and brewed coffee,' replied Kelly after giving Andrew a warm and loving smile.

'Fried tomato, French toast and brewed coffee,' repeated Andrew, having leaned over, closed his eyes and sniffed the cooked food. 'What a star you are!'

'Oh, go on with you!' objected Kelly with a chuckle as she gave Andrew a soft pat on his behind. 'You and your cupboard love, but how about a little squeeze for a dear little old mother who cooks for you?'

Andrew obligingly gave Kelly a quick one-armed squeeze around her shoulders and with a cheerful smile, headed to the dining room table, where she served him a breakfast fit for a king.

'Easy does it, Son!' scolded Kelly, having watched Andrew start shovelling fried tomato into his mouth and then take a fair-sized bite of French toast. 'You *do* want to taste your food don't you?'

'Sorry, Mom,' apologised Andrew, blushing a little and having quickly slowed his pace. 'I'm just thinking about the hiking trip, and the fact that Tim will be here soon. We don't want to be late. Has Dad eaten yet?'

'Yes, your father has eaten,' replied Kelly, 'and he has already packed the cooler box with your supplies for the second night's stayover at the canyon, so you are running behind, but it won't help you much if you struggle with indigestion, now will it? I know Tim hates waiting, and you don't want to be late, but eat slowly!'

Kelly's animated facial expression caused Andrew to laugh, and he almost choked on a piece of French toast.

'I see that you've fetched your fishing tackle,' observed Kelly with interest, coming back to the dining room after having left Andrew to quietly eat for a while, 'so I presume that you and Tim are still intending to fish on Saturday?'

'Yes,' replied Andrew before taking another mouthful of food, 'I discussed it with him last night, and he's still keen. You know how much we love fishing! After the hike we thought it would be nice to just sit and relax, and see if we could catch a fish or two. We decided that it would be enjoyable to stop off at Misty's for lunch on the way back.'

'Misty's, hey?' said Kelly with raised eyebrows. 'I'll bet you thought of that! Isn't that where June and July have started waitressing?' She asked, pronouncing July as "Julie".

'You're ahead of me on this one!' exclaimed Andrew, looking up in disbelief and dropping fried tomato off his fork. 'How did you know, for they only start this morning!' Just then the doorbell rang.

'Never mind,' replied Kelly, patting him on the head as she walked past on her way to the front door, 'I'm sure they'll both be pleased to have you stop by. That must be Tim. Finish up while I let him in.'

Andrew promptly turned his attention back to his plate, eager to finish the remainder of his French toast and the few sips of coffee that were left.

'Good morning, Rin Tim Tim,' greeted Kelly when she opened the front door.

Timothy Nicholls, who was fondly called Tim, was Kelly's nephew, the son of her older sister, Gloria. Tim was twenty-one years old, a little shorter in height than Andrew but broader at the shoulders. With deep dark-brown eyes and hair to match, he had somewhat Italian features, which was understandable as he resembled his father who was of Italian decent. Tim too, like

Andrew, loved the outdoors. He was also enrolled at Ailensbury University and was studying structural engineering. Life for Tim had not always been easy. Sadly, his father had been a reprobate and had left Gloria when Tim was only four years old. Gloria would only attend church on the very rare occasion, and although she was not completely averse to biblical dialogue, would certainly not engage the topic of her own accord nor liked it if the discussion addressed her personally. She left Tim to find his own way regarding such matters. Because Gloria was working as an events manager for Irving & Baxter, a large multinational concern, she was often away on business. When Tim was younger, Gloria had left him at these times to the care of her brother-in-law, George and sister, Kelly.

'Morning, Aunt Kelly,' greeted Tim, who then beamed a sly smile. 'I brought you something because you're the best aunt.' He brought out a drooping yellow flower from behind his back and started laughing heartily. 'You should see your expression,' boomed Tim and laughed some more.

'Tim, I'm grateful,' responded Kelly with a straight face. 'A flower is a flower. Now let me give you a kiss in appreciation.' Before Tim had a chance to object, Kelly had reached forward, taken hold of Tim's head and given him a big kiss on his forehead, leaving a big red lipstick print. 'Thanks, Tim,' continued Kelly with a mischievous grin. 'Now you go and enjoy yourself on this hiking trip, but as always, be careful. Oh – and I approve of you taking lunch at Misty's on Saturday, it's just a pity you cannot stop there now, before you start your hike from Ailen Oak Lake!'

Kelly chuckled lightly as she turned and came inside.

'Morning, Tim,' spluttered Andrew as he came nonchalantly out of the dining room into the hall way, still chewing on some

French toast. He suddenly stopped, and his eyelids widened and narrowed again as he fixed his gaze on Tim's forehead. 'That would go down well at Misty's for sure!'

It suddenly dawned on Tim, who was at first taken aback, that his aunt had done something. He shot off like a lightning bolt towards the wall mirror with such speed that he crumpled the entrance hall rug under his feet.

'Man!' exclaimed Tim in horror. 'Aunt Kelly you sly thing; that was really nasty!' Tim quickly disappeared into the bathroom, leaving Kelly and Andrew enjoying a good laugh.

'And this?' came the words of a mature and strong voice from the direction of the staircase. 'Who've you stuck away this time?'

It was George Renshaw, Kelly's husband. He was a tall man and it was easy to see that he was Andrew's father, although he was not as athletic looking as Andrew. He was two years older than Kelly and equalled her friendly nature. He was a microbiologist by profession and worked at Microlab Industries, one of the downtown laboratories. Andrew often enjoyed visiting there as he was not only studying biology but found the workings of the lab fascinating.

Tim returned from the bathroom, a big grin on his face and the skin on his forehead bearing the marks of vigorous rubbing.

'Good morning, King George, how are we?' greeted Tim lively, promptly sticking out his hand and doing a dance-type handshake move.

'Be gone with you,' objected George light-heartedly, 'before I really make you dance!' Tim chuckled and jumped out of the way of his uncle's slow swipe.

'Are you ready, George?' asked Kelly, putting her arm around his waist. 'You don't want to keep Michael and his sons waiting!'

'We're going hiking, my dear,' replied George with a smile,

reciprocating Kelly's embrace, 'not catching a flight somewhere, but yes, I'm ready – and raring to go!'

'Oh, go on,' responded Kelly, giving George a loving nudge with her hip, 'you know what I mean. You're being too practical, but that doesn't mean you shouldn't be punctual. Off you go then, and enjoy your adventure!'

After kissing Kelly goodbye, George and Andrew picked up their backpacks, with Tim taking Andrew's fishing gear and their cooler box, and the three of them headed out the front door. They packed their stuff in the trunk of Tim's car and drove off, leaving Kelly standing alone on the front porch waving goodbye to them, having come out into the relative warmth of the dawn of the new spring season sunshine to see them off.

Chapter 2

The adventure begins

TIM had a relatively new cream-coloured sedan thanks to his hard-working mother, who saw to it that he was adequately provided for. Tim, however, never took this for granted and like Andrew, always saw to it that he pulled his weight when it came to home chores and his efforts at university and study.

The threesome drove down the street, through town and eventually past the urban edge where the more densely populated suburb began to thin out, giving way to fields with housing interspersed. Andrew watched the scenery as it flashed by, the fresh spring breeze, accentuated by the moving vehicle, blowing in his face and the sun drawing nature to life from its sleepy hibernation. Andrew noticed life sprouting again – butterflies and birds flittering here and there and the back and forth flapping of cows' tails. In the not too distant past these pasturelands and fields had lain barren and bare, a void of silence from the resultant winter cold.

'It's hard to believe,' said Tim as he continued to drive on a little further, the houses now having completely given way to fields on the one side and forests on the other, 'that I've never yet been on the Smoking Gorge hike or been to Charon Canyon! Until now sports activities have always prevented me from accompanying you on these hiking trips. This is going to be a journey for me for sure!'

'More like an adventure!' said Andrew lively as they neared an old rusty signpost just off to the right-hand side of the road, its faded and peeling brown lettering reading, "Ailen Oak Lake". 'Here we are – and time for the adventure to start!'

Ailen Oak Lake, to which they were headed, was not far from the main centre of town, about a 10-minute drive on a day when the roads were quiet. A large wooded forest surrounded the lake, and it was a popular place for picnics, day camping, sailing and fishing, with a number of mountain biking and hiking trails extending out into the woodlands. It was a pleasant area for a respite from the humdrum of daily work activity. It was also the starting point for the gruelling 2-day Smoking Gorge hike that wound its way through the extending forests and over the hilly terrain to the frightening and eerie Charon Canyon.

Tim slowed his car, flicked on the indicator and turned right, onto a gravel road that seemed to be smothered by the tall, densely populated and imposing forest trees. The air suddenly changed as they drove along the partially rugged terrain, a slight shudder and hum coming from the car as it transported them with ease to their desired destination.

The season had only recently passed the depths of winter and spring was now emerging, revealing its long awaited presence. Whereas the suburb and surrounding pastures gladly embraced the dawn of the new season, the forest trees seemed to clutch to the end of the past season and hold onto it for as long as possible. There was still the cold, yet fresh air within the forest branches and the early morning mist was still within its grasp.

The gravel roadway wound its way between the trees and then straightened. Light began to appear and grow bigger and brighter as the destination area, Ailen Oak Lake, drew nearer. The car emerged from the forest into the lake area clearing like an object hurled from a catapult as the automobile in motion contrasted the stationary surrounds.

'Ailen Oak Lake,' said Tim in a satisfied tone.

'Indeed!' replied Andrew with equal satisfaction.

'Come on, you two,' chirped George with a chuckle, who up until then had been sitting quietly in the back. 'A person would think that you'd never been here before!'

Although the two lads only lived a short distance from the lake area, the winter coupled with academic and extra mural activities kept them from visiting the lake as often as they would have liked to.

Tim drove into the large parking area and parked his car as close as he could get to the administration office, which was at the far right-hand side of the parking area at the edge of the forest. They all climbed out. Andrew scanned the area taking in all the familiar beauty and serenity of what was before him, and what was behind him too, while George went to look for their hiking companions. There were already many cars there, with a colourful collection of hikers and mountain bikers standing round in groups near the front of the administration office.

The administration office was a large log cabin, with the logs protected with a dark coat of sealant, giving it a very old appearance. Its dark-green corrugated roofing matched the colour of the trees' leaves and needles, causing it to be pleasantly inconspicuous just in front of the edge of the forest as it blended in beautifully. The only noticeable oddity was the communication antenna mounted atop it, but as it was located on the back side of the roof, it was partially hidden. Inside was a large reception counter also made of logs. On the walls were photos of the lake area and surrounding forests, along with pictures and maps of all the different routes spreading out from or near to the office. There were also tourist brochures and leaflets in racks mounted upon the wall or in display units on the counter, along with rules and safety guides. Ceiling fans kept the cabin cool in summer.

'It's good to see you, George,' called Michael Aldenberg with his strong brogue accent, having stepped out of the office, his two sons, Michael Jnr and Matthew, following him. 'Everything's set,' he continued, shaking George's hand energetically after walking up to him. 'We all paid in advance, so we just need to sign in and hand in our supplies to be dropped off for us at Charon Canyon. There's a queue at present, as it's the first day that the closed routes during the winter have been reopened and many, like us, seem eager to stretch their legs and get out into the back forests. However, the admin staff are working efficiently and processing all forms quickly, so it won't take long.'

'That's great to hear,' said George, happy to see Mike. 'Are there many going on the Smoking Gorge trail?'

'No,' replied Mike with a smile, 'but apparently tomorrow and Saturday the huts and tree houses have been fully booked. It should be relatively quiet for us – we seem to have beaten the crowds!'

'That's unusual,' observed George, surprised, 'I would have thought today would have been just as full, being the opener?'

'Apparently there's an 80% chance of a storm this evening,' replied Mike. 'I overheard one of the admin staff members telling a hiker who made the same observation as you did. Small groups of three or less have to join up with others if they want to go – precautionary measures.'

'We checked the weather forecast five days ago,' said George, a little startled, 'and the storm was only due on Sunday evening!'

'There's one due on Sunday evening,' confirmed Mike, 'but apparently this one arose from nowhere – it was a surprise that began to show on the monitors three days ago. The huts are sturdy, so we should be fine. Hopefully it doesn't hang around past the morning.'

'We had better get a move on then,' said George thoughtfully, a concerned look on his face and not sure what to expect. 'We still have 15 miles of hiking to do before we reach camp. I don't think it will be pleasant to be caught in a storm! Neither myself, Andrew or Tim were aware of this, but thankfully we've all brought warm thermal underwear and waterproof jackets.' George promptly turned and headed purposefully back to Tim's car, Mike and his boys following him.

Michael Aldenberg was a geologist who held to a creationist perspective. He had spent much time researching various aspects surrounding the whole evolution versus creation debate. He was a short man, of medium build, with his mix of brown and grey hair covering his ears and touching the back of his collar. He was the same age as George, forty-five, and a friendly, quiet man, but he knew his facts about his topics of interest and firmly held to his standpoint. Michael's two sons were quiet and respectful boys. Junior, aged 16, and Matty, aged 14, both attended a private Christian senior high school in Ailensbury, El-Elyon Senior High School. Both had thick brown hair and brown eyes. They had small builds, but were strong and handsome youths.

'We need to get a move on lads,' informed George

purposefully as he walked up to Andrew and Tim. 'Mike informs me that there's an 80% possibility of a storm this evening, and the authorities are concerned enough that they are not permitting groups of three or less people to go out. For safety sake, they have to group with others.'

'This is news to me!' exclaimed Andrew, shocked. 'When did—'

'It apparently began showing its ugly face three days ago,' interjected George, 'and we for some reason never bothered to check, but let's not worry about it, let's just get going and not waste any time hanging around here!'

Andrew cordially greeted Mike and his two sons and introduced Tim to them, before the Aldenberg's went to fetch their hiking stuff. Tim quickly put up the sunscreen on his car's dashboard while George and Andrew removed the backpacks from the trunk of his car, including the cooler box. Tim locked his car, and they all headed to the administrative office, meeting up with their hiking companions at the door.

'Come, Tim,' called George, beckoning with his hand to Tim, who was reading some of the hiking information on the wall, 'you need to fill in the form, so get back in line behind Andrew.' Tim promptly obeyed.

'This is what I call life!' said Tim to Andrew, picking up one of the hiking trail brochures lying on the counter and opening it. 'It's wh—' Tim stopped speaking, his attention being drawn to a small handwritten note affixed to the inside of the brochure by means of a paperclip. *"He who has the <u>Son</u> has life (1 John 5:12)"* it read.

Tim looked at it with shock and partly recoiled. It was unnerving, almost as though it was countering the very proclamation that he had made only seconds before, "This is what I call life!". It pricked Tim's conscience, and he felt it. His mind suddenly whirled with questions as he looked at it a second time. Who had written it? Was it purposefully put there? Did someone write it and forget to take the brochure with them? What did it mean, and was it by some force or divine influence meant for him?

Tim quickly looked about him to see if anyone was watching, but there was no-one specifically taking note of him. Andrew had not really been paying attention to him either, as he had been handed a form to fill in just as Tim had begun speaking. Tim would normally have brushed such an occurrence off without a second thought, but it seemed too real, too coincidental, too direct an opposition to what he had just said. What's more, the words spoke loudly to him, almost as though he had not read them but heard them being spoken!

Tim shut the brochure, covering it with the palm of his hand, but the words remained as a picture in his mind, and he could read them as clearly as if the note was before his eyes. Just then one of the admin staff handed him a form to fill in and sign, diverting his attention.

Tim filled in the form as quickly as he could, not realising that for him a journey of conflict between the two proclamations had just begun, and there was no turning back!

Chapter 3

Satisfaction on Smoking Gorge trail

'**I** CERTAINLY hope we make the huts before a storm hits!' said George, pressing forward at the head of the group after just having begun on the Smoking Gorge trail. 'We have 15 miles to cover today, so there's still a lot of daylight between us and the campsite – many hours and many obstacles!'

'I wouldn't worry about it, Dad,' responded Andrew, a little surprised at his father's concern. 'We should manage okay even if a storm hits. We must just keep to the path and all keep together.'

The sun was shining brightly, and although the mist was still present in the thick of the trees, it was slowly being torn free and evaporating under the confident and strong muscle of the sun's influence. There was not a cloud above, the deep-blue sky evenly painted and brilliant across its entire expanse.

At the start of the long trek, Tim hung at the back of the group, his thoughts having returned to the odd occurrence that had transpired at the administration office, causing his heart to beat faster than needed. His attention was diverted by what had happened, and he was trying to figure it out, but he could not. In the past, he had never given so much as a consideration to anything that had come from the Bible, so why was he now? Why was he allowing it to consume his thoughts? He had always switched off before, even when his relatives had spoken to him, why not now, why did it bother him so?

'Hey, Tim!' called Andrew, turning round and seeing Tim more than a dozen paces behind them as they climbed steeply to the top of the first hill. 'Giddy up, old fellow, you're already lagging behind! We haven't even covered half a mile yet!'

'Buried in thought,' said Tim, having looked up and immediately picked up his pace, 'sorry.'

Tim was soon on Andrew's heels, having snapped out of his contemplations. He determined that he was not going to allow what had transpired to spoil the hike that he had so long desired to do, nor was he going to allow it to wreck his hike from being an adventure, as Andrew had said. He wanted to live it, enjoy it, and above all, savour every moment and not miss sight nor sound of what was all new to him. They reached the summit of the first hill a few minutes later and paused, a small clearing having been made for people to be able to enjoy the view from there.

'Isn't that a sight!' exclaimed George with satisfaction, scanning the panorama, the sun's rays bouncing off the hilltops before them and lighting the hikers as they stood gazing in awe and pleasure.

'It's stunningly beautiful!' agreed Tim, enjoying both the view and warmth of the sun. 'I really missed a lot not having come on this trail before, but at least I'm here now!'

'There, Tim, is our end destination,' said Mike, pointing in the direction of the sun in the far distance, 'that last hill that stands above the rest. It doesn't seem like it from here, but it's 30 miles away. At this time of year, you just set your bearings on the rising sun and walk!'

'Come on,' perked up George, leading by example, 'let's get walking then! We still want to stop for a break at Stream's Edge. No point in using all our rest time up before we've even walked half a mile!'

They set off again, walking single file, but Tim held back and just absorbed the sights before him, a feeling of satisfaction filling his being. He was struck by the beauty of nature, its colours, contours, vibrant condition, all feeding abundantly from the life-giving source that shone upon it majestically.

'Come on, Tim!' hailed Andrew, having glanced back and seen Tim still standing at the top of the hill. 'Are you intending to set up camp there? There's still more to see, so come on!' Tim did not answer, he just began his descent down the hill, following the path between the tall, woody trees and was soon on the tail end of the hiking party.

In the valley the mist was still quite thick and cool but pleasant and refreshing. They hiked on, George ensuring that they kept to a calculated schedule but not pressing harder than what the weakest in the group could manage. The two Aldenberg boys were young but strong and fit and able to keep pace without a problem. The path wound its way between the trees, up the slopes and down again. There was a vast amount of elevation and in one or two places some rocky terrain that had to be crossed. From time to time they caught a glimpse of the stream that meandered between the forested hills, its lively flow over rocky outcrops often announcing its whereabouts. The hiking party pressed on, water bottles often in hand to quench their thirst and ensure they remained properly hydrated. They only stopped briefly at certain points to have a quick breather or to enjoy the sights from the top of the hills they had summited.

'Ah, wonderful!' exclaimed Mike from the head of the group upon seeing the clearing alongside the stream. 'Almost halfway. We've reached Stream's Edge. Time for our lunch break.'

'Right on cue!' informed George, pleased with their progress. 'We can rest nicely here now. Although we cannot dawdle,' he added, looking up at the sky, trying to see as much as he could between the thick tree branches, 'there's no need to rush our lunch.'

Right by the edge of the stream there was a clearing with a dozen or so short, cut logs that doubled as stools. The only manmade items present were a small, wooden hand-painted sign, that read "Stream's Edge", nailed to a tree and a large dustbin that had a special locking mechanism on it to prevent animals from being able to scavenge in it. The stream's crystal water burbled as it passed by, its calming melody constant and clear. The six hikers removed their backpacks, instant relief being felt, and sat down on the logs. It was the first proper rest that they had taken, and their feet were equally pleased to be able to rest awhile. Bananas, peanut butter crackers and energy bars were the main makeup of their lunches, no junk food having been brought along. They all sat chatting quietly and eating, the feint call of eagles and piercing, loud cry of hawks joining in from time to time. When they were halfway through their lunch, another group arrived and joined them. The tops of the trees began to gently sway just as they were finishing, to George's voiced concern. The group promptly finished up, threw wrappers and other rubbish in the dustbin and filled their water bottles from the cool, refreshing water that flowed abundantly down past the edge of the rest spot. With their backpacks remounted upon their backs, they returned to the trail. The trail immediately began an ascent up a hill, taking them away from the stream, which now cut through the hills and ran almost parallel to the hiking trail nearly all the way to the midway campsite, turning away only at the end. Twenty minutes later they summited the hill into a clearing at the top.

'Oh, dear!' groaned George, looking out before him, having been the first to arrive. 'Just look at that!'

The others in the group soon joined him and looked on thoughtfully. In the distance, the wind that had slowly been picking up was carrying along a heavy wrack of ominous looking deep-grey cloud. Although it was still far away, it seemed to be moving quickly across the sky, erasing the deep-blue hue that had graced the heavenly expanse for hours.

'It does look like trouble brewing,' affirmed Mike, his mind trying to calculate what was before them. 'There's no turning back though, we must just press on! Come on!'

Mike took the lead, and with his boys in tow he began descending the hill, disappearing from the clearing back into the thick of the forest trees. George, Andrew and Tim promptly followed suit, not wasting time to linger on the impending storm. They enjoyed the hike, making steady progress, but as the hours moved on, so the skies above clouded over and darkened. The wind harassed the tops of the trees, but thankfully for them, they were sheltered from its effects. With about an hour to go before reaching the campsite, the heavens began to let loose, and the rain started to fall. At first, the thick forest trees reduced its effects, and it was hardly noticeable, but it steadily increased in intensity. With about 15 minutes to go before reaching camp, they arrived at the plain that led to Granite Gorge, a small gorge, and the hanging bridge they had to cross near to the campsite.

The wind suddenly rose in strength, bringing with it a dark wall of rain that rushed at the hikers face on. The driving rain came thundering down upon the unshielded group, pelting them with thick, soaking drops. Thankfully their backpacks, jackets and trail shoes were waterproof, so only their caps and short pants were drenched. The unpleasantness of the downpour was felt upon their faces and legs, with the cold liquid almost stinging at times as they hastened along. The water splashed onto the path and muddied their shoes and legs, but they had to press on.

'Cross carefully,' called George, leading the way as they reached the hanging bridge, which was swaying as a result of the wild wind blowing across the plain and down the gorge, 'and hold tight to the ropes! It should be safe if we proceed with caution.'

They all filed behind George, walking steadily but slowly across the bridge, gripping tightly the side ropes that were part of the safety railing, as they moved along. A gust of wind caught the bridge as they neared the other side, causing them to have to quickly brace themselves, but Matty, who was just in front of Tim, lost his balance. Tim managed to reach forward and grab his arm, preventing him from falling, helping him to quickly regain his footing and move on without delay. They all crossed the hanging bridge safely and wasted no time pressing on towards the campsite that lay within sight only a few hundred yards ahead, a feeling of triumphant satisfaction pounding in their chests with every heartbeat!

Chapter 4

Tough going

'THAT last section was some going,' said George, breathing heavily as he quickly closed the door of the hut after they had all entered, the wind swirling and blowing the rain in. 'I cannot say we just made it, but I'm thankful we're all safely inside!'

'Even though it was some going,' said Andrew, taking off his jacket and hanging it on the coat rack, 'it was still exciting and an adventure – got the heart pumping and blood flowing that's for sure!'

'Oh, go on,' objected George with a chuckle. 'Youthful nonsense – skin like a rhino! It sounds like you knew the weather report beforehand but weren't saying anything. You make it seem like you were glad to have the storm catch us short and would relish going back out there into it now!'

'And I'd join him,' joked Tim as he hung up his coat next to Andrew's, the others laughing. 'Satisfying stuff – I'd have paid extra for it!'

'We'll leave you to it then,' said George just as thunder pealed through the thick clouds above the hut. 'Later on we'll need some water, so I'll volunteer the two of you to go and fetch it! In the meantime, let's get ourselves settled. I need something warm to drink!' He promptly looked around the hut to familiarise himself with what was inside.

The midway campsite on the Smoking Gorge trail sat in a clearing along the edge of the plain and forest. It was located just behind a large area of protruding granite rock. There were 10 stone huts, with pitched roofs that had dark-green corrugated sheeting. The huts had one large lattice window with rectangular panes, located next to the door. Each hut had an outside water closet, its cistern supplied by a large water tank that was fed rainwater from the roof of the hut or topped up from the river. The huts were partially shielded by the tall forest trees but not when the wind swirled. Inside, there were five double bunkbeds closely placed, blankets, a small kitchen unit with the basics, foldup chairs, a small wooden table, a large gas heater, gas bottle with accessories so that food could be cooked or water heated, two oil lamps and a fire extinguisher. Water had to be fetched from the stream that ran past the back of the huts, for there was no running water available. Although the huts were small, they were well-built, resilient to the forces of nature and adequate for an overnight stay along the hiking trail. The Ailensbury Forestry Foundation managed the huts and saw to it that they were serviced on a daily basis during the open season.

The six hikers settled quickly, each taking a lower bed, with Matty being assigned the top bunk above his brother, Junior. Mike got the gas heater going without delay so that they could all warm up and get their wet pants and caps dried as soon as possible.

Before changing into dry clothes, Andrew and Tim darted back out into the rain, having put on their waterproof jackets, and quickly made their way to the back of the huts to fetch water from the stream. They were back in no time at all, dripping wet from the continuing heavy downpour but as bright and excited as when they had first entered the hut, enjoying every minute of the outdoor wonders.

'It's hard to believe,' stated Tim matter-of-factly while taking off his trail shoes, 'that those granite rocks out front are estimated to be anything between 1.6–2.6 billion years old! But then to me, they look it!'

'You're absolutely correct,' responded Mike wittily, placing a pot of water on the cooker top of the gas bottle, everyone eager for a hot mug of coffee, 'it's certainly hard to believe – because they cannot be more than 6000 years old!'

'I did not mean it in the sense of disbelief,' said Tim quickly, stopping what he was doing and looking at Mike, 'but in the sense that it's incredible to consider it!'

'I know what you meant,' responded Mike, turning up the gas flame, 'I was just using the play on words. Meaning no disrespect though, you have been provided with misinformation if that's what you believe the age of the rocks to be. I'm aware that it's commonly taught in evolution-based education, but that doesn't necessarily make it correct.'

There was temporary silence.

Tim finishing taking off his shoes and wet pants and put on another pair of pants. All the hikers' wet caps and pants were soon strung up around the gas heater drying quickly.

Thunder continued to roll in, closer and closer, the storm being driven along by the powerful wind.

The hikers remained in their shelter, warm and contented, all having enjoyed a warming mug of coffee. A pot of steaming hot vegetable soup was prepared, filling the small hut with a homely winter smell, while they all sat round chatting about the hike, laughing and enjoying the sweet taste of oranges.

Darkness soon fell upon the land, the stormy weather aiding its early arrival. The two gas lamps were lit, providing the little hut with dim but sufficient light that enabled everyone to operate comfortably. A hush fell upon the group as they began to eat their dinner – protein bars and more peanut butter crackers being enjoyed along with mugs of thick vegetable soup.

Tim's thoughts returned to what Mike had said, and instead of just brushing it off like he would normally have done, he pondered on it.

'Mike,' said Tim, having just received a mug of coffee and two oat biscuits from Andrew, dinner having been finished, 'with regard to what you said earlier, what about carbon dating, which has established the age of rocks? That cannot be denied!'

'It actually can,' replied Mike, his brogue accent distinct from the rest, 'and I'll explain to you why. If the dating methods *are* an objective and reliable means of determining ages they should not have to ask you a) what age you would like, or what age you think it is – which is what is done by labs before testing, and b) they should agree. However, with radiometric dating the different techniques often give quite different results.[1] There are even cases where the age of the objects under examination are known to be no older than fifty years, for example andesite lava flows from Mt Ngauruhoe in New Zealand, and they have been calculated to be millions of years old using such methods.[2] Mount St. Helens is another example. Samples gathered there have been dated using the potassium-argon method. According to radioisotope dating, certain minerals in the lava dome are up to 2.4 million years old. However, we know that these minerals and the rocks that contain them cooled within lava between the years 1980 and 1986.[3] This is not a source I would dare trust.

'Most members of the public still think, as a result of years of conditioning, that the formation of fossils is somehow associated with long time-spans. However, there is an exquisitely preserved fossil of an extinct marine reptile called an ichthyosaur. The mother ichthyosaur is shown having almost completed giving birth to a live infant – the beak of the young reptile is still inside the mother's birth canal. There is another fossilised mother ichthyosaur with several unborn in her abdomen, and with what appears to be a new-born juvenile a short distance away, which could perhaps be her own. There are two issues represented here; firstly, it is not possible or feasible that the mother just lay on the bottom of the ocean floor giving birth for thousands of years while being slowly covered up by accumulating sediments.'

'Of course not!' sniggered Tim, interjecting. 'That would be absurd!'

'But that would not be inconsistent with the evolutionary model!' responded Andrew, laying the blame at the foot of the door where such possible reasoning stemmed from.

'The second issue,' continued Mike unfazed by the interjections, being a person who enjoyed controlled, lively interchange and debate, 'is that the beautiful state of preservation of the fossils defies the idea that long time spans were involved in their formation; it is just not possible. Their formation must have been swift and would be more consistent with an overwhelming catastrophic rapid burial, like the aspects surrounding the flood of Noah's day.' [4]

'Then what about the formation of the Grand Canyon?' questioned Tim, sarcastically objecting. 'I suppose that was also rapid formation and not millions of years?'

'I get the point of your question,' said Mike matter-of-factly, 'but let me not answer it directly for you. The evolutionists use what is called uniformitarianism, which means that what happened in the past is what is happening today. With that reasoning, the Colorado River that flows through the Grand Canyon is what flowed through it in the past and is what carved it out. However, this is not what has been observed by us at all. In May 1980, Mount St. Helens in Oregon blew her top and in a short space of time had created a "Grand Canyon" in a 1/40th scale, with all the strata layers and everything. In March 1982, a small summit eruption melted snow within the crater and displaced water, forming a 32-kilometre long mudflow. The mudflow pooled within the big stream explosion pit behind the debris dam. Mud quickly overtopped the west end of the big stream pit and cut back and downward, producing a 43-meter deep canyon where before there was no canyon at all. In a single day the new drainage channel was established by a catastrophic mudflow, and we were able to observe it happen.[5] So why was this not possibly the case for the Grand Canyon?'

'You're inferring,' responded Tim disbelievingly as thunder ripped through the night's sky, 'that the flood of Noah's day is what created the Grand Canyon. What happened then to all the water and how was it possible for water to cover the entire earth?'

'That's an interesting point,' replied Mike with a brief smile, aware of the logical progression of the question. 'There are a number of issues to mention here. Firstly, if the entire Earth's surface were levelled by smoothing out the topography of not only the land surface, but also the rock surface on the ocean floor, the waters of the ocean would cover the Earth's surface to a depth of 3 kilometres, about 1.8 miles. We need to remember that about 70% of the Earth's surface is still covered by water.

Secondly, Psalm 104 tells us concerning the flood that God rebuked the waters, and they fled; the mountains rose, the valleys sank down and God set a boundary so that they will never again cover the earth. The waters that we have today are the same waters. Thirdly, the layers that form the uppermost parts of Mt Everest are themselves composed of fossil-bearing, water-deposited layers.[6] This would not be possible if the ground had not been covered by water.'

'There's another part to that,' said George, not afraid to lay down on the table what he considered sound and sensible reasoning. 'We have an earth that is 70% covered by water, which if levelled would cover it to a depth of 3 kilometres, but the possibility of a worldwide flood is frowned upon. Yet the evolutionists are baffled by all the water on the earth because according to the evolutionary model the earth should not contain water[7] but it does – and their explanations are considered credible and to be accepted! This is illogical. In fact, evolutionists say the earth should have formed with practically no water at all. They assumed that comets bombarded the earth providing it with water as these were understood to be large ice balls. However, after properly investigating comets they realised this was not a feasible possibility because although comets do have small amounts of water their chemical make-up is different to what we find here on earth. A report in a science magazine once said concerning this that there was one thing on which most geochemists and astronomers agree, and that being that the celestial pantry was now empty of a key ingredient in the recipe for earth.'[8]

'And how the heck,' asked Tim sceptically, 'are you going to obtain seven billion people in just four and a half thousand years after the flood?'

'Actually,' replied Mike after sipping some of his coffee, 'quite easily!'

'What!' spat Tim in astonishment. 'You've got to be kidding me!'

'No,' replied Mike, unmoved by Tim's response. 'Let me give you the mathematical figures; they're very realistic.'

'I'm listening,' said Tim with a smirk on his face as he folded his arms.

'The world's population,' began Mike without hesitation, having mentioned this bit of information on many prior occasions, 'was approximately 600 million in the year 1650 and increased to about 2,400 million by 1950. This means that it would have doubled twice in 300 years, at an average rate of once every 150 years. We can calculate the rate of population growth starting from about 4,500 years ago when, from the historical details found in the Bible, Noah and his family – eight in total – survived the deluge. That population has to double 29½ times to get a world population of about 6.5 billion, at an average doubling rate of once every 152 years.'[9]

'Interesting, isn't it, Tim?' said George as Mike paused momentarily. 'It certainly bears thinking about, don't you agree?'

'Interesting, yes,' replied Tim with a cheeky look, 'but at the moment I'm a little tired to want to think too hard about it!'

'What is additionally interesting,' said Mike, the rain suddenly beating hard against the hut's corrugated roof, 'is that the Bible's timeframe of history fits the data. A number of years back a popular British science magazine answered the question – how soon could Adam and Eve have populated the world? They said that if one believed in the Biblical account of the Creation, it was possible to get a rough estimate of the time when Adam and Eve existed. They said the only trouble would be the assumptions about birth and death rates, which could have a dramatic effect on the final estimate. However, they assumed an average net rate of population growth of 0.5%, which was one-third of the then growth rate, and calculated it would take about 4400 years to get to the then population figure of six billion people.[10] So you see, it's not an impossibility, it actually fits rather well – so well, in fact, that it should cause people to doubt claims that man has been around for hundreds of thousands of years.'

There was momentary silence amongst the group as they all sat sipping coffee and nibbling oat biscuits.

'During my investigations for a project earlier this year,' said Andrew suddenly jumping up and heading across to where his backpack sat leaning against his bunkbed, 'I came across an article by a plant geneticist, who was part inventor of some gene machine or other. The important thing is what he said, and I have it on my phone, so I can read it to you verbatim.'

Andrew unzipped one of his backpack's side pockets and pulled out his smartphone. He scrolled through his phone while returning to where he was sitting, the others waiting in anticipation.

'The geneticist said the following,' continued Andrew, 'and I quote: "Institutional science has systematically 'evolutionized' every aspect of human thought. Contrary to popular thinking, this is not because evolution is central to all human understanding, but rather has arisen due to a primarily political and ideological process. Consequently, in the present intellectual climate, to reject evolutionary theory has the appearance of rejecting science itself. This is totally upside down. An axiomatic statement often repeated by biologists is: 'Nothing makes sense in biology, except in the light of evolution'. However, nothing could be further from the truth! I believe that apart from ideology, the truth is exactly the opposite: 'Nothing makes sense in biology except in the light of design.'"" [11]

'That reminds me of Isaiah 29:16,' said George, 'which says, "You turn things upside down, as if the potter were thought to be like the clay! Shall what is formed say to him who formed it, 'He did not make me?' Can the pot say of the potter, 'He knows nothing?'" That is what is happening today with evolution.'

'That's quite a remarkable parallel,' said Mike thoughtfully. 'I also remember reading a comment made by an atheistic evolutionist who heads one of the largest national science education institutions. She said that in her opinion, using creation and evolution as topics for critical-thinking exercises in primary and secondary schools would be virtually guaranteed to confuse students about evolution and could even lead them to reject one of the major themes in science.' [12]

'I thought that all noteworthy scientists were evolutionists!' said Tim, a puzzled look on his face.

'That's what the institutions and evolutionists want you to believe,' responded George, 'but it's not true at all. Nor will you hear from them that Copernicus, Galileo, Kepler, Newton and others like them, who were proponents of science, were all young-earth creationists.'

'So if this is the case,' asked Tim, 'why is little being said about it?'

'The reason,' replied Mike, 'is that they don't want you to hear about it. A former Nobel Prize winner once said, "Science today is locked into paradigms. Every avenue is blocked by beliefs that are wrong, and if you try to get anything published by a journal today, you will run up against a paradigm, and the editors will turn it down." [13] It's not that little has been said, it's that it is kept suppressed!'

'I'm not quick to bite into a creationist's apple,' said Tim, standing his ground on his beliefs and perspectives, as he stood up and went to his bunkbed, 'but if that's accurate, that truly is tough going!'

Chapter 5

The mysterious note

TIM'S move towards his bunkbed ended all conversation for the night and stirred the others to follow suit and head for bed. They had had a long day and wanted to get up at the crack of dawn, an early start planned as the second leg of the trail would be more demanding due to elevation and undulating surfaces at places. They also wanted to reach the next campsite with enough time to enjoy the remaining sunlight while relaxing around a barbeque.

It was a cold, blustery night, with the rain continuing unabated right into the early hours of the morning. Thankfully for the group, the thunder ceased not long after they had all gone to bed, and they all managed to sleep relatively easily on the unfamiliar beds.

'Rise and shine everyone,' called Mike, who was the first of the group to climb out of bed, 'it's 06:30 and we need to be out of here within an hour.'

There were a few moans and groans, but they were all out of bed and fully dressed within minutes.

Feeling a nip in the air, Andrew peered out the window to see what the weather looked like. A light mist drifted past, so they all put on their thermal wear, knowing that they would be descending into cold valleys, with the trees hugging affectionately onto the mist.

Mike had a pot of water boiling shortly after they had all risen, and they soon all enjoyed a hot mug of coffee.

Tim was the first to venture outside, eager to get to the water closet. He hastened out the door while the others were busy packing their backpacks and preparing for breakfast. He soon returned, and as he neared the door of the hut, he suddenly stopped. There before him, fastened to the wooden door with two pieces of yellow masking tape was a piece of white paper with a handwritten note on it. He realised that it had been there when he exited but had been in such a hurry that it had not drawn his attention. Tim walked slowly up to the door, focusing on the note, and reading it as he drew near. *"Proceed with caution to Wrath Canyon"* it read.

'Who affixed it there?' thought Tim, a little troubled, as they had not heard anyone outside, and the note was not wet from the rain, so it could only have been placed there recently. He quickly ripped it off the door and went inside.

'I found this stuck to the door,' informed Tim, holding out the note to George, who was nearest to him when he entered, 'but I don't know what it means.'

'What's this?' asked George, taking the paper from Tim. 'A note. I wonder who put it there?'

'That's what I was thinking too,' said Tim, still a little troubled by it. 'What's meant by "Wrath Canyon"?'

'Mike, take a look,' asked George, handing the note to him. 'What do you make of it?'

'Charon Canyon is sometimes referred to as Wrath Canyon by locals who frequent the area,' replied Mike, having quickly read the note. 'Whoever wrote the note must be a local, who's mentioned that we need to be careful on our way to it – maybe because of the overnight rain?'

'Why Wrath Canyon?' ask Tim.

'The word Charon,' replied Mike, quite familiar with the whole area, 'is a Hebrew word for a burning anger – sore displeasure, fierceness, fury or wrath! The locals have just converted to using its English meaning.'

'Rather odd,' said Andrew, walking up and looking at the note. 'I never heard anyone arrive outside, except for the two other hiking parties that arrived after we did, but that was late yesterday afternoon. Both parties are made up of foreigners, so they would not likely know the local name used, surely! Did you notice a note on the doors of their huts, Tim?' asked Andrew thoughtfully.

'I didn't look,' replied Tim, realising that if there had been, it would definitely rule them out as having placed the note, 'but then they are already up. I saw members of both groups outside, so if there were notes on their doors, they may have already taken them down.'

'Never mind who it was,' said George, looking at his watch, 'we had better sit down to breakfast if we want to leave on time. We'll just proceed with caution as the note has advised us to do, that's all.'

Breakfast, consisting of bananas, oat biscuits and granola bars, was soon over, and within the hour they had all visited the water closet, washed their hands and faces, cleared up and packed away everything they needed to in the hut.

'Everyone's looking bright and lively this morning,' observed

Mike after they had filled their water bottles from the stream behind the huts and were ready to go.

'Not so sure about that,' complained George, rubbing his thighs, 'but I'll blame it on the bunkbed!'

'Couldn't be anything else, now could it!' chirped Andrew as they all laughed.

'Ah, go on with you!' groaned George light-heartedly, grabbing Andrew and ruffling his hair. 'Where's some support from my son!'

They promptly began stage two of their hike. Andrew quickly took a short video with his smartphone, checked that the shoelaces of his trail shoes were tight and joined the others.

The air was crisp, the condensation of their breath strong, and the sun had already placed its hands on the hilltops and was lifting itself up quickly. A small bank of cloud hung just above the horizon, sitting atop the sun like one of Napoleon's bicorne hats, with a bright glow of red and orange hue bursting forth and penetrating deep into the early morning soft-blue expanse. The green, forested hills and plain looked lush and lively from the night's rain. It was a beautiful sight, clean and fresh, calm and tranquil, and it lifted the spirits of the six hikers as they trekked along.

The party descended a short while after departure into a valley, the pathway being mushy from the heavy rainfall and a bit slippery in places, so they proceeded carefully.

They soon entered a thick mist clutched firmly by the branches and pressed down by a temperature inversion above. The hikers' thermal wear came into its own, keeping their bodies shielded and warm, for the mist was cold but invigorating. Tim and Andrew particularly enjoyed the feel of it against their faces, their skin being made a lively colour. They eventually climbed out of the valley and up to the summit of another hill.

The going was tough, with the wet and mushy ground adding to the difficulty in certain irregular areas and rocky sections. A few small cuts and a couple of bruises were recorded amongst the hikers but nothing that warranted immediate medical attention.

They continued on unabated, the sun rising steadily in uniform harmony with time as it so faithfully did day after day, year after year, and was soon pitched high in the sky, strong and hot. The forest, however, was still damp from the overnight rain, and in the shadows of the trees it was still cool and fresh, with the slightest of breezes shuffling through, keeping the temperature down.

Just as they crested a small mound, they came across three forestry workers sitting on a fallen tree and eating their lunch. They were easily recognisable by their blue outfits with yellow reflective ribbon above and below the knees of their pants and on the chest, back and around the arms of their jackets.

'Hard at work we see,' said George jokingly as they walked up to them, causing them all to laugh.

'Indeed,' replied the one, his bright blue eyes lighting up at the friendly jest, 'it's why we all love this job! Managing okay on the trail?' he added, standing up and coming closer to the group of hikers. 'The rain has made it a little more difficult, but nonetheless it should still be a pleasant hike. I left a note on the door of your hut, did you get it?'

'Yes,' replied George, turning towards Tim, 'my nephew found it, thank you. We wondered where it came from but took the warning. We were a little confused about Wrath Canyon, but thankfully Mike here was familiar with it. The trail has been a little difficult at places, as the few bruises and cuts will testify, but as you say, pleasant nonetheless.'

'Sorry for writing Wrath Canyon,' apologised the worker, 'I realised after I had left that I had used the local word for the canyon, not thinking at the time that it may confuse you – just habit with us locals at times I guess!' 'You're not far now from Boulders Rest,' informed the worker, momentarily turning and looking down the path. 'It's about another half a mile. The water in the stream is running strongly from the night's rainfall. You'll get yourselves wet if you sit too close to it! The animal kingdom has been a little livelier today as well, probably from the rain, so please take care and watch your step.'

'We've already noticed that,' said Mike, 'with raccoons, porcupines, a mongoose and a couple of deer being spotted along the way thus far. Yesterday we hardly saw anything, other than the odd lizard scuttling across the rocks.'

'That's how it goes,' said the forestry worker with a smile. 'Anyway, let me not detain you. We also have to get this tree cut up and out of the way before nightfall!'

'Just one question,' spoke up Andrew. 'How did you get that note to us? We didn't hear anyone arrive at the huts this morning!'

'Those are the culprits!' said the worker with a bright face, chuckling as he pointed to scarcely visible objects behind the large fallen tree. 'We've all received new electric dirt bikes. They've only recently been launched by the manufacturer, and they're a wonder – you can hardly hear them. That's how I snuck up on you and disappeared equally as fast without disturbing you. Not only can we now check the trails quickly, but it's great fun to do so. Before we had the dirt bikes, we used to fight about who had the task of checking the trails, and now that we have them, we still fight about who has the task – the only difference is that now we all want the task! The headlights make it easy for us to operate in the dark as well. As a motocross fan, I love my bike to bits!'

'That's wonderful,' said Andrew, all of them laughing heartily at what the worker had told them, including his two fellow assistants, whose guilty looks seemed to affirm the story.

'Much obliged to you,' said George amiably as they started moving on again. 'Keep up the effort; we all appreciate it.'

'You're welcome, Sir,' responded the forestry worker, tipping his hard hat, his two fellow workers doing the same. 'Happy to be obliging. Enjoy the rest of your hike.'

The hiking party made the detour round the fallen tree, Andrew and Tim taking the opportunity to quickly look at the new electric dirt bikes, and were back on the path and on their way without much delay.

They soon arrived at Boulders Rest, which was a clearing alongside a stream much like Stream's Edge, with the only manmade items present also being a small, wooden hand-painted sign nailed to a tree and a large lockable dustbin. There was no need for short, cut logs though, as the area was part of a rocky outcrop and natural, grey boulders in plentiful supply could be used to sit on. The outcrop created a miniature waterfall right at the side of the rest area, crafting a picturesque setting for a short rest.

As the forestry worker had said, the stream was running strongly, with the boisterous waters cascading down the rocky slope, bickering and jostling for position over the smooth rocks.

They all sat quietly, blissfully eating their rations of peanut butter crackers, nuts, raisins and energy bars, just enjoying the pleasant ambience.

Everyone was eager to get going once lunch was finished.

With backpacks on, having already filled their water bottles from the stream, they set off without delay. Tim chose to lead the group for a while this time, and they pressed ahead steadily, Charon Canyon and a nice, hearty barbeque awaiting.

Tim walked happily along, his mind in neutral, just enjoying the fresh, clean air and pleasantness of the forest. Suddenly, to his great surprise, he felt someone grab his backpack, the straps quickly pulling against his shoulders.

'Hold it, Tim!' exclaimed Mike quietly, having brought him to an almost immediate halt in absolute bewilderment, the others having stopped behind Mike. 'Look, on the right!'

Tim half recoiled, looking in shock as a large, ugly brown snake slithered out of the underbrush less than two meters in front of him, across the path and into the underbrush on the other side.

'That was close,' said Tim, letting out a heavy sigh as Mike let go of his backpack. 'I never saw it at all, but then my mind was elsewhere. I wasn't alert or paying attention!'

'No worries,' said Mike reassuringly, 'that one was harmless, but I couldn't be sure at first sight of it.'

The group pressed on again, enjoying the hike through the forests. They eventually made the campsite late in the afternoon, about an hour after schedule.

They climbed the wooden steps to their tree houses, Mike and his sons sharing one and George, Andrew and Tim sharing another. After entering, Andrew and George took off their backpacks and flopped down on beds, happy to just be able to let their bodies relax awhile.

Tim was tired too but pleased with the hike and satisfied that he had now had a chance to go on it. He made his way slowly to one of the beds and put his backpack down next to it. Having never seen the place before, Tim returned to the doorway to scan the area, but on his way his eye caught sight of two brochures lying on the small kitchen counter. They drew his attention as he glanced at them and seeing that there was no paperclip on either of them, he opened the one that took his interest. Tim immediately went cold and stared in disbelief!

Chapter 6

A repentant heart

"**T**HE *wrath of God is being revealed from heaven against all the godlessness and wickedness of men who suppress the truth by their wickedness (Romans 1:18)*" read Tim, handwritten on a small white piece of paper similar to the one at the administration office. This one, however, was not affixed with a paperclip, it was just lying loose inside the brochure.

Tim shut the brochure and looked up, regretful and penitent for having opened it. Who was doing this? What were they doing it for? Tim was indignant. He had not expected it, but again, where he would normally have shrugged off such an occurrence without batting an eyelid, he was troubled by it. He did not need to read the note again, he knew what it said!

Tim turned and looked at Andrew and George lying restfully on their beds, then quickly moved to the open door of the treehouse and stepped outside.

What did it all mean? Did it actually have any significance, or was it just plain coincidence? Tim's spirit was disturbed as he leaned against the balcony's railing considering it.

Tim could not rationalise away the occurrence at the administration office as just being coincidence; it had been too close to his thoughts at the time, too real, too impactful for him, and he got goosebumps at the thought of it. He did not want to consider this second occurrence though so shoved the whole thing out of his mind. Tim drew in a deep breath, and let out a heavy sigh as he began to scan his surrounds.

The campsite at Charon Canyon was located right on the edge of the Canyon's precipice. It was at one of the highest points and looked out over the expanse of the canyon that stretched and meandered for miles into the distance. The water in the canyon was still and blue, the tapered slopes green and lush. Just to the right of the camp's location, it cut steeply down with large rocky outcrops on either side of the canyon at that point. There were two vents within each rock face, right at the bottom just above the waterline, from which smoke rose in columns high into the sky for approximately one minute periods at about ten minute intervals. Soft, white cotton-wool clouds drifted through the canyon, below the level of the campsite, and made for interesting viewing. The area was quiet, apart from the occasional screech or cry of an eagle or hawk soaring high above, effortlessly floating on thermal columns.

There were twenty small, round treehouses, all about 5-metres above the ground, neatly built into the trees of the forest's edge. They all had balconies and were joined to one another with gangways. They were accessed by means of two sets of steps, one on either side of the group of treehouses. Each treehouse had sleeping facilities for five persons and basic amenities. An area in front of them, right at the edge of the cliff face, had been cleared and replaced with barbeque facilities and small fire pits for the travellers to utilise. A sturdy safety railing was fixed across the front so that people could get up close to the edge without danger and enjoy the scenic panorama the location offered. A paid service was provided by the management, whereupon hikers could provide them with a cooler box or parcel of food, and they would ensure that it was waiting for the hikers in their treehouse when they arrived at the campsite. A shuttle service was also provided to ferry hikers back to Ailen Oak Lake the day after the hike had been completed.

'What's up?' asked Andrew, coming out of the treehouse and seeing Tim leaning with his elbows on the balcony railing. 'You have a serious look about you.'

'Just viewing the surrounds and scenery,' replied Tim, standing upright and looking at Andrew. 'We had better get started with the barbeque if we want to eat before it's pitch dark!'

'I agree with that,' said Mike, coming up behind Tim along the gangway, having just exited the treehouse next door. 'Besides, I'm starting to feel rather hungry after the great trek!'

Mike and Tim made their way down to the entertainment area, leaving Andrew to quickly make another short film with his smartphone, for June and July, before joining them to assist with getting a fire going. George, Junior and Matty soon arrived as well and before long, a healthy fire was raging.

As the sun gradually faded so too did the fierceness of the fire's flames, leaving glowing embers as the sun slipped silently behind the edge of the canyon. Junior and Andrew fetched their supplies that the management team had dropped off for them. Juicy steaks along with spicy beef sausage were soon sizzling on the barbeque under the watchful eyes of oil lamps, torches and distant starlight. Smoke billowed up each time fat dripped onto the red hot embers. To the pleasure of all, a tantalising smell permeated the area while they sat round on camping chairs, brought down from the treehouses, talking about the hike in a lively and animated fashion while sipping soft drinks.

With the full moon, silvery and bright, well established in the heavens above, all the meat, along with grilled cheese and tomato sandwiches, had been cooked. Quietness fell upon the group as they began eating their dinner, fresh salads and potato chips being a welcome addition. An occasional drip from the grid onto the fading embers revealed a faint show of red as a puff of smoke instantly rose, with the odd comment amongst the hikers also breaking the stillness of the night.

After dinner, Andrew and Tim filled one of the fire pits with chopped wood and got a healthy fire going. They all sat round it relaxing and engaging in further conversation, drawing from its warmth as it crackled, spitting sparks now and again up into the air. Junior and Matty did not stay up too long, for although they had managed well on the hike, they were both quite weary so retired to their treehouse for the night.

'Oh!' exclaimed Andrew, pulling out a note from his pocket as he watched Junior and Matty climb the wooden steps to the treehouses. 'I forgot that I found this in one of the brochures on the counter in our treehouse! It's a note with Romans 1:18 written on it, *"The wrath of God is being revealed from heaven against all the godlessness and wickedness of men who suppress the truth by their wickedness."'*

'Can I see that?' asked Mike with interest, holding out his hand. Andrew promptly gave the note to him.

'Oh, this is mine,' laughed Mike. 'There should have been another note attached to it. I took three brochures from the rack at the administration office and wrote two scripture verses down on notes of paper, fastening them to one of the brochures with a paperclip. I forgot them on the counter at the office. One of the staff members must have just put them with our food parcels and dropped them off.'

Tim was quite taken aback. He sat silently listening, his mind alert and ears attentive to every word spoken.

'There were only two brochures on the counter in our treehouse,' informed Andrew, 'but neither of them had a paperclip nor was there another note.'

'May have been mislaid or something,' responded Mike. 'Not to worry, I'll get another brochure from the office tomorrow when we get back to Ailen Oak Lake. I remember the other scripture verse I wrote down so that's okay too.'

'Tell me something,' said Tim thoughtfully, looking into the heart of the crackling fire before him, having not mentioned what had transpired with the notes. 'What has Christianity actually done for man? What has it actually done for society and civilisation? In my opinion, it tends to hold onto the past and keep people in bondage!'

There was momentary silence as the question seemed to stun the others, being thrown at them totally unexpectedly.

'The main issue is not what Christianity has done for man, society or civilisation per say,' said George, having gathered his thoughts, 'but what God has done and continues to do for man, which then impacts upon society and civilisation. From that you have the development of Judeo-Christian values and ethics as an established way of life. To first take your question as you asked it, Proverbs 31 talks about a virtuous wife and describes an industrious woman who buys and sells, including property, works and trades – and this was written at least 2500 years ago. About 2000 years ago the apostle Peter said to husbands that they were to be considerate as they lived with their wives, and to treat them with respect and honour as the weaker partner and as heirs together of the grace of life so that their prayers may not be hindered.[14] However, this does not change the role of the husband and wife in God's economy, an aspect of importance that today's society is seeking to overthrow, to their own detriment! Christianity never brought bondage to people or societies.

'To take South Korea as an example of what Christianity did for society,' continued George, pulling up a note that he had on his phone, 'Christian influence played a big part in their development and growth. Many of the Korean Christians are under the impression that their principles have had a positive impact on various social relationships. A semi-divine emperor, under which society was hierarchically arranged according to Confucius principle was what made up traditional Korean culture. Rights were not available to women, children were totally subservient to parents, and except as defined by the overall social system, individuals had no rights either! The Bible's indication that we are created in the image of God with equal rights and worth challenged the traditional structure. This brought about emancipation for the people, not further bondage. Wives were no longer treated as chattel and the neglect of children, particularly girls, was no longer accepted. Furthermore, there was a study done that apparently suggested that societies with high levels of belief in heaven and high levels of church attendance exhibited high rates of economic growth. To some, this study has been used to support the belief that Christianity played a major role in South Korea's economic success. Christian missionaries also started nearly 300 schools and 40 universities, having a significant influence on the educational upliftment in that country.[15] In countries where Christianity is suppressed, there is oppression of the people and bondage, not liberty. This is an example of what has been done, but the main issue is not that, it's the need for salvation through Jesus Christ. We need to have a repentant heart, and the word of God reveals this to us!'

Chapter 7

Wrath revealed at Charon Canyon

'**M**ANY people see Christianity as a whole lot of rules,' said Andrew, throwing a few logs on the fire, 'which they feel just creates bondage, as you mentioned, Tim. What's hypocritical is that they'll accept rules and regulations in other areas of their lives on a daily basis and actually find stability in the fact that they have them. Interestingly, I was reading through the *Rules of Golf* one day. At the beginning of the booklet there was a picture of the silhouette of one of the world's best golfers hitting a golf ball. The caption above said, "*It takes a lot of rules to create such freedom*". How can we accept this but shun God's requirements as being burdensome and bondage? Mankind can understand the need for this in their daily lives and activities in order to create stability, safety and standards, yet Christianity is considered bondage! The apostle James tells us that the perfect law gives freedom.[16] The Psalmist tells us that rebelling against the word of God and despising His counsel is what puts people into bondage, deepest gloom and distress! [17] Christianity does not bring bondage to man or society, it actually brings freedom.

It's a deception and lie to believe otherwise!'

Anger rose rapidly in Tim's being, and he took a deep breath as he almost wanted to fume. He did not personally like what he was being told, but what annoyed him more was that something internally said that he needed to listen. Something stirred within him, but he did not know what it was. He opposed what he was hearing, yet at present, found that he also did not want to switch off from hearing it. Tim tussled internally, and he hated his own feelings and preparedness to pay attention. He made every effort not to vent his frustration.

'Indeed, what you say is so!' agreed Mike, scrolling on his smartphone to a particular book of the Bible. 'One of the reasons for having written the verse that Andrew found was to remind me of a certain aspect. Men willingly suppress the truth, and the ultimate outcome is God's wrath and judgement. Babylon and Nineveh are two examples. King Nebuchadnezzar was king of Babylon's vast empire. Pride rose in his heart and in his own eyes he exalted himself saying, "Is not this the great Babylon I have built as the royal residence, by my mighty power and for the glory of my majesty?" The words had not left his lips when God spoke proclaiming his judgement. His royal authority was stripped for seven years, after which he acknowledged that God Most High was sovereign over the kingdoms of men and gave them to anyone He wished. God had mercy on Nebuchadnezzar and restored his kingdom to him, after which the man praised, exalted and glorified the King of heaven, the LORD Most High.

'However, a later descendant – either his son or grandson – Belshazzar, paid no respect to this and it resulted in the origination of what is known as "the writing's on the wall". The prophet Daniel was summoned to the king. After mentioning to Belshazzar all that God had done with Nebuchadnezzar, Daniel spoke further and said, "But you his son (descendant), O Belshazzar, have not humbled yourself though you knew all this. Instead, you have set yourself up against the Lord of heaven. You had the goblets from His temple brought to you, and you and your nobles, your wives and your concubines drank wine from them. You praised the gods of silver and gold, of bronze, iron, wood and stone, which cannot see or hear or understand. But you did not honour the God who holds in His hand your life and all your ways." That very night the king was slain, and the kingdom given to the Medes and Persians.[18] God had had mercy on Nebuchadnezzar, by teaching him his lesson and then restoring his kingdom to him, but his son – or grandson – knew it all; he was without excuse. God's wrath and judgement were proclaimed and executed, for he had been weighed on the scales and found wanting.'

Mike scrolled on his phone to another book of the Bible.

'Nineveh was the same,' continued Mike, having quickly found the book that he wanted. 'God was about to destroy Nineveh, for their wickedness had come up before Him. He sent Jonah to proclaim to them their destruction, and when they heard it, they believed God, humbled themselves and repented of their evil ways and violence. When God saw what they had done, He had compassion on them and did not bring upon them the destruction he had threatened. Jonah was angry with God for doing so, but God told him that He was concerned for that great city, for there were 120,000 people and many cattle as well.[19] Yet, less than 150 years later that great city was completely destroyed. It's not likely that they didn't know about what had happened at the time of their forefathers, when Jonah declared to them their destruction, for it had been such a massive event and turnaround of the people. The latter generation must have conveniently walked passed it and carried out their evil ways. Therefore, the LORD's anger burned against them.

'The prophet Nahum says the following,' continued Mike, having scrolled to another book and checked the different verses that he wanted to read, '"The LORD takes vengeance on His foes and maintains His wrath against His enemies. The earth trembles at His presence, the world and all who live in it. Who can withstand His indignation? Who can endure His fierce anger? His wrath is poured out like fire; the rocks are shattered before Him. He cares for those who trust in Him, but with an overwhelming flood He will make an end of [Nineveh]; He will pursue His foes into darkness. The LORD has given a command concerning you, [Nineveh]: 'You will have no descendants to bear your name. I will destroy the carved images and cast idols that are in the temple of your gods. I will prepare your grave, for you are vile.'" [20] God had once been gracious to Nineveh, for He declared to Jonah that they were a people who were ignorant, not being able to tell their right hand from their left. [21] In his prayer to God, Jonah had said, "Those who cling to worthless idols forfeit the grace that could be theirs," and that "Salvation comes from the LORD." [22] Nineveh were now not ignorant nor were they humble or repentant. They knew the truth but suppressed it, and God's wrath was kindled!'

Tim listened, the fire crackling before him as varieties and shades of red and orange flame leapt and twisted, but he started to erect an internal barrier, feeling that what was being said had personal implications. He wondered if it had merit but did not want to stop and consider it.

'That's so true!' agreed George. 'As said, the main issue is not what Christianity has done for society but what God has done for humanity – for man is perishing and cannot save himself! We need a saviour, and God has provided one in the person of Jesus Christ! Does man accept Him is the question, or does man's pride and arrogance stand in the way? Nebuchadnezzar was humbled, but he also humbled himself and repented. His son did not, although he was knowledgeable of the truth. The people of Nineveh humbled themselves and repented, but a later generation did not, although they would have been knowledgeable of the truth.

'Where does our society stand today? We have seen what God has done in the past in our country, in the lives of the people – parents, grandparents or even earlier generations. We are not without knowledge, we are not without His Word! Are we turning to Him or away from Him in our pride and arrogance? Today we have pride parades, where people are brazenly flaunting their self-importance, their choices and their rights to do their own thing. They are flaunting their sin and dissipation with shameless hearts, while shaking their fists in the face of God. God's wrath and judgement will fall upon the nations who do this, particularly where they have received a knowledge of the truth and have seen His merciful hand outstretched. They will bring about their own demise and destruction!'

George scrolled on his smartphone, seeking a particular section of scripture.

'The book of Matthew,' continued George without much delay, 'tells us that Jesus denounced the cities in which most of His mighty works, or miracles, had been performed, because they did not repent. Jesus said, "Woe unto thee, Chorazin! Woe unto thee, Bethsaida! For if the mighty works, which were done in you, had been done in Tyre and Sidon, they would have repented long ago in sackcloth and ashes. But I say unto you, It shall be more tolerable for Tyre and Sidon at the day of judgement, than for you. And thou, Capernaum, which are exalted unto heaven, shalt be brought down to hell: for if the mighty works, which have been done in thee, had been done in Sodom, it would have remained to this day. But I say unto you, That it shall be more tolerable for the land of Sodom in the day of judgement, than for thee." [23] Proverbs tells us that pride goes before destruction, a haughty spirit before a fall.' [24]

'In speaking about wrath,' said Andrew, having looked up a verse on his phone, 'the Bible speaks about a time when the Antichrist will rule the world – a topic and issue that has become increasingly prevalent around the world in recent times, not just in conversation but also in practical outworking. It will be a time when God's wrath is let loose in judgement. However, the Bible also tells us that God's saints, His children, are not appointed unto wrath.[25] Listen to what it says about those who align themselves with the Antichrist: "And the third angel followed them, saying with a loud voice, If any man worship the beast and his image, and receive his mark in his forehead, or in his hand, the same shall drink of the wine of the wrath of God, which is poured out without mixture into the cup of His indignation; and he shall be tormented with fire and brimstone in the presence of the holy angels, and in the presence of the Lamb: and the smoke of their torment ascendeth up for ever and ever: and they have no rest day nor night, who worship the beast and his image, and whosoever receiveth the mark of his name." [26] This is not a nice prospect, but God in His faithfulness has warned mankind in advance about His wrath upon those who are disobedient and turn away from Him.'

'I mean this in all kindness, Tim,' said Mike, concern in his heart for the young man sitting opposite him on the other side of the fire. 'We have seen and heard. We have no excuse and are not ignorant of God's hand of mercy, salvation and provision. Man is automatically an object of God's wrath and only comes out from underneath that wrath through repentance and acceptance of Jesus Christ as Lord and Saviour, for Scripture tells us that, "Whoever believes in the Son has eternal life, but whoever rejects the Son will not see life, for God's wrath remains on him." [27] If you turn your back and spurn God's grace, the outworking of God's wrath in your life will not be unwarranted!'

'I hear you,' said Tim a little disgruntled as he got up and threw another log on the fire. He walked over to the railing and leaned on it, looking out into the dark open sky, the concept of what he considered life and what the Bible declared as having life fighting in his spirit like a tug of war.

Conversation quickly changed to a different topic with Tim having gone over to the railing. He returned and sat down some minutes later, when they began discussion their schedule for the morning. General conversation on various things was then engaged until the fire died down, leaving only glowing embers and little heat.

Tim's spirit, however, was raging. He went back to the railing when the others called it a night, standing alone to look out across the expanse. This was something he always loved doing at home from his second story bedroom window, where he could look out over the bay area below and into the vast, black ocean distance.

The air was crisp, clean and clear; the silvery moon, bright in the night's sky, cast a glossy light on the still waters below; and owls hooted softly in the forest behind the treehouses.

Tim stood and watched the thick columns of smoke from the rocky vents rise high into the sky, the moon as a backdrop. His questions and concerns about the two notes had been answered, but he still could not reconcile what had happened at the administration office.

Tim reflected further on what had been presented to him in answer to his question about Christianity and the immediate follow through. George had revealed a need, and Mike had nailed those two verses to his conscience. However, none of it was clear to him, and a fog of doubt in his inner being added to the already blurry vision. Besides that, he did not like it at all. He did not like what he had heard nor the concept of what it represented. He felt ill at ease and in no way wanting to embrace what he considered trouble or change, why should he? Did it truly have merit? Was it truly justified? Was it not just religion handed down from generations past? What had spoken to his conscience, what had pricked it? None of this had ever been an issue before, why now? Why did it now present itself as though it may be real, that there may be some truth to it?

Tim looked out, the torment of the deep rising eerily up and its smoky presence imposing. The connection between it and the wrath revealed in Scripture was troubling, almost terrifying. Tim shuddered. This tore at his thoughts, but he resisted it. He turned and walked away, leaving his thoughts behind, balancing dangerously on the edge of the safety railing!

Chapter 8

Fishing at Ailen Oak Lake

THE sun kissed the horizon good morning and awakened the dawn, the six hikers rising early to enjoy a hot, cooked breakfast of eggs, beef sausages, fried tomatoes and fried toast prepared outside on a griddle atop one of the barbeques before the shuttle was to ferry them back to Ailen Oak Lake. The air was fresh and invigorating, and although there were a few stiff bodies amongst the group, they were all upbeat and energetic.

Tim returned to the safety railing where he had left his thoughts the night before. Once again he pondered on them while the group waited for the fire to die down so that they could cook their food. The day was clear and bright but his thoughts foggy and dull. His upbringing had not placed a high value on Christianity; therefore, there was no critical emphasis placed on the need for salvation in Jesus through repentance. Yes, his relatives had spoken to him, taught him certain aspects when they could, even demonstrating it continually in the conduct of their lives. However, he had never been open to it, and it had never penetrated his heart. The lack of his father at home, the early years of struggle that his mother had gone through, and her total indifference to the things of God and Christianity as a whole had until then overridden all external influence. Besides, Tim had always reasoned that he was a good person, a respectable individual, who conducted his life and activities for the most part in what could be termed as social decency, which he believed counted for much and would weigh in his favour. This was the first time in his life that his conscience had been pricked, his spirit troubled and his ears open – albeit only slightly – to what had been said. He did not like it, and if he could not see or understand it clearly, he was not going to be grasping at it. At present, he could not so did not linger long in contemplation, dismissing the issues as not being highly relevant in his perspective. Tim returned to the others and engaged heartily in the lively chat, leaving the issues raised, his prior thoughts and contemplations sacrificed on the fire before him and going up in white, eye-watering smoke into the heavens above.

Breakfast was soon over, having been thoroughly enjoyed by all out in the fresh, open air. The robust shuttle bus arrived just as they were clearing up, and it was not long before they were underway, the two other hiking groups also catching the lift back to Ailen Oak Lake. A lively ambience filled the bus as they bounced along a gravel road. The route took them away from the campsite and trail that they had walked along, taking them to a main tarred road. They turned onto it, and with windows down and a fresh breeze swirling around their heads, they had a smooth ride all the way back to the turnoff leading to Ailen Oak Lake. The bus pulled strongly up the gravel road to the lake, the driver skilled but cautious, navigating the twists with care, and they arrived safely at the parking area outside the administration office. With chatting never seeming to end amongst the foreigners, they all climbed out and went their separate ways, having thoroughly enjoyed their two-day hike.

'Enjoy yourselves lads,' called George, heading off with Mike and his sons as Andrew and Tim had planned to do some fishing at the lake. 'Bring home the big one – ten bucks to the one who catches the biggest fish!' With big grins Andrew and Tim waved before heading to Tim's car.

'So, cousin,' said Andrew, his thoughts turning to fishing as they neared Tim's car, 'what's the game plan for today?'

'Fish for one hour and lunch at Misty's for three hours!' replied Tim with a straight face.

'Nice plans, nincompoop,' said Andrew as they both began to laugh, 'but it's not going to happen.'

'Then the only thing I'm planning on doing is to relax,' responded Tim, promptly pulling his sunglasses down off his head and onto his face.

'Lovely!' said Andrew, stretching in his customary fashion with his hands extended to the sky, after having reached Tim's car and put his backpack down.

'Great, eh!' responded Tim as he too was drawn by what lay before him.

'It always is,' affirmed Andrew, soaking up the warmth and beauty of the surrounds.

'Come on!' perked up Tim after a moment as he suddenly caught himself day dreaming. 'If we stand here all day we won't get any fishing done!'

'That's true,' agreed Andrew, awakening from his brief slumber. 'Let's get fishing, for I also want to get to Misty's to show June and July my videos but first want to get some fishing in!'

Tim had his car unlocked, trunk open and backpack stowed

inside in seconds. He grabbed his fishing gear, Andrew following Tim's lead and doing the same, and they were soon marching off together with great expectation and intent towards their fishing spot.

Andrew and Tim seated themselves on their light-brown coloured camping chairs and began to bait up. The randomly dispersed trees created a contrast of light and dark dancing images all around them as the branches moved slightly in the gentle breeze. They held off as much sunlight as they could, providing the lads with enough shade, but could not resist the entire onslaught of the rising sun whose rays managed to breach their leafy armour in places.

'This brings back memories of the good old days,' said Tim as he mused a little while prepping his line.

'At twenty-one years of age, Tim, what "good old days" are you referring to?' responded Andrew, who found his own comment rather amusing. 'You sound like Gramps sitting on the porch in his rocking chair!'

'Okay, okay,' defended Tim, smiling. 'You know what I mean. I'm referring to last summer.'

'Of course, Timothy *old* boy,' joked Andrew in a funny, mocking tone. 'I knew exactly what you meant, *old* pal.'

Andrew burst into laughter, his voice carrying across the lake and dispersing into the awaiting greenery that had majestically looked down upon the lake area for centuries. Tim, with his good sense of humour, saw the funny side and joined Andrew in providing the rather quiet and restful area with a melody of echoes. A few "elderlies", fishing not too far from the pair, scolded and waved their hands in a gesture that the boys should rather disappear, telling them they would scare off the fish. The lads muffled their laughter and tried hard to contain themselves at this added irony, quietness quickly returning to the tranquil area.

The air was still fresh, and the sun shone down on the lake creating a golden shimmer that pulsed every time a hook, line and sinker penetrated the glassy surface of the lake. In the far distance, colourful sailboats were heeling as they drew strength from the breeze blowing in over the tops of the forested expanse. The boys sat idly, almost mesmerized by the golden warmth radiating around them, not even fully aware that others were there too.

'Maybe we did scare the fish away,' mentioned Andrew thoughtfully. 'We've been fishing for a whole hour, and I haven't even had a nibble yet!'

'Not a chance!' responded Tim while lifting his hat a little in order to see Andrew better. 'They're there. I've had a few nibbles. It's early season, give them some time.' Tim reclined back in his camping chair and pulled his hat back down over his eyes. 'We've got to catch something though,' added Tim. 'How else will one of us gain a whole ten bucks!'

Andrew, remembering their "friendly" fishing neighbours, stemmed his inevitable laughter as he turned and quickly looked in their direction. He continued casting and reeling, casting and reeling, while Tim took an early nap.

'Hey, Tim,' said Andrew a little hesitantly, seeing him beginning to stir a while later, 'I know that you're not one for going to church and have never wanted to go in the past, but how about joining me tomorrow evening and come along to the evening service? It may just be a message that you need to hear!'

'No, Andy,' replied Tim resistantly, 'there's nothing there that I want!'

'I just thought I'd ask,' responded Andrew. 'The invitation's always open to you though.'

'Yeah, thanks,' mumbled Tim, 'but no thanks!'

They continued fishing, silence ruling the hour, casting and reeling in an attempt to lure the fish, but there was very little action. They nevertheless enjoyed the calm, tranquil ambience and the pleasant warmth that encompassed them.

'You know what, Andy,' said Tim, eventually breaking the silence while reeling in his line. 'I'll go with you.'

'Go with me?' questioned Andrew, stopping reeling as he looked at Tim. 'Do you mean to church tomorrow evening?'

'Yes,' replied Tim, a little unsure of himself. 'I don't know why I'm agreeing to go, but I'll go. Maybe it's about time I went to see this nonsense for myself – not that I need to be convinced that this religious rubbish is a bit far-fetched, but I'll go with you. I just hope I don't regret the decision.' Tim looked a little out of sorts as he stared at the gently rippling water, his facial expression clearly showing signs of internal conflict.

'That's a positively negative acceptance,' said Andrew, a little surprised at Tim's change of mind, 'but an acceptance nevertheless. I don't expect you to regret it.'

'I think I'm regretting it already,' mumbled Tim, reeling in his line more aggressively, 'but we'll see tomorrow evening. Just this once though!'

'Okay, Tim,' responded Andrew, reeling in his line again, 'as you— I've got a bite! I've got a bite!' Andrew jumped up with excitement, his face completely illuminated. Upon seeing Andrew, Tim's facial expression also changed, from one of seriousness to one of excited anticipation.

'Hang on, Andy!' shouted Tim, forgetting at that moment the restriction on noise levels imposed by the "friendly fishing fraternity" camping a little further down the bank. 'Don't let it get away!'

Andrew overemphasised his effort in fighting the fish, the dramatization even capturing the interest of those fishing nearby. When Andrew thought he had put on enough of a show, he hauled out a relatively small fish.

'Woohoo!' hollered Tim as he began to laugh. 'Not bad, not bad. You're fighting hard for the ten bucks, aren't you? You surely cannot lose with that!'

'Says you!' responded Andrew with a chuckle. 'Considering what you *haven't* caught thus far, it's bound to win! Come on, see what you can hall in, it's nearly time for us to pack up and head off to Misty's!'

Chapter 9

Misty's and the end to a good trip

MISTY'S was a smallish, informal dinette on the outskirts of Ailensbury, only a short detour from the main route the lads would be taking home. The restaurant could be viewed from the main highway, up high, hugging the hillside. It seemed to drape the hill around its sides like a shawl around a lady's shoulders and often floated upon the mist that smothered the valleys below on cold mornings. The panorama from there, across the meadows and into the distance, was like that of a majestic painting with its iridescent array of colours smudged into each other as the scenery merged from the fields to the distant landscape to the skyline. The shimmering light from the sun did the trick of creating a kaleidoscopic effect as it appeared to move along its path of perpetual bliss. The owners of Misty's had captured this perspective beautifully through their blend of colours in the interior decoration and design.

Andrew and Tim arrived at Misty's soon after departing Ailen Oak Lake. They had spent an hour and a half there, enjoying tasty food, warm sunshine and pleasant service from the Harris twins.

'I think it's time we headed North, Tim,' said Andrew, patting his stomach, the warming rays of sunshine beaming down upon him from high in the sky as they sat outside on the terrace. 'We've enjoyed plenty, I would say!'

'We've definitely enjoyed plenty,' agreed Tim, his face bright in the sunlight. 'Wow, I was ravenous! A soft drink, malted ice-cream, not to mention two cheese, tomato and lettuce sand–'

'Which you savagely assaulted, I might add,' interjected Andrew, chuckling.

'The pot calling the kettle black!' countered Tim. 'You forget that you finished your sandwiches before I finished mine!'

'True,' admitted Andrew, loving the occasion, 'but I enjoyed every mouthful. I think I had to eat quickly, otherwise I wouldn't have been able to tell the girls about our hiking trip! I don't know how I fitted it in to tell you the truth!'

'You told them quickly if you don't recall,' observed Tim, 'for they only had a few minutes to stop and listen! But it didn't stop you from swallowing your food while they watched your videos!'

'I was trying to give some running commentary,' defended Andrew, a little conscious stricken, remembering his mother stopping him from shovelling his food down his throat on the morning they left to go on the hike.

'Never mind, Andy,' joked Tim, seeing his face, 'we all love and appreciate you! You'll learn some manners as you get older!' Andrew just laughed, knowing that he was usually quite disciplined at the table, with these two occasions actually being rare occurrences despite their close proximity.

'Are you finally done, boys?' came the sweet soprano voice of June, one of the Harris twins with whom Andrew was particularly friendly, as they attended the same church –

Ailensbury Christian Fellowship.

'Absolutely!' replied Andrew, palming his stomach.

'Andy boy, have you had enough?' came the sarcastic question from the other Harris twin, July, as she walked past them on her way to serve tea and marmalade scones to an elderly English couple two tables down. Andrew shot her a mocking look, to which she just laughed in her peculiar yet pleasant to the ear, rapid machinegun-fire laughter.

The girls were Andrew's age, twenty. They had healthy complexions and animated expressions and were both of medium height and delicate in build. Both had bright blue eyes and long, golden-brown hair – June with locks and July with straight hair. Although June and July had bubbly characters, they were not in any way brash, gushy, forward or attention seekers. Even July's peculiar laughter never drew outside attention. They were both studying physiotherapy together at Ailensbury Medical College, a division of Ailensbury University, and were thoroughly enjoying it. The twins had the rare privilege of not only celebrating their birthdays on separate days but also in different months – being born 10 minutes apart across the midnight divide of the departing and dawning sixth and seventh month, June being the firstborn.

'Will we see you at church tomorrow evening, Andy?' asked June as she cleared the table, Andrew assisting her, her golden-brown locks glistening in the sunlight and bright blue eyes sparkling.

'Yes,' replied Andrew, 'I certainly plan to be there, and—' Andrew stopped himself, realising that it may not be wise to mention Tim's agreement to join him.

'And what, Andy?' asked June, looking at him as she began wiping off the table with a damp cloth.

'Oh, nothing,' answered Andrew casually, 'just that I hope the weather will still be warm and agreeable.' Andrew glanced at Tim who was looking at him a little anxiously.

'Oh,' said June with a little smile, 'so do I actually, but a storm has been forecast for tomorrow evening – maybe it will hold out until after the service?' In cheeky jest, she promptly wiped the cloth over Andrew's hand and forearm.

The two cousins packed it in, said their goodbyes to the twins and headed for home. They made their way down the winding roadway on the side of the hill, out of the green meadows with their livestock, birds and butterflies, and turned onto the main road where they had made the detour just more than an hour and a half earlier.

'Home, James!' exclaimed Andrew quite happily as Tim pressed the accelerator, causing the car to steadily gain speed for the homeward bound.

Tim pulled into Andrew's driveway and brought his car abruptly to a halt, causing both of them to be thrust forward, the seat belts pulling tight across their chests as the car rocked forward.

'That was a neat stop, Tim,' said Andrew sarcastically. 'You need some lessons, *old* boy!'

'Definitely!' replied Tim with a grin. 'Maybe July could help!'

'What an opportunistic thought,' responded Andrew as he hopped out of the car. 'Trust you to think of that!'

Andrew was soon removing his backpack, fishing gear and lone fish from the trunk of Tim's car.

'Thanks, Tim,' said Andrew with gratitude as he popped his head back in the car through the passenger window, all his possessions placed on the well-manicured grass behind him. 'That was good fun and a nice break!'

'Certainly was,' agreed Tim. 'I'm pleased that I eventually got a chance to do the Smoking Gorge trail and get some fishing in as well. It wouldn't have been much fun without you though.'

'Sorry you lost the ten bucks to my big catch,' apologised Andrew jokingly, lifting up the fish.

'What!' exclaimed Tim in disgust. 'With a fish like that I'd be embarrassed to take the ten bucks!' Tim and Andrew chuckled.

'Still on for tomorrow evening?' asked Andrew.

'Sure,' replied Tim somewhat reservedly. 'I'll see you then, but I hope it's not going to be too long. Sunday night is happy hour at Down and Out's,' added Tim assertively, 'so I don't really want to miss it!'

'I'll pick you up at 18:30 tomorrow evening,' responded Andrew as he patted the roof of Tim's car, producing a hollow, tinny sound that caused Tim to look up. Tim gave Andrew the thumbs up, reversed out of the driveway and was heading down the street in seconds.

Andrew picked up his backpack and fishing gear and headed for the house.

The surrounding flower beds produced an array of colourful beauty, matching that of a rainbow, and removed any feeling of melancholy that beset anyone entering onto the property. Kelly was a green-fingered lady who spent much time in her garden and took great pride in it.

'I thought I heard Tim's car pull up,' said Kelly, having come out the front door and seeing Andrew.

'Indeed you did!' confirmed Andrew with a smile as he walked towards her.

'He left so quickly!' teased Kelly, knowing that they had just come from Misty's. 'Didn't he want a bite to eat? Did you have a good time?'

'Absolutely!' said Andrew energetically, lifting his catch to show his mom.

'My, O my,' responded Kelly with animation, placing her hand briefly over her mouth. 'Is that the winning fish? Your father told me that he had put up ten bucks to the one who caught the biggest fish.'

'Yip,' answered Andrew proudly, 'but then it was the only catch too!'

'When your father sees that fish,' joked Kelly, 'he's likely to give you twenty bucks!'

'More likely to classify it as an invalid entry,' responded Andrew. 'but I'm sure you could make a wonderful kedgeree with it.'

'With that!' exclaimed Kelly. 'Oh, definitely! I'll just have to increase the amount of rice and hard-boiled eggs in the dish. Meal for one coming up!'

'Oh, Mom!' said Andrew enthusiastically as he suddenly had a recollection while the two of them ambled towards the front door. 'Believe it or not, but I'm picking Tim up tomorrow evening for church – he's going to be joining us!'

'What!' exclaimed Kelly in disbelief. 'Timothy Nicholls?'

'Who else do you think I'm talking about?' replied Andrew a little condescendingly. 'Yes – your nephew, my cousin, Timothy Nich—'

'What brought that about?' asked Kelly, not waiting for Andrew to finish his sentence and nearly stumbling in the process.

'Careful, Mom!' called out Andrew as he spontaneously reached out to steady her, wiping his slimy fish across her dress and arm in the process. Andrew had placed the fish in Tim's cooler box for transport, but in the excitement and preparation for the hike, they had forgotten to take newspaper with them, so he could not wrap it.

'Yucky!' protested Kelly with a screwed up face, a slight shiver running through her body. 'That felt horrible! Let's get that thing inside first, then you can answer me.' They promptly entered the house.

'Now you can tell me what brought about Tim joining us tomorrow evening,' said Kelly, happy that the fish was now lying harmlessly in the sink.

'We spoke about Christian issues last night,' replied Andrew, 'and at times while we were fishing, Tim looked thoughtful. I felt it impressed upon my heart to ask him if he wanted to join us, so I asked.'

'Your father told me about the discussion you all had,' said Kelly. 'I hope it touched Tim's heart.'

'I don't know if it did or not,' said Andrew thoughtfully, 'but I invited him. At first he flatly declined but later on changed his mind and accepted the invitation – said it was about time he came to see this nonsense for himself!'

'Was Tim actually serious in answering yes?' asked Kelly, still doubtful at Tim's agreement to go.

'You know Tim, Mom,' replied Andrew. 'He doesn't normally joke foolishly on such issues, particularly not when accepting such an invitation!'

'That's true,' considered Kelly, looking thoughtfully out the bay window. 'Well,' she concluded after a short while, having gathered her thoughts together, 'time will tell, won't it?'

'Indeed it will!' agreed Andrew, Kelly having turned from the window and headed for the kitchen, leaving him to sort out his backpack and pack his fishing gear away. 'Only time will tell what the outcome will be in the end!'

Chapter 10

Off to church

ANDREW bounded down the staircase, nimbly and confident, the banister shuddering and the steps moaning as usual in objection to his abusive treatment of them.

'See you later at church, Mom and Dad,' called Andrew as he passed the large, sunken living room where George and Kelly were relaxing for a while before church. Andrew caught Kelly by surprise and she stirred, looking up quickly in astonishment.

'What's the rush, Andy?' asked Kelly with bewilderment. 'It's still early!'

'I've got to pick up Tim, remember?' replied Andrew without slowing his pace as he continued to head for the front door. 'It's already 18:15 and I told Tim that I'd pick him up at 18:30.'

'Oh, yes,' responded Kelly quietly, looking at George. 'I forgot about the snow in summer. Drive carefully, please,' she called to Andrew in a little more energetic fashion, her mind having properly clicked into gear.

'Always do, Mom,' was the faint reply she received from Andrew, who was already half way out the front door. 'Bye!'

'Snow in summer, indeed!' exclaimed George with a grin, lowering the local weekend paper he was reading and peering over the top of it.

'In Tim's case it's snow in summer,' responded Kelly, meeting George's look as she leaned over and took hold of his hand. 'And I hope it snows for a while too!'

'So do I, my dear,' said George warmly as he put down his paper and smothered Kelly's hand with his other big hand, 'so do I!'

*   *   *

'Come on, Tim!' called Andrew in frustration as he honked the car horn for a second time, knowing though that no-one could actually hear him speak. 'For someone who hates being made to wait, you're not doing too badly yourself!'

Andrew, looking at his watch, was about to jump out of his car and go and see what was holding Tim up, when the hand-carved wooden front door with its picturesque inlays swung open, and the familiar face of Tim appeared.

'At last,' sighed Andrew, mumbling under his breath. He promptly turned the key in the ignition and had his car comfortably idling just as Tim ambled up and climbed in. 'What's the matter, Tim?' asked Andrew, stopping himself from giving Tim the quick sarcastic "welcome" he had planned. 'You look a little down in the mouth.'

'I'm just not sure this is a good idea,' answered Tim miserably. 'I know that I said I would go, but it's just not really my kind of scene. Mom's away and—'

'Okay, Tim,' interjected Andrew without hesitation, 'you're free to stay at home and go to Down and Out's later on if you so wish. There was no catch, excuse the pun, to me asking you yesterday, so the call is yours.'

Tim was taken a little by surprise at Andrew's quick response to give him the freedom to withdraw his agreement to go, thinking that he would strongly object in an attempt to get him to church. He felt flustered, ill at ease, in a state of war in his mind and turmoil was raging in the depths of his being. He had wrestled all night and all day over agreeing to go, trying to find a way out of it but coming up short of providing a descent excuse every time. Yet, something still plagued him – an appeal in the depths of his being to go. Tim glanced at Andrew, his conscience being pricking with a thousand needles to honour his agreement but his flesh fighting hard to resist it. The call to avoid what he considered trouble was deafening and strong and the enticement of a night at Down and Out's viciously attractive.

Andrew waited for Tim's reply, and to him it felt as though an eternity had passed before Tim finally answered.

'Okay, I'll go,' agreed Tim, albeit hesitantly, the two scriptures that he had seen, which Mike had unintentionally mislaid, having entered the internal battle, and he could not overrule their decisive impact. 'I don't know why I changed my mind yesterday and agreed to go, but I'll honour my word.'

'Are you now sure, Tim?' asked Andrew, looking questioningly at him. 'You have the choice.'

'Get going before I change my mind again,' protested Tim. 'Don't ask me stupid questions – I already feel that I'm going to regret it!'

Andrew wasted no further time at all in backing his car out of the driveway and heading South West – next stop, the church!

Andrew pulled into the cobbled parking area belonging to Ailensbury Christian Fellowship and spotted a vacant parking bay. He headed for it as though it was the last one available and if hesitant, would be swamped by a multitude of savages following suit behind him. This was, however, not the case as there was ample parking available. With them being late, hounding traffic anxiously seeking parking bays was also not an issue, although they were not the last to arrive.

'Come on, Tim,' said Andrew energetically as he sprung from the driver's seat. 'We're quite late now!'

Tim slowly undid his seat belt and removed himself from the car with the speed of an old man, still evidently unsure of his agreement to attend the church service.

'How long is this going to take anyway?' asked Tim gruffly, resistant defiance clearly visible in his manner. 'I don't want to be here and preached to all night!'

Andrew turned and briefly looked at Tim but did not answer him.

'I'll be honest,' spat Tim as an addition to his objecting manner, 'if I miss happy hour at Down and Out's, I'm not going to be happy!'

'The only thing you'll be is drunk, not happy!' snapped Andrew offhandedly. 'You were given the choice and you made it – now get moving, we're late!'

Andrew started to march off with purpose only to stop suddenly as he realised that Tim was not doing likewise.

'If you don't stop delaying,' warned Andrew sternly, having turned round, 'I'm going to kick your "whatsitsname", then you *really* won't be happy! Now get moving, we're late!'

Andrew almost seemed to forget that there may be people within ear shot of him speaking, and that church and Bible teachings were to Tim like a splinter in someone's finger – an object of discomfort that a person did not want possession of.

'Hey!' objected Tim, quite taken aback by the reprimand. 'You're supposed to be the goody-goody!'

Andrew caught himself, realizing that his cordiality was falling short of acceptability and his stern reprimand was not necessary.

'Sorry, Tim,' apologised Andrew, speaking in a quieter, calmer manner, having gone over to him. 'I didn't mean to reproach you like that. However, just because I'm a Christian doesn't mean I can't kick your "whatsitsname", you know! Now please, make a final decision – are you coming inside or not? But I would encourage you to do so.'

'Okay, okay,' answered Tim with a heaving sigh, 'I'm inside!'

The two lads directed their attention at the two wooden church doors without further ado, from where they could hear the buzzing tone of voices and see the silhouette of people sitting in pews as the light from inside penetrated the outer darkness.

The church was not a huge structure or imposing building, neither dull nor flashy in its presentation; it was comfortable and spacious. Wooden pews and a few beautiful, stained-glass windows along with sepia-coloured carpeting and tan-coloured surrounds seemed to provide a mix of old tradition and new styling. It was warm yet practical as far as possible and in no way had the presentation of a theatrical show. The freshly picked flowers placed at the sides of the church added colour and brightness to the surrounds, but it was not there for the allurement of people. Nothing seemed to distract or detract from the purpose of what the building was for – the presentation of the scriptures in fullness and truth for the uplifting, correcting, teaching and edification of the congregation, and for the unifying glory of the Lord.

Andrew strode hastily inside with Tim lazily and a little

arrogantly lagging behind. The sudden change from darkness to light caused him to squint a little as he scanned the church for his parents. A few seconds later he had them in his sights.

Although the lads were late, the service was also a little late in starting, so Andrew had a few minutes to greet known faces. Some of the congregants knew and liked Tim, as he was a very likeable and normally respectful and respectable young man, but they were surprised to see him there. Tim felt awkward.

'I'm very glad,' said Andrew to June and July, having sought them out, 'to see that we have warm, amenable weather at present.'

June and July were dressed in beautiful green and yellow dresses respectively. They always dressed beautifully but not in a way that would attract undue attention. They always kept propriety and would have been unhappy to think that they were in any way presenting themselves inappropriately at church – a place of worship – or in general for that matter. The twins also always looked radiant, but in Andrew's perspective, June always seemed to bloom a little more with her golden-brown locks.

'I see that Tim's here with you, Andy,' remarked June after greeting him, a little bewildered and surprised. Tim took no notice.

'Evening, Tim,' greeted July, but she did not receive a response from him either.

'I asked Tim yesterday,' said Andrew, nudging Tim with his elbow, 'while we were fishing if he would like to join us for this evening's service.'

'What?' said Tim abruptly, looking at Andrew.

'July greeted you, Tim,' informed Andrew.

'Oh, hi,' greeted Tim in quite a disinterested fashion, not actually wanting to talk to anyone at that time and particularly not wanting to have to answer questions as to why he had decided to attend the church service. He quickly turned away and looked at some of the building's internal architecture.

July looked at Andrew a little puzzled, shrugged her shoulders and just kept quiet. June had a relatively discerning disposition and felt for Tim, as she realized that he might be feeling uneasy and out of place.

'Come on, Sis,' said June after having briefly glanced at Tim and then at Andrew, 'it's time we were seated. We'll speak to you later, Andy; nice seeing you here, Tim.'

The two girls shifted in with their parents across the aisle and one row back from where Andrew and Tim would be seated.

'Come on, Tim,' said Andrew, 'it's time we were seated too. My parents are just ahead and are keeping space for us.'

'Yeah, sure,' said Tim, not showing much enthusiasm at all.

Kelly and George were seated on the left side of the church, against the aisle, about midway forward.

'You're squeezing it a bit, aren't you?' mentioned Kelly as she and George shifted up to give the lads seating room.

'You know old Tim here, don't you?' answered Andrew with a droll look. 'Early for fishing and late for church! Besides, we stopped to chat to a few people as the service was delayed in starting.'

'Better late than never,' reasoned George in a sensible and fatherly manner.

'Evening, Aunt Kelly, Uncle George,' greeted Tim, the first purposeful words uttered by him since passing through the church doors. 'Andy boy kept me waiting and then said he wouldn't rush.' Tim rolled his eyes and forced a wry smile, causing Kelly and George to chuckle a little.

'No problem, Tim,' said Kelly, having leaned across Andrew

and put her hand on Tim's knee. 'We understand perfectly.'

'We're glad that you came,' added George warmly. 'We just hope—'

'Sh, Dad,' interrupted Andrew. 'The service is starting!'

Tim looked quickly forward, but it was clear from his demeanour that he was switched off to church!

Chapter 11

Mark's message

THEY all looked forward in time to see the minister, Mark Marsh, take his place at the rather bland box-shaped pulpit.

Mark was a middle-aged man, in his early forties and married to an attractive and quiet lady named Annabelle. He himself was somewhat on the quiet side too, even when he preached, yet he always came across with authority and purpose and never seemed to bore. He was an athletic person, enjoying outdoor sports and exercise, and had a good sense of humour that accompanied his composed manner.

Mark announced the programme for the evening and then stepped aside as the praise and worship was about to begin, the beginning of his sermon to follow.

Tim seemed to stare at him, as though trying to make out some of his character from a distance without any acquaintance. Apart from being able to see that he was dressed in the same fashion style as his uncle, Tim could not glean much from what he saw – clean shaven, short-trimmed brown hair and upright posture. It was not much to go by, but he still tried to x-ray as much as possible. Andrew noticed Tim staring but let him be.

During praise and worship, Tim's interest swung from the pianist to the singing leaders to the on-screen songs, even to Andrew. He never partook of the singing but took note of the words of the songs.

'What on earth am I doing here?' thought Tim, the question continually infesting his thoughts throughout the praise and worship. He was not drawn in by any of it at all and hoped that it would not go on for too long. Tim was already anxious not to spend more time there than was necessary.

The people sang and praised and worshiped the Lord in a joyous yet reverent way. The music was never rowdy and remained an accompaniment to the singing, carrying the congregation along purposefully. One aspect that hit Tim quite strongly about the people when they sang was that it seemed to be an outward action from within their beings, not just a shallow mouthing of words.

'Poor people,' thought Tim sympathetically, rationalising this all as being emotionalism. 'What do they actually see in all this?'

The praise and worship eventually came to an end, not too soon from Tim's perspective. Those who had been standing sat back down and settled while the accompanying musicians and two singing leaders also found their places.

Mark Marsh returned to the modest pulpit, looked at his notes and cleared his throat. He looked up just as the final murmurs of noise petered out, and silence fell upon the congregants in anticipation of the evening's sermon. Mark looked out across the congregation for a few seconds, the pews teeming with eager fish waiting for their nourishment and the bright, teardrop-shaped hanging lights shining from above on the colourful group below.

'Well, here we go,' thought Tim, first glancing at his watch and then at Andrew, whose attention at this stage was fixed on the minister, not noticing Tim's sideward glance. 'Hopefully I can still make happy hour!'

'Evening once again, folks,' said Mark calmly as Tim looked on with curiosity rather than genuine interest, but he gave the man his attention. 'I start by saying that man's own pride and arrogance has caused him to walk and operate in total ignorance. Ignorance, dear friends, is a lack of knowledge. I want to tell you a story that is a perfect illustration of what we, as people, do all the time. A young Jewish man went to his father and told him that he did not believe the Torah – that is the five books of Moses, the first five books of the Bible – and that he was rejecting his Jewish roots in favour of becoming an atheist. The young man's father was distressed so took his son to the local Rabbi and told him what his son had said. The Rabbi asked the young man if this was true, to which the young man said yes. The Rabbi thought for a few moments then said to the young man, "Ah! You have been listening to someone speak about communism and have done some research and decided to accept their ways?" to which the young man said no. The Rabbi sat back in his chair and thought for a few moments more, then said to the young man, "Ah! Then you must have had some input from Darwinian proponents and have decided to accept the evolutionary teachings?" to which the young man again said no.'

Tim had heard both the communistic thought, delivered through socialistic structures, and the evolutionary thought that was a great opponent to the very existence of the church under which he currently sat. He was interested in the outcome and continued to listen.

'The Rabbi sat back in his chair once again,' continued Mark, 'puzzled at the situation before him. He then sat forward and looked the young man in the eye. "Son," he said, "tell me what input *has* influenced you in this way?" The young man very proudly acknowledged no input other than his own opinion and decision. The Rabbi responded, "*Now* I understand! Son, you are mistaken and deceived, you are not an atheist – you are an ignoramus!"'

Laughter erupted from the congregation, and Tim could hear July's peculiar yet pleasant to the ear, rapid machinegun-fire laughter as she was sitting not too far from him.

'Ha, ha,' mumbled Tim sarcastically under his breath, loud enough that Andrew could hear, who gave him a quick glance. Tim was astute enough to realise that the minister was also referring to people who use their own opinions about God and the Bible. He knew that in this regard he was guilty.

'This folks,' said Mark, resuming his message after the laughter had ended, 'is true of our life's walk, not just with spiritual and scriptural aspects – although with regard to Scripture and God it probably manifests itself the most.'

This was what Tim had picked up, and he did not enjoy being poked in the ribs.

'How many times do we say much about that which we don't know?' asked Mark rhetorically. 'How often do we argue about that which we don't understand? And how regularly do we disregard and ignore fact and truth for the sake of our own comfort and convenience? Despite this my friends, reality and truth do not change. Neither does God's Word change to conform to our whims and fancies – truth is truth, reality is reality!

'If I had to ask you about the events surrounding Jesus' birth, you all would be able to give me pretty much the same story – the Virgin Mary gave birth to Jesus in Bethlehem, wise men brought gifts, He was born in a manger and an angel appeared to shepherds to tell them the good news. It's all pretty straight forward, isn't it? We hear about these events every year. The same old Christmas carols get sung and played over and over in our homes and malls, etc. But have we missed the very essence and purpose to which God was pointing? I believe we have. I believe the Jewish people missed the very point, and the Gentiles up to and including present time are doing the very same thing.'

Mark hesitated momentarily, either to gather his thoughts for the following points or to allow the preceding rhetorical question and answer to sink in.

'Let me substantiate my point,' continued Mark calmly. 'Let's read the first and second chapters of Matthew, followed by Luke 2:1–20.'

'Oh, boy!' thought Tim, having now become a little fidgety and disinterested. 'The whole Bible in one sitting, how wonderful!'

Tim had never really listened to more than one verse at a sitting, let alone almost three chapters! He was shocked to see that neither Andrew nor his uncle and aunt seemed to mind the reading of such a long passage, for they opened their Bibles and followed along as Mark read carefully and concisely with neither slur nor haste. He read the first two chapters of Matthew, which Tim thought took an age and was rather inappropriate, not to mention trivial, and followed it with further discourse.

'Let us now read Luke 2:1–20,' said Mark, who according to Tim's perception seemed to think the importance of conveying his message was far more important than finishing on time. This was not something he fancied much with happy hour approaching at Down and Out's!

Tim looked at his watch again and though the hands had moved closer to happy hour, he shot a second glance as he felt that they had already been sitting in church for an eternity. While Mark was paging in his Bible, Tim glanced over his right shoulder in the direction of where the twins, June and July, were seated. He spotted them diagonally behind him also ready to follow in their Bibles. Tim's glance caught July's attention as she was nearest the aisle. She gave him a quick smile, her bright cheeks puffing slightly at the sides as she did so, illuminating her expression. Tim turned abruptly forward again, just as Mark began reading from the book of Luke.

'Luke 2:1–20,' said Mark in a monotone and then with a slightly raised voice began. "'In those days Caesar Augustus issued a decree that a census should be taken of the entire Roman world. (This was the first census that took place while Quirinius was governor of Syria.) And everyone went to his own town to register. So Joseph also went up from the town of Nazareth in Galilee to Judea, to Bethlehem the town of David, because he belonged to the house and line of David. He went there to register with Mary, who was pledged to be married to him and was expecting a child. While they were there, the time came for the baby to be born, and she gave birth to her firstborn, a son. She wrapped him in cloths and placed him in a manger, because there was no room for them in the inn. And there were shepherds living out in the fields nearby, keeping watch over their flocks at night. An angel of the Lord appeared to them, and the glory of the Lord shone around them, and they were terrified. But the angel said to them, 'Do not be afraid. I bring you good news of great joy that will be for all the people. Today in the town of David a Saviour has been born to you; he is Christ [or Messiah] the Lord. This will be a sign to you: You will find a baby wrapped in cloths and lying in a manger.' Suddenly a great company of the heavenly host appeared with the angel, praising God and saying, 'Glory to God in the highest, and on earth peace to men on whom his favour rests.' When the angels had left them and gone into heaven, the shepherds said to one another, 'Let's go to Bethlehem and see this thing that has happened, which the Lord has told us about.' So they hurried off and found Mary and Joseph, and the baby, who was lying in the manger. When they had seen him, they spread the word concerning what had been told them about this child, and all who heard it were amazed at what the shepherds said to them. But Mary treasured up all these things and pondered them in her heart. The shepherds returned, glorifying and praising God for all the things they had heard and seen, which were just as they had been told.'" Mark slowed, emphasising the last few words of the passage. He stopped and looked up, about to deliver a powerful point that would leave Tim shocked!

Chapter 12

The sermon continues

'**YEAH**, so what, you might say!' boomed Mark in a tone that shook Tim from his slumbering, and expressed the possible sarcastic ridicule that a person might direct at what he was saying and reading. 'You have just read the same story that we already know!'

'Been there, heard that,' thought Tim with amusement, having been revived by the change in Mark's speech and relating to what he had just said as those were his exact sentiments.

'Well, that's not entirely true,' continued Mark, changing his tone back to what it was before he woke Tim, 'because what I've just read is not just an event recorded in the annals of history. It's not just a period of time in the history of mankind. It *is* the fulfilment of prophecy – prophecy made more than 600 years before its time!'

'Surely you don't believe that!' thought Tim, shocked by the statement. 'Six hundred years before its time – not possible! I think I'm now hearing the nonsense that I alluded to at Ailen Oak Lake!'

'In these few chapters,' continued Mark steadfastly, 'we have the fulfilment of seven prophecies, which are only a small amount of the many. What we need to understand is that all the prophecies surrounding the Messiah, Jesus, were recorded in the Old Testament. In those days there was no New Testament.'

Mark paused and took a breath, giving the impression that he was about to deliver a profound statement.

'The New Testament,' said Mark with distinct clarity, 'is in the Old Testament contained, and the Old Testament is in the New Testament expounded and explained. The Jewish people had the Old Testament that contained everything they needed in order to recognise who the Messiah was, or is. The Christ, also called Messiah or Saviour, had to come from the line of David. Here we have an account of the genealogy of Jesus – fourteen generations from Abraham to David; fourteen generations from David to the exile to Babylon; and fourteen generations from the exile to the Christ, Jesus. For those of you who have done some study in Bible numerics, you will know that the number seven is God's number, and the number six is man's number. Three groups of fourteen generations equals forty-two generations – from Abraham, the beginning of the Jews, to Jesus, the beginning of redemption. This is interesting, because seven multiplied by six equals forty-two, and we know that Jesus is both God and man!'

Tim had heard this kind of talk from the Renshaws but had not paid much attention to it. He now listened a little more closely and with more interest, but he was sure it was nothing more than far-fetched foolishness.

'A question we also need to ask is this,' said Mark. 'How could any baby influence such circumstances? A baby cannot choose where they are born or what their name will be. This occurrence had to be God sovereignly working and moving.'

'That's at least fair comment,' thought Tim, who was listening with definite reservation.

'Let's now have a look at the physical impact the birth of Jesus had on the people of Israel,' said Mark calmly, continuing with more analysis and intent on going through the rest of his message without hesitation or pause.

'Point number one,' said Mark, starting his analysis and beginning to read from his Bible. 'Matthew 2:1–3, "After Jesus was born in Bethlehem in Judea, during the time of King Herod, Magi [wise men] from the east came to Jerusalem and asked, 'Where is the one who has been born king of the Jews? We saw His star in the east and have come to worship Him.' When King Herod heard this he was disturbed, and all Jerusalem with him."

'How often do you think wise men came asking – "Where is the one who has been born king of the Jews? We saw His star and have come to worship Him."? Obviously not often enough, because when Herod heard this he was disturbed and *all* Jerusalem with him. This visit by the wise men and the purpose thereof must have been the talk of the entire area. The people were probably talking about it, arguing about it, questioning it – to anyone and everyone and probably all day! The circumstance was so disturbing that Herod had *all* the peoples' chief priests and teachers of the law brought in to find out where the Christ, the Messiah or Saviour, was to be born. This is like the American president bringing in all the F.B.I. agents, C.I.A. agents and Chiefs of Staff!

'Herod learned that the Christ was to be born in Bethlehem in Judea,' said Mark, looking back down at his Bible and continuing to read verse five and six. '"For this is what the prophet has written: 'But you, Bethlehem, in the land of Judah, are by no means least among the rulers of Judah; for out of you will come a ruler who will be the shepherd of my people Israel." This is referenced from Micah 5:2.'

Mark did not seem to take a breath and went straight into his next point, firing away.

'Point number two,' said Mark. 'Luke 2:8–18, "And there were shepherds living out in the fields nearby, keeping watch over their flocks at night. An angel of the Lord appeared to them, and the glory of the Lord shone around them, and they were terrified. But the angel said to them, 'Do not be afraid. I bring you good news of great joy that will be for all the people. Today in the town of David a Saviour has been born to you; He is Christ the Lord [or Messiah]. This will be a sign to you: you will find a baby wrapped in cloths and lying in a manger.' Suddenly a great company of the heavenly host appeared with the angel, praising God and saying, 'Glory to God in the highest, and on earth peace to men on whom His favour rests.' When the angels had left them and gone into heaven, the shepherds said to one another, 'Let's go to Bethlehem and see this thing that has happened, which the Lord has told us about.' So they hurried off and found Mary and Joseph, and the baby, who was lying in the manger. When they had seen Him, they spread the word concerning what had been told them about this child, and all who heard it were amazed at what the shepherds said to them." This too, connected with the wise men, must have had all the people talking. The second extraordinary and separate happening proclaiming a King, a Messiah, a Saviour – and both similar. Both claim a new born baby and both directing to Bethlehem in Judea!

'Point number three,' said Mark purposefully, a look of concentration on his face as he moved straight on, as though any form of break would disrupt continuity and sabotage what was being said. 'Even a lapse in time did not dampen the events that had taken place, especially not in the mind of Herod! But even if it had amongst the people, a cataclysmic devastation was about to hit them that was initiated, or ordered, as a result of the events that had taken place. Bethlehem was again about to become the talk of the land and again in connection with the Christ.'

Tim sat listening, his heart beating strongly. He had never stopped to really listen to this stuff before, certainly not in a way that he would have considered the truthfulness of what people claimed it to be nor what it would have meant to those directly affected by it at the time. He hated what he was hearing, for if real, it could not be overridden by his own opinion about it. Just like in front of the crackling fire at Charon Canyon, he felt that what he was hearing had personal implications attached, an undesirable aspect that warred in his spirit.

'Matthew 2:7–8,12,16–18 reads,' said Mark, continuing unflinchingly and transitioning seamlessly back to reading from his Bible again, '"Then Herod called the Magi secretly and found out from them the exact time the star had appeared. He sent them to Bethlehem and said, 'Go and make a careful search for the child. As soon as you find him, report to me, so that I too may go and worship him'. And having been warned in a dream not to go back to Herod, they returned to their country by another route. When Herod realised that he had been outwitted by the Magi, he was furious, and he gave orders to kill all the boys in Bethlehem and its vicinity who were two years old and under, in accordance with the time he had learned from the Magi. Then what was said through the prophet Jeremiah was fulfilled: 'A voice is heard in Ramah, weeping and great mourning, Rachel weeping for her children and refusing to be comforted, because they are no more.'" This is referenced from Jeremiah 31:15.'

'This must be what he had said earlier,' thought Tim, recognising the possible connection, as the verse was written in the New Testament but had been taken and quoted from the Old Testament. 'The New Testament is in the Old Testament contained, and the Old Testament is in the New Testament expounded and explained.'

'Can you imagine the devastation this must have had on the people of that area!' said Mark. 'I don't think many of us have truly stopped to think about the effect or impact this must have had on the lives of the people. For the entire earthly walk of Jesus the effect of this destruction must have still been evident in Bethlehem and the surrounding areas. Why then did the Jews reject Jesus as the Messiah? Why after the visit by the wise men, the word of the Lord to the shepherds telling them that a Saviour has been born to them, He is Christ the Lord, and the fulfilment of prophecy – why did they not recognise Jesus as the Saviour?

'Firstly, they did not recognise Him as the Saviour because they did not understand the requirements, purpose and plan that God had laid out that the Saviour was to fulfil. Secondly, they were religious but did not know the ways of God. The high-minded arrogance and pride of the religious hierarchy could not and would not see the truth of Scripture revealed before their very eyes. Had they done so, Jesus would have toppled their status quo, and they wanted the recognition, the money, the power and the seats of distinction and honour for themselves. Thirdly, if they had studied the prophecies of Scripture regarding the Christ in relation to Jesus, instead of trying to downplay and eventually destroy Him, they might have recognised Him for who and what He was. Fourthly, they obviously rationalised away the events that had taken place – the very announcement by God that He had sent the Messiah, the Saviour!'

Tim recoiled at hearing this, for if this religion was true, salvation a requirement and Jesus the Redeemer, all four points could be tacked to his chest. He had never bothered to understand the requirements, for he had never seen them as being relevant. He was not religious but knew that he put himself first and did not want someone taking his seat of honour. He had never studied Scripture, having ignored it completely. And lastly, he too, even while sitting listening to Mark speak, had downplayed the events as being irrelevant. Tim put his hand on his nose and closed his eyes, his chest burning with conflict. He felt that he had heard enough.

'But remember,' added Mark, not tiring and remaining focused on the purpose of his message, 'Jesus' disciples only grasped and fully understood all the issues after Jesus had risen from the dead – and they had been around Him for three years!'

Mark now took a breath and looked seriously at the attentive congregation, the bright and illuminating lights still beaming upon them from on high.

'Why am I telling you all this, my dear friends?' said Mark as he began presenting his concluding remarks. 'Surely, you say, what have the Jews rejecting Jesus got to do with us? Surely you don't put us in the same boat? We haven't rejected Jesus! My friends,' continued Mark, having lowered the tone of his voice a little, 'listen carefully. If you haven't accepted Jesus as your Lord and Saviour, you've rejected Him. Acknowledgement of who He is, is not good enough. We, folks, have the New Testament, which the Jews didn't have at the time. The understanding of salvation – it's been explained to us. The purpose of God's working – it's been clearly revealed to us in the New Testament, although it's all present in the Old Testament as well. Am I saying that God rejected the Jewish people and the nation of Israel as a result?

Not at all, for Paul says in Romans 1:16 that salvation is first for the Jew, then for the Gentile. But what I *am* asking and saying is this – are the Gentiles not making the same mistakes? Are we not also missing it? Are we not conducting ourselves with the same high-minded arrogance and pride of the religious hierarchy of that time? I believe we are! I believe that we're doing worse than what they did, because we have more than what they had. Jesus *is* the Messiah. He *is* the Saviour. You must be born again!'

Chapter 13

Contention brewing at Roccocoa's

MARK folded his notes and closed his Bible, having ended his message.

'Hallelujah and good night!' thought Tim with deep sarcasm, desperately wanting to leave. He had listened but could not put it all together. His spirit was troubled, for what he had felt would end up having personal implications did have – that you must be born again! He could not understand this nor wanted to, for it would mean a change in his life, but for what? So Christianity had had an impact on the societies that had fully embraced it, but was it not just another religion? Tim could not see the difference and even though, according to Andrew, Christianity did not bring bondage upon mankind but rather liberty, there would no doubt be aspects attached. Again, what he could not grasp he would not go for, and what he could not see he would not surrender to. Tim stood defiant. He looked at his watch and realised there was no point in trying to make Down and Out's, as happy hour was nearly halfway through and by the time he would manage to get there, it would almost be over. Nevertheless, he wanted to get out of there, and fast!

Andrew looked at Tim after Mark had concluded with a short prayer, everyone now starting to stir and buzz as they had done before the message began. He could see that Tim did not look too impressed, a stubborn look on his face, and he seemed to be a little hot under the collar. The Renshaws and Tim stood up and moved out of the pew, with George and Kelly immediately heading off to help with the refreshments. Tim turned to speak to Andrew but heard the beautiful, clear voice of June from over his shoulder.

'I hope you didn't find the message too much to your disliking, Tim?' said June politely, she and July having come up behind them. 'Andy, do you and Tim want to join July and I in the hall for some tea or coffee?'

'No!' spat Tim, whirling around in a flash. 'We're just leaving. I have no more business here and have things to do! So, no, but thanks anyway for asking,' added Tim more respectfully, suddenly realising the harshness of his response.

'Absolutely fine, Tim,' said June quickly, diffusing any conflict in a flash as she could see that Andrew looked disturbed and unappreciative of Tim's response to her. June glanced at Andrew and indicated with her facial expression that it was okay.

'Please do me a favour, June,' asked Andrew. 'Give my folks the message that I'll see them at home – Tim and I decided to leave early!' Andrew gave June a little smile, which she seemed to be able to interpret.

'Certainly, Andy,' replied June agreeably, 'no problem at all, and have a good week.'

'You too, Tim,' added July quickly, and she disappeared with the fleet-footedness of a doe before a response from Tim could be given, her sister in tow.

Andrew and Tim weaved their way through the mingling congregation and headed for the doorway, which seemed to draw Tim like a magnet as they transitioned from the light of the church into the darkness of the night. Andrew hesitated for a few seconds once outside, his eyes having to adjust to the darkness that now surrounded them. To Andrew's surprise, the clouds had come in swiftly, severing the bond of heaven's bright and brilliantly illuminated expanse from them. Only the pathway lamps and parking bay lights provided illumination to their steps.

'Wow!' exclaimed Andrew, looking up. 'I wasn't expecting this. I know that a storm was forecast, but from the weather we had before church, I thought it would hold off and be a clear night. Where did all the heavy cloud suddenly come from? Tim, did you expect to see such threatening clouds tonight?'

Tim did not answer, he just kept walking towards Andrew's car, eager to have the fading chatter coming from the church building behind him lessen even more.

Andrew pressed the central-locking button on his car key upon reaching his car, but Tim was in such a hurry to open the door that he yanked on the handle before the door had been properly unlocked, jamming the lock as a result.

'Patience, dear cousin,' said Andrew, pressing the button a second time to release the jam. 'You won't get in that way.'

Tim was in no mood for joking and again did not answer. He was in Andrew's car and buckled up in seconds, the complete opposite of what had transpired when he had climbed in to come to church.

They were soon out of Ailensbury Christian Fellowship's parking lot and onto the lonely auxiliary road that led to the central part of town. For Tim, it could not have been too soon, and he sat staring out the passenger window brooding, his elbow on the armrest and chin in hand.

'"If you haven't accepted Jesus as your Lord and Saviour, you've rejected Him!"' groused Tim sarcastically, breaking the silence as he repeated Mark's words. '"Jesus *is* the Messiah. He *is* the Saviour. You must be born again!" And for that I gave up happy hour!'

'Come, Tim,' said Andrew, realising that something had not jelled well with him. 'I'll take you to Roccocoa's for coffee and for whatever else you would like.'

'I don't need coffee, nitwit,' moaned Tim, a degree of irritation noticeably evident even though he was now trying to make a joke. 'I missed happy hour!'

'I said I was buying!' responded Andrew coaxingly, glad that Tim had not lost his sense of humour altogether.

'Sure, why not,' accepted Tim with disgruntlement. 'You've ruined my evening already. What could be better than an alcohol-free, acorn-tasting hot drink! Come, come, step on it a little, will you!'

Andrew soon pulled into the parking lot of the Sunny Valley shopping complex, the main shopping hub for the community of Ailensbury. It was a large, double story shopping mall with multiple entrances that radiated their existence into the dark night. Joined to the shopping complex was an annex housing a number of bistros and coffee shops that had external access to them. Although they were part of the complex, they were able to operate independently.

Andrew did not have to scout for an empty parking bay, as being a Sunday evening, the only places open were the restaurants, coffee shops and the two main grocery stores. There was an open parking bay in front of the neatly paved walkway, just to the left of Roccocoa's, and Andrew carefully navigated his way in, bringing his car to a stop with the front spoiler only an inch from the edge of the walkway.

'The clouds have really rolled in, Tim,' said Andrew with a degree of concern, looking up at the heavens. 'Looks like a big storm brewing. At least we're parked here by the walkway, not far from Roccocoa's.' Tim did not answer, he just climbed out the car and shut the door with a little more force than Andrew thought was necessary.

The outside temperature had dropped substantially, and there was quite a nip in the air. The evergreen trees lining the walkway were swaying slightly in the light breeze that now blew in from the North. They seemed to shiver as if cold and ill at ease, almost anticipating the brewing storm.

'Despite the looks,' said Andrew, pulling the collar of his jacket up to shield his neck, the light breeze having caught him on the back of his neck just as he climbed out his car, sending an instant shiver down his spine, 'I hope we aren't going to have too much of a storm! Anyway, Roccocoa's is warm and sheltered. Ah, Roccocoa's! I can smell the coffee and double thick ice-cream malts already!' Tim just glanced at Andrew, not really interested in the weather or Roccocoa's, being indifferent and distant in his thoughts.

The two lads reached the warm, enticing bistro with its old-fashioned style windows and arched shade covers over them. The lights from inside were creating shadows on the walkway outside as they beamed out, only hindered by the latticed window frames. The cast-iron tables outside had already been cleared and cleaned and the wooden umbrellas closed and tied, the store-branded printing being obscured by the folds in the canvas. To Andrew, this place always reminded him of what a bistro must have been like many decades ago, and he thought it much like the landscape of a French sidewalk that also belonged in a puzzle.

'Bonjour,' greeted the friendly waiter as the two lads entered, the old-fashioned doorbells tingling. 'Can I see you to a table, sirs?' The waiter's black, curly hair that was slightly greying at the sides added character to his beaming smile and facial characteristics.

From over Tim's shoulder Andrew responded, giving the waiter a hearty smile of his own. The waiter motioned with his hand and led the lads to a table at the side, near one of the windows.

Andrew always found the warmth of service at Roccocoa's complemented the warm, drawing character the bistro provided, with its exquisite Imbuia cabinets and bamboo and woven-reed tables and chairs all stained dark to match the cabinets.

'This is quite pleasant,' commented Andrew after the waiter had left, 'it's not crowed at all.'

'Yeah, I suppose so,' mumbled Tim gruffly as he looked about, taking in the fact that the bistro was less than half full.

Tim cased a little once they were seated, and for the first time since marching out of the church earlier that evening, took notice of his surroundings, glancing particularly across at the counter where the mouth-watering bakes were nicely displayed on round cake stands or in glass dishes.

'You're welcome to whatever you would like,' offered Andrew generously, noticing Tim's interest.

'Thanks, Andy,' responded Tim with a clipped smile. 'I am a little hungry so would like something, but I'm not yet sure what I would like.'

'Well, look at the menu,' said Andrew with a chuckle, 'or go and take a look at the display, that should help the indigestion – I mean indecision!' They promptly looked at the menu.

Tim, who seemed to be staring at the menu, suddenly put it down and leaned forward.

'So what if Jesus is the Saviour, Christ, Messiah, whatever you call Him!' burst out Tim in a low voice but quite aggressively, much to Andrew's surprise. 'This religious nonsense has made me nauseous!'

Tim sat up again because the waiter returned to take their order, much to Andrew's relief as he had been caught off guard. He felt that the comment was contentious and did not quite know how to respond immediately. A peal of thunder suddenly ripped through the sky causing the windows to rattle and everyone to look up.

'Good gracious!' said the waiter. 'I did not expect a storm this evening after the earlier weather conditions, despite the predictions!'

'Neither did I!' exclaimed Andrew, his heart pounding quite rapidly from the surprise as he briefly looked out the window. 'It was most unexpected!'

'Ready to order, gents?' asked the waiter politely after the brief interruption, resuming his original intent and looking from one to the other, his manner resembling that of a well-educated butler.

'I'll have a strawberry double thick ice-cream malt, please,' requested Andrew quickly, 'with cream and a marshmallow.'

'A marshmallow!' exclaimed Tim in amazement.

'Yes, a marshmallow,' returned Andrew, producing a friendly smile. 'Why not?'

'And for you, Sir?' asked the waiter without flinching at what Tim seemed to think was a bizarre and juvenile request from

Andrew, his professional objectiveness holding steady.

'I'll have a standard cappuccino – with an acorn, please,' requested Tim with a wry grin.

'Excuse me?' said the waiter, looking up from his order book, not quite believing what he had just heard. 'Please repeat that!'

'Don't mind him,' responded Andrew, laughing. 'He just wants a plain cappuccino, thanks.'

'Very good, Sir,' said the waiter, nodding his head once. He repeated the order before gathering the menus from the table and leaving. Andrew and Tim gave him a quick glance upon his departure, enough to see him shaking his head as he ripped the order sheet from his book and headed for the kitchen.

'Getting back to your statement, Tim,' said Andrew after a brief moment's contemplation. 'Christ and Messiah both mean Saviour. This isn't religious nonsense. It has no jargon or ambiguity at all. God doesn't want religious people, He wants righteous people! We can only be made righteous by accepting the atoning work that Jesus accomplished on the Cross of Calvary and then by walking in the ways that God instructs us through His Word, the Bible. It was probably the mushroom, salami and *escargot* pizza you ate for lunch that's made you feel nauseous,' quickly added Andrew with a brief chuckle.

'Smart Aleck!' retorted Tim gruffly. 'Funny ha–ha! Religious and righteous also mean the same thing, so why separate them?'

'Nope,' replied Andrew, 'the words religious and righteous don't mean the same thing. Religious – it's a habitual, ritualistic practise. Righteous – it's a way of life, a behaviour, a lifestyle through a relationship that is in right standing with God. In Jesus' time the Pharisees and Sadducees were the leaders of the people and the rulers of the Temple. They were highly revered by all the towns' people, yet John the Baptist called them a brood of vipers, and Jesus warned of their hypocrisy and poison. Being religious and being righteous are two completely separate things!'

Tim leaned back against the woven-reed back of his chair, making it flex slightly and offer an objecting squeak. He sat quiet for a few seconds.

Andrew suddenly leaned forward and started to look intently out one of the windows. A light rain having now started could be seen as it steadily fell gracefully past the shopping centre's glowing lights placed strategically along the pathways and in the parking lot.

'Never seen a light rain before, Andy boy?' joked Tim as he looked to see what had attracted Andrew's attention. 'Hmmm,' mumbled Tim, going on with the analysis of his thoughts. 'Okay, so let's say, for argument sake—'

'Wait, Tim!' interrupted Andrew, jumping up and heading for the door. 'There goes Mark Marsh! I wonder if he would like to join us?'

'But, wait!' cried Tim in objection, stretching forth his hand as he half stood up, the thought of seeing Mark Marsh for a second time that night churning his stomach and already creating a brew of contention stronger than the coffee Roccocoa's could offer!

Enter Mark Marsh

TIM'S objection was to no avail as Andrew had darted out the door in an instant, not noticing his protest. He flopped back in his chair, the bamboo and woven-reed echoing his objecting sentiments loud and clear.

'This is all I need!' moaned Tim lamentingly as he combed his fingers through his dark-brown hair. 'More archaic "Greek" from this donkey and twice in one night!'

In frustration Tim called to their waiter, who was standing nearby, and he promptly came over.

'You don't perhaps have any gin or whiskey do you?' asked Tim sarcastically.

'Sorry, Sir,' replied the waiter with sharp wit, looking at Tim with a raised eyebrow, 'we only serve what is needed *after* gin or whiskey – care to add another cup to your order?'

'Sure, why not,' replied Tim, amused by the cool and collected reply he received. 'My cousin's paying – and I'll have one of your chocolate chip muffins along with it, please.'

'Certainly, Sir – coming up,' responded the waiter, shaking

his head again after leaving Tim. On his way to the kitchen he pulled a face and made some sort of gesture to a fellow waitress.

In the meantime, Andrew had caught up to Mark. They had stopped just inside the entrance of one of the large, illuminated entrances, out of the rain, which had now started to come down at a much harder rate. Andrew had been explaining the situation to Mark, not going into much detail about Tim's behaviour, other than to mention that he had been irritated by Mark's message but had now started asking questions.

'So, if you have some spare time available to join us,' said Andrew, 'it would be well appreciated, at least from my side! You may be better able to answer the questions or put the information in a more understandable manner than I could.'

'Certainly,' agreed Mark after looking at his watch. 'I just need to pop into Sunny Valley supermarket. We're running out of dog food for Machie, so Annabelle asked me to stop in here on the way home from church. I'll give Anna a call and let her know that I'll be delayed.'

'That will be fantastic!' exclaimed Andrew, well pleased.

'I'll meet you at Roccocoa's in a minute or two,' said Mark, who started to move off in the direction of the supermarket, nearly bumping into someone as he was still looking at Andrew.

'If you don't mind,' called Andrew, 'I'll wait here for you, the rain's bucketing down now and maybe it will have subsided a little by the time you've finished your shopping.'

Mark gave Andrew a thumbs up as he turned and headed off down the walkway.

'Where the heck is Andrew?' thought Tim as he looked at his watch. He turned and began peering through the window, the presenting picture a blur of smudged images as a result of the heavy rain.

Just as he was about to turn back, he was able to make out the familiar figure of Andrew, who was accompanied by someone carrying a shopping bag. They were moving quickly along the pathway. They entered Roccocoa's, immediately losing their hunchbacks. Andrew's eyes lit up when he saw Tim, but Tim did not seem to share the same feeling. Nonetheless, he was glad to see Andrew as he was his lift home and the sponsor of his intended indulgence.

'Have you ever heard of the saying, "Two's company, three's a crowd", Andy boy?' asked Tim sarcastically, not caring if he came across as offensive to anyone who heard him. 'I've been waiting for you for ages!'

Mark did not hear Tim as he was a few paces behind Andrew, for which Andrew was rather glad.

'Mark, this is Timothy Nicholls, my cousin,' introduced Andrew, having ignored Tim's comment but given him a sharp look. 'Tim, meet Mark Marsh, Ailensbury Christian Fellowship's senior pastor.'

'Please, sit down,' said Tim rudely, giving a half wave in a totally disinterested manner, not bothering to get up. 'The way the night's been going for me, I couldn't have asked for a more pleasant surprise!'

'Come on, Tim!' objected Andrew as he looked at him, a pained and dissatisfied look clearly evident. 'That's not quite like you!' Andrew was immediately on tender hooks as he knew that Tim, who was normally an easy going and accommodating person, could be really difficult and otherwise when he wanted to be.

Mark and Andrew sat down just as the waiter arrived with their order, including Tim's additional request. He placed Andrew's strawberry double thick ice-cream malt before him, for which he received a grateful thanks, and turned to Tim.

'Here you are, Sir,' said the waiter, placing Tim's order on the table. 'One cappuccino, one after gin tonic and a chocolate chip muffin to go along with it.'

Andrew and Mark first looked at the waiter, who maintained a straight face, then at Tim.

'Don't ask me to explain,' said Tim, having burst out laughing, loud enough to draw the attention of the nearby patrons.

'Nor I,' said the waiter, still maintaining a straight face, 'as I could not! Anything for you, Sir?' he asked, immediately turning the spotlight onto Mark.

'What would you like, Mark?' asked Andrew quickly. 'A cappuccino or ice-cream malt, or would you like the menu?'

'A hot cappuccino would be lovely, thanks,' replied Mark with a smile. 'In this weather I couldn't think of eating ice-cream!'

'Anything more for you, Sir?' asked the waiter as he noticed Tim looking slyly at him. 'An after whiskey pick-me-up perhaps?'

'No thanks,' replied Tim, promptly pointed at Mark, 'but perhaps you could also bring Mr Marsh here a *marsh*mallow with his cappuccino. He may just be a *mellow* kind of guy.'

'I don't mind laughing at myself,' said Mark, joining Tim's chuckle with a chuckle of his own. 'I like a good sense of humour.'

The waiter went off shaking his head once more, returning a minute later with Mark's cappuccino.

'Tim, aren't we fortunate that Mark was able to join us?' said Andrew a little hesitantly.

'Oh brother,' snorted Tim under his breath, 'aren't we!'

'Mark's wife, Annabelle, was running out of dog food,' continued Andrew uneasily, having heard Tim's snorted comment, 'so he just popped down to Sunny Valley on his way home from church to buy some for her.'

'Your wife eats dog food?' remarked Tim quickly as he sat up in his chair, a naughty look on his face.

'That did sound a bit funny, didn't it?' replied Mark as he started to laugh. 'Andy, you'd better be careful. If people start declining Anna's dinner invitations, I'll know why!'

Andrew placed his hand on his forehead and just shook his head.

'As I was saying, cousin, before you so rudely interrupted me,' suddenly started Tim with a raised voice, startling both Andrew and Mark after the light-hearted banter, 'was that let's say for argument sake that Jesus is the Messiah, the Saviour, what difference does it make to me, and why should I care?'

Andrew was quite taken aback at the forthrightness of Tim and his preparedness to boldly continue the discussion, but something had stirred within Tim once again, and he wanted an answer even if he was not going to agree with it. He hated the sight of Mark and did not want to hear from him but fought to put down his pride, a small voice telling him that he did not know all things.

'Do you mind if I answer?' asked Mark, looking at Andrew and then at Tim.

'Not at all, not at all,' responded Tim quickly. 'This discussion wouldn't be a discussion if you weren't permitted your penny's worth!'

'Thanks, Tim,' said Mark, Andrew having hung his head and covered his brow with his hand again. 'Who needs a more welcoming invitation to speak than that!'

Tim produced a disdainful smile, knowing that he was being offhand and downright rude. His tongue had unleashed an ugly comment, despite his decision to put down his pride only seconds before. Tim was suddenly convicted and recoiled at the realisation of his conduct, tussling within himself to be self-controlled and maintain civility.

'The word Saviour is being used,' continued Mark, climbing straight in without waiting for a further response, 'but what is a saviour? The word saved is used by people when they get out of trouble. For example – saved by the skin of my teeth; I was saved by the bell; he saved me from embarrassment; you saved my life. Something or someone has been the role player in preventing death, destruction or trouble. An unwanted situation or circumstance has been eliminated or avoided. The same is true of the biblical term, Saviour. That's why born again Christians use the term, "I'm saved". So to answer your question, let's look into what it is that we are saved from and why Jesus plays the central part in this.'

Tim was a little taken by Mark's firm and decisive confidence. Helped by his own resolve, he started to listen without trying to make any further wisecracks, although inside, he still had an aversion to Mark and to what he was hearing.

'Andrew, do you perhaps have a Bible with you?' asked Mark.

'I should have,' replied Andrew as he leaned down next to him and unzipped his small, blue carry bag. 'Yes, here it is!' said Andrew triumphantly as he brought it out after scratching in the small bag for a few seconds. 'This is my Bible that I take with me to church.'

'Ah, that's good news indeed!' said Mark in a satisfied tone of voice. 'Please read for us John 1:1,2 and John 1:14, will you?'

'Certainly,' agreed Andrew, 'no problem.' He swiftly found the verses Mark had mentioned and prepared to read.

Chapter 15

Law and Grace

'JOHN 1:1,2,' said Andrew and began reading. "'In the beginning was the Word, and the Word was with God, and the Word was God. He was with God in the beginning.'" Andrew paused for a second then continued with verse fourteen. "'The Word became flesh and made His dwelling among us. We have seen His glory, the glory of the One and Only, who came from the Father, full of grace and truth.'"

'Ha!' remarked Tim quite loudly as Andrew stopped reading and looked up at Mark. 'It sounds like John was confused!'

'Actually,' said Mark calmly as he began to expound these verses carefully, 'these two verses are quite amazing, for they reveal a fundamental aspect about Jesus and the Bible, the Word of God. Firstly, "In the beginning was the Word" – this means that it has always been there. Secondly, "the Word was with God" – implies two separate entities. And thirdly, "the Word was God" – means that God is made up of more than one person. Verse fourteen expounds this mystery and makes it clear. It says, firstly, "the Word became flesh" – which means He became human. Secondly, "and made His dwelling among us" – which means lived on earth. And thirdly, "We have seen His glory" – whose glory? "the glory of the One and Only, who came from the Father, full of grace and truth". Jesus is, therefore, the Living Word and, therefore, is also God. If the Son is full of grace and truth, then the Word is full of grace and truth. Let's find this grace and truth in the Word of God.'

'So what you're trying to tell me,' remarked Tim in astonishment, leaning back in his chair, his one arm hanging limp over the side of the backrest, 'and wanting me to believe, is that *this* Bible is Jesus!'

'What John is saying, not me,' countered Mark, 'is that the very principles, concepts, precepts, commands and laws that make up the Bible are not only words spoken by God but in very essence of nature and character *is* God. Jesus, who is also God, has revealed this through becoming a man and demonstrating it to us. The very truth of the Word was shown, and the very grace of God was given. Andrew, please read Ephesians 2:8,9 for us.'

Andrew nimbly paged in his Bible and in a few seconds was at the requested verses.

'This Paul is saying to the saved,' added Mark quickly before Andrew began reading.

'Ephesians 2:8,9,' began Andrew. '"For it is by grace you have been saved, through faith – and this not from yourselves, it is the gift of God – not by works, so that no-one can boast."'

'Paul says,' continued Mark in his exegesis, '"it is by *grace* you have been saved" and John says – we have just read it – "we have seen His glory, the glory of the One and Only, who came from the Father, full of *grace* and truth." Therefore, with confidence we can say that Jesus is this grace, and that it is by Jesus we have been saved.'

'Yeah, so what!' snorted Tim rather rudely. 'What do I need to be saved from?'

'Sin!' replied Andrew instantly, somewhat surprised at the question, having thought the answer would have been obvious.

'Who's to determine what is sin and what is not?' countered Tim defiantly, his chair squeaking with objection as he rocked against the backrest.

'Another way of putting it,' said Mark, who seemed to understand the question, 'is like this. Sin is the breaking of the law. It's the committing of an offence against a set standard. When you drive through a stoplight, you break the law. Why do you break the law? Because you know that the law says that if the robot is red, you must stop. If a traffic officer is there when you commit the offence against the law, what do you think will happen?'

'He'll obviously give you a fine,' replied Tim, a little bemused by the simplicity of the question.

'Exactly!' confirmed Mark, keeping focus on the purpose of his question. 'He'll fine you according to the offence you committed. God works on the same principle. He too has established law – the Ten Commandments. Every principle, precept and character trait of God fits within His commandments, and every possible sin under heaven will fall within the classification of one of the Ten Commandments. Romans 3:19,20 says, "Now we know that whatever the law says, it says to those who are under the law, so that every mouth may be silenced and the whole world held accountable to God. Therefore no-one will be declared righteous in His sight by observing the law; rather, through the law we become conscious of sin." You see, God's standard is so high that it's impossible for us on our own to match up to it. In Romans 3:23 it continues, "for all have sinned and fall short of the glory of God."'

'Ah!' said Tim, who seemed to be interested in what Mark had just said. 'So, what is God's fine then?'

'Paul tells us the answer in Romans 6:23,' replied Mark, 'where he says, "For the wages of sin is death". This is the penalty, or fine, for breaking God's law. But, this is where the mercy of God and the grace of Jesus come in because God makes a way out for us. Paul continues in this verse and says, "For the wages of sin is death, but the gift of God is eternal life in Christ Jesus our Lord."'

'Great!' exclaimed Tim, sitting up and flinging his hands in the air, animated triumph written all over his face. 'Why then do I need to worry about the wages of sin?'

'God doesn't ignore or excuse the sin,' answered Andrew. 'Jesus Christ paid the price on our behalf because the fine for the offence of sin is too great for us to pay. But, if we'll not accept His payment on our behalf, God will not credit us with it.'

This was some food for thought and Tim pondered it for a few seconds.

'But who says I can't and don't keep the Ten Commandments?' asked Tim with a feeling of confident victory.

'The Word of God says and proves you can't and don't!' answered Mark.

'Oh, sure!' challenged Tim boldly. 'How?'

'Andrew,' said Mark in a level tone of voice that Tim recognised from earlier that evening, 'please read Exodus 20:13,14.'

Andrew hastily paged through his Bible, with Mark and Tim silently waiting for him.

'This is two of the Commandments,' said Andrew and began reading, '"You shall not murder. You shall not commit adultery."'

'So far, so good,' commented Tim with a cheeky and self-confident smirk on his face before laughing lightly.

'I'm glad—,' said Mark, and just as he was about to continue, a flash of lightning lit up the car park and sent a piercing bright light through the bistro's windows, making the interior look as though the lights had been dimmed.

Everyone stopped and looked, a deafening crack of thunder closely following that sounded like a number of fighter jets passing through the sound barrier at the same time. The windows and lights shook, causing a few patrons to gasp. Andrew also felt his heartbeat climb once again at the sudden change in ambience. There was silence for a few seconds, people not stirring in anticipation of more, but there was nothing coming. The rain then started pelting down with the bistro's roof taking a beating from on high. Everyone looked up, grateful there were thick clay tiles between them and the onslaught. In a matter of a minute the intensity was over, the downpour steadily slowing as though being reigned in from above.

'Wow!' exclaimed Andrew, who had been speechless during the spectacular event, just marvelling at its sheer power. 'That was quite something!'

'It sure was,' agreed Mark, his gaze still fixed on the window, the rain having returned to a soft, mild filtering down that would soon stop for the evening.

'You were saying, Mark?' questioned Andrew, turning the attention and focus back to the discussion they were having.

'Oh! Yes!' said Mark, looking at Tim again after thinking for a few seconds. 'I'm glad you could answer that way. You'll be surprised at how many people cringe when the latter commandment is read. However, Jesus clarifies these two commandments and reveals the depth of their meaning and the height of God's righteousness, His standard, in the book of Matthew.'

'More reading I suppose?' commented Tim cheekily.

'Indeed!' replied Mark with a smile. 'Andrew, please read for us Matthew 5:21,22.'

'This is Jesus speaking,' said Andrew after finding the place in his Bible, '"You have heard that it was said to the people long ago, 'do not murder' [with reference to Exodus 20:13] and anyone who murders will be subject to judgement. But I tell you that anyone who is angry with his brother without cause, will be subject to judgement. Again, anyone who says to his brother, 'Raca' [an Aramaic term of contempt] is answerable to the Sanhedrin. But anyone who says 'you fool' will be in danger of the fire of hell."' Andrew looked up the moment he had finished reading the passage.

'Please continue with Matthew 5:27,28,' requested Mark as he picked up his cup of cappuccino to take a sip.

'Matthew 5:27,28,' echoed Andrew as he flicked the pages in search of the scriptures. '"You have heard that it was said – 'do not commit adultery' [with reference to Exodus 20:14], but I tell you that anyone who looks at a woman lustfully has already committed adultery with her in his heart." So far, *not* so good,' blurted out Andrew before anyone could say anything, a sleek, sly smile spread across his face in light jest of Tim's cheeky and self-confident comment made earlier on.

'Oh, shush man!' snapped Tim somewhat seriously, a little troubled by what had just been presented to him as he had no answer for it and could not escape the depth to which it penetrated his heart!

Chapter 16

The confabulation continues

'**R**EMEMBER what Romans 3:19,20 says?' mentioned Mark quickly, realising that any further comment would just be fuel on a fire. '"Now we know that whatever the law says, it says to those who are under the law, so that every mouth may be silenced and the whole world held accountable to God. Therefore no-one will be declared righteous in His sight by observing the law; rather, through the law we become conscious of sin."'

Mark paused momentarily and seemed to contemplate the verse himself.

'If we are honest with ourselves,' continued Mark, 'and understand the law of God, we will not be able to brag about how much we keep but should shrink at how often we break it! God's standard is so holy and so high that it's impossible for us to match up to it on our own − we need help, we need a Saviour. How about analysing the other Commandments?'

Mark gave Tim a closed-lip smile and Andrew, understanding that it was actually no laughing matter, had to contain himself as he compared the two opposing facial expressions.

'It's getting late,' groused Tim. 'Two's enough, thanks!'

'Sure, Tim,' said Mark understandingly, 'but let me just clarify what Scripture reveals about our ability, or inability I should say, to match God on His turf without a Saviour. Andrew,' asked Mark, maintaining focus as he turned to him, 'please read Galatians 2:16, if you will?'

'"Know that a man is not justified by observing the law,"' read Andrew, having located the scriptures quickly, '"but by faith in Jesus Christ. So we, too, have put our faith in Christ Jesus that we may be justified by faith in Christ and not by observing the law, because by observing the law, no one will be justified."'

Tim was not pleased with what he was hearing and was again sitting slouched over the backrest of his chair. His chocolate chip muffin lay half eaten, its mottled inside and partly gnawed chocolate chips exposed to everyone. Tim had managed to finish one cup of cappuccino almost before the main discussion began, but the other cup remained untouched. Some of the milky froth was still clinging to the sides of the cup, but the majority had begun sinking to the bottom. Andrew on the other hand, who was basically playing the role of virtual spectator except for his Scripture reading, had steadily worked away at his ice-cream malt with both a spoon and a straw.

'The word justified,' said Mark after a brief distraction while Andrew shifted his chair slightly so that one of the waiters could clear the table behind him more easily, 'means – "just as if I had never sinned" and the law is the Ten Commandments. God has no sin, and His Kingdom has no sin in it. God will *not* allow sin into His Kingdom, therefore, only people who have been made just as if they have never sinned will be allowed into His Kingdom. As Galatians 2:16 reveals, it is only through faith in

Christ Jesus that we are made like this and not by our own efforts in trying to keep the Ten Commandments. Galatians 3:10 clarifies this when it says, "All who rely on observing the law are under a curse, for it is written, [with reference to Deuteronomy 27:26]: 'Cursed is everyone who does not continue to do everything written in the book of the law.'"" Mark suddenly sat up.

'Anything further for you gents?' asked the waiter, now standing at Mark's side.

'Not for me, thanks,' answered Mark amiably, while Tim just raised his hand in a gesture of "No".

'I'm also okay for the moment,' replied Andrew agreeably, 'thank you.'

'Very good then,' said the waiter with a friendly smile, and he turned and headed off.

'Andrew,' said Mark, picking up from before the short interruption, 'please continue in Galatians and read Galatians 3:11.'

The attention once again shifted to Andrew, who was methodically paging in his Bible, having closed it after the last reading.

'Ah, here we are!' said Andrew. 'Galatians 3:11, "Clearly no-one is justified before God by the law, because, 'The righteous will live by faith'" – with reference to Habakkuk 2:4.'

'God can't lower His standard of justice,' said Mark. 'Isaiah 55:8,9 says, '"For my thoughts are not your thoughts, neither are your ways My ways,' declares the LORD. 'As the heavens are higher than the earth, so are My ways higher than your ways and My thoughts than your thoughts.'""

'Yeah,' objected Tim, 'but surely there must be a line of acceptability?'

'Like what?' asked Andrew.

'Like a pass mark of fifty or sixty percent,' replied Tim. 'Surely God must grant us some leeway? Anyway,' added Tim defiantly, 'what kind of a God is He – if there is a God – who says you can choose and then punishes you when you don't choose Him?'

'Whoever told you that God said you could choose?' asked Mark curiously but knowledgeable of what Tim was referring to.

'Well,' stammered Tim, a little unsure and astounded by the question, 'uh— that's what Christians say! They say that God gave us a free will so that we could choose, and that He wants us to choose Him!'

'Unfortunately,' confirmed Mark, 'what you say is true. However, the premise is incorrect. God has never given man a choice, only a command and a consequence. Take Genesis 2:16,17 for example. It says, "And the LORD God commanded the man, 'You are free to eat from any tree in the garden; but you must not eat from the tree of the knowledge of good and evil, for when you eat of it you will surely die.'" This was not a choice, it was a command and a consequence if not heeded. Take the Ten Commandments; they were not choices, they were – You shall not! Take the conditions given to the Israelites about the promised land of Canaan. They were not choices either but commands and consequences. The same applies today, and the message is the same. It goes as follows: Our ancestor, Adam, sinned and as a result was separated from God. This sin is continued from generation to generation. The Bible says *all* have sinned and fallen short of God's Glory. As a result, God made a plan and a way to redeem man from his fall, and this was through the sacrifice of His Son, Jesus, taking the consequences of our disobedience in our place. Today there is still no choice, only the consequences of our obedience or disobedience to God. Our free will allows us to choose to obey or disobey, that is all. God is the LORD, the King, the Creator of the heavens and the earth. He doesn't run a democracy but a theocracy.'

'If God didn't want Adam to eat from a tree,' queried Andrew wide-eyed, a little stunned by what he had just heard, 'why didn't He just remove the tree or place a fence around it? Was it to test Adam?'

'Fair comment and question,' replied Mark. 'With such consequences at stake, I don't think God was testing Adam. The tree was not a magical tree but a sacramental tree, just like the Tree of Life that was also there. God can appoint physical channels to communicate spiritual blessings or curses to us. God uses the physical to communicate the spiritual. So why did God put such a tree within their reach? It was His way of saying, "I retain moral authority over you." In other words, "You don't decide for yourself what is right and wrong, you trust Me to tell you what's right and what's wrong." God is saying to the human beings He has created, "You are not landlords on earth, you are the tenants and I am the Landlord, and I retain the right to tell you what's good for you and what isn't." The trouble is that all of us in some way or another won't be told, we're going to try it for ourselves to see whether it's good or bad!' [28]

Mark paused for a second and seemed to gather his thoughts together like he had done a short while ago from behind the pulpit. Andrew, and even Tim, waited in anticipation for further explanation.

'Besides the reason just given for the tree being there,' continued Mark, 'the fact is, it was there! An additional lesson to be learned is that God warned Adam about it and gave him the consequence of disobedience. He did not just tell Adam that he was not to eat from it. That's faithfulness on God's part, and He has done the same for all humanity by giving us His Word and in it, forewarning. In the end, man will be without excuse. Personally, I think that God placed a lot of faith and trust in Adam, and He did not want Adam to disobey. Can you imagine a doctor at a hospital telling an orderly that he may not enter a certain room, for if he does so he will become infected and die and then locks the door and takes the key with him? How would the orderly feel? He would ask himself why the doctor bothered to tell him in the first place and think to himself that the doctor didn't trust him or place much value in his integrity. In such an instance, the orderly should have faith in the doctor that he has spoken the truth, and what has been instructed is for his own good and not harm. With God it should *definitely* be that way, and with the command and warning given to Adam, it definitely was! Faith is defined as having complete trust or confidence in something or someone.'

'That's all good and well,' said Tim abruptly, 'but everything is faith. You've just mentioned "faith", and I often hear it said, "You need to accept it by faith, just have faith and believe." I don't buy it at all!'

Chapter 17

The pass mark

'FAIR comment,' responded Mark, not troubled at all by what was said, 'but let me ask you the following: In your life, do you not act on faith? Must all things first be proven and understood?'

Tim raised his eyebrows and looked at Mark for a second, a little surprised at the question. Andrew too was astonished and had no idea what the purpose of it was, thinking that up until then it should have been obvious that Tim did not accept "faith".

'I'm not a faith man,' replied Tim confidently, not flinching in response despite having paused for a second before answering, 'I like things to be proven and understood!'

'Let me highlight a few "faiths" for you,' said Mark calmly, having anticipated the response, 'which you exercise on a regular basis.'

Andrew sat up a little more attentively, realising that although there were no hostilities there was definitely tension and friction present, recalling with a half-smile the lightning and thunder that had recently entertained them.

'This will be interesting,' remarked Tim scoffingly, not

believing that Mark could possibly show him any such thing.

'When you enter a lift and start moving up,' reasoned Mark, 'are you not putting faith in an object and someone else's hands? Did you examine the cable or the pulleys or check that the person doing the installation was qualified and did the job properly?'

'Well, no,' answered Tim with slight recoil, 'but—'

'And in the past,' interrupted Mark, shutting off Tim's stumbled attempt at an objection, 'when you have flown across the country, did you check that the plane had been properly manufactured? Did you check that the workers who had made the engines had followed procedures correctly? Were you not also, in faith, to a large degree placing your life in the hands of the pilots – people you didn't know and had probably never seen or even heard of before? You probably didn't even see them on the plane!'

Tim stared silently at Mark, not attempting to question his reasoning.

'Take the chair you're sitting on,' continued Mark without hesitation. 'You may have never sat on that chair before, but did you examine the chair or its legs before you sat on it? You probably just pulled it away from the table and sat on it without a second thought! The chocolate chip muffin you're eating – did you send it to a laboratory for testing? You just started eating it! These are just a few examples from a myriad of circumstances, events and activities where you place "faith" in something or someone – not bad for a guy who likes things proven! Faith can also mean trust, and we need to trust God that what He says, He will do!'

'Yeah, okay,' defended Tim, although he was a little taken aback, having never thought about things in such a light, 'but with the current life examples that you've just given we have experiences and proof to back the faith or trust we place there.'

'What you seem to be indirectly saying,' said Mark after drinking the last of his cappuccino and placing the cup carefully back on its saucer, 'is that the Bible can provide no proof and, therefore, it requires much more faith?'

'Yes,' confirmed Tim thoughtfully, 'pretty much so.'

'Okay,' said Mark and then paused, Tim hoping that he was about to surrender.

'Here's a little proof,' continued Mark after a moment, to Tim's despair and slight annoyance. 'Were you perhaps listening to the message I gave earlier this evening?'

'Somewhat,' replied Tim, a little rebelliously.

'Then you would have heard some of what was said about the circumstances surrounding the birth of Jesus,' questioned Mark purposefully, 'is this correct?'

'Yeah,' answered Tim, retaining his rebellious tone, 'some of it.'

'Well, those are proofs,' said Mark. 'In fact, you will never be able to obtain in any human structure or person those proofs. At the time the Old Testament was being written, how much evidence did man have for believing God was God, what He said He meant and what He promised He would do?'

'In a manner of speaking,' replied Andrew, who had been side-lined for a while, 'not too much really.'

'That's exactly it,' said Mark, 'initially anyway — although there were two catastrophic circumstances in the form of the fall of man and the Flood, not forgetting Creation itself which testifies to God. However, because of disobedience, the people had to learn by experience, but what we have is their experience coupled with prophecy that was written during their time. Let's get back to your fifty or sixty percent pass mark, shall we, Tim?'

said Mark, wanting to elaborate on this.

'Sure, whatever,' mumbled Tim as he began tapping on the table with his fingers, having started to get a little uneasy.

'Not *too* much more now,' reassured Mark, who sensed Tim's uneasiness and noticed his fidgetiness, 'just a few pertinent points that will wrap up the whole discussion properly and provide a complete panorama for you of what it all means.'

'Sure, sure,' chirped Tim abruptly, 'might as well.'

'The book of James,' said Mark, 'answers your very queries as to there being a line of acceptability, like a pass mark of fifty or sixty percent, and with regards to God granting us some leeway. Well, there is no line of acceptability and no leeway! In James 2:10 it says, "For whoever keeps the whole law, and yet stumbles at just one point, is guilty of breaking all of it." Scripture can't say it plainer or simpler than that. We need help, we need a Saviour! You see, it links together like a bicycle chain. It doesn't matter which link gets broken to make the whole chain useless!'

'So we are sinners,' responded Tim a little aggressively, 'so we are separated from God because of our sin, so we can't reconcile with God on our own, so a person is apparently saved "through faith in Jesus Christ" by this *grace* that's a free gift from God – great! What's the significance of Jesus then, and what's this faith?'

'Not bad!' complimented Andrew, quite amazed at Tim having accurately summarised the points and main issues that had been addressed up to that point, whether or not he accepted it all. 'You've put it in a nutshell quite well. Quite astute, I must say!'

Tim gave a snort but said nothing.

'It's the very thing we've now come to,' replied Mark, 'why

Jesus is the central part to us being saved and reconciled to God. Do you remember that in Galatians 3 it says, "Cursed is everyone who does not continue to do everything written in the book of the law"?'

'Yes,' replied Tim, 'I do.'

'It continues to say in verse thirteen,' added Mark, '"Christ redeemed us from the curse of the law by becoming a curse for us." Let's see how this works then. Paul says in 1 Corinthians 2:2, "For I resolved to know nothing while I was with you except Jesus Christ and Him crucified." Obviously, "Jesus Christ and Him crucified" was very important to Paul, but what about it? What's the significance of it? Paul clarifies this statement in 1 Corinthians 15:1–4. Andrew, please read it.'

'*Okay!*' said Andrew enthusiastically, happy to get into the action again, and promptly began reading after locating the scriptures. '"Now, brothers, I want to remind you of the gospel I preached to you, which you received and on which you have taken your stand. By this gospel you are saved, if you hold firmly to the word I preached to you, otherwise you have believed in vain. For what I received, I passed on to you as of first importance: that Christ died for our sins according to the scriptures, that He was buried, that He was raised on the third day according to the scriptures."'

'We can now understand,' said Mark as he began his dissection of this passage, 'that what Paul is saying is that the Cross of Calvary is the absolute centre and foundation of our faith, around which everything else must focus.'

'I see,' said Tim casually.

'Paul starts 1 Corinthians 15,' continued Mark, wanting to emphasise certain key words, 'by saying, "I want to remind you of the gospel I preached to you". What gospel was this? The very gospel in 1 Corinthians 2:2 where he said, "for I resolved to know nothing while I was with you *except* Jesus Christ and Him crucified." Jesus Christ and Him crucified, therefore, must be the gospel that they received and on which they took their stand. It continues in 1 Corinthians 15, "by this gospel you are saved", which means by Jesus Christ and Him crucified you are saved, "*if* you hold firmly to the word I preached to you". Why? Because, "otherwise you have believed in vain." We have to grasp with both hands this very gospel that Paul is talking about and keep it the central focus of our lives and lifestyles without shifting our stand on it. Paul continues, "For what I received I passed on to you as of", what? – "as of *first* importance". And what is it? It is 1 Corinthians 2:2 – Jesus Christ and Him crucified. But Paul now clarifies and specifies that it consists of three aspects. Firstly, that Christ died for our sins according to the scriptures; secondly, that He was buried; and thirdly, that He was raised on the third day according to the scriptures. Paul gives us one focus, one central point, which is Jesus Christ and Him crucified, divided into three aspects – death, burial and resurrection, upon which our faith is founded and functions.'

Chapter 18

The prophecies

'**W**HAT scriptures is Paul referring to,' asked Andrew, 'when he says, "Christ died for us according to the scriptures"? Is that what you referred to earlier this evening being the Old Testament?'

'Yeah,' perked up Tim, 'I heard that much this evening from your sermon! However, Paul is probably referring to New Testament scriptures where Jesus predicted His death or is finding something that was written after the fact!' Tim leaned back in his chair, satisfied with his remark.

'Actually, not at all,' replied Mark, who never seemed to get overly irritated with peoples' opinions or remarks. 'They didn't have the New Testament like we do, for it was only written during their time and put together a while after that. Paul was also not one of Jesus' disciples so wouldn't have been able to quote Him directly. They only had the Old Testament and Paul is referring to scriptures that were prophecies written more than 600 years before their time! This is some of the proof that I mentioned to you earlier – prophecies I mean. They form a major part of the credibility of the Bible.'

'Can you show us some prophecies?' asked Andrew, feeling that it may be of benefit for Tim to hear some of them, apart from which he always found them moving and attention grabbing anyway so did not mind hearing them again.

'Come on, Andy,' prodded Tim quickly, not sharing Andrew's enthusiasm for such things nor fully believing they were true or accurate anyway, 'it's time we went home!'

'Let me quickly give you just three prophecies,' said Mark, understanding that it had already been quite a discussion.

'Just three,' said Tim sharply, 'no more!'

'Agreed,' replied Mark with his customary cheerful smile and wasted no time in getting stuck in by quoting from memory. 'Isaiah 52:14 says, "Just as there were many who were appalled at Him, His appearance was so disfigured beyond that of any man and His form marred beyond human likeness."'

'I remember someone talking about this scripture,' said Andrew, 'and saying that Jesus' appearance was so bad that He literally looked like a hamburger!'

'Oh, come on!' protested Tim disbelievingly as he sat up from his slouching position, lifting his hands in the air. 'He had a few lashes!'

'It's true what Andrew said,' responded Mark. 'Jesus literally looked like a hamburger. He took thirty-nine stripes, but the whip that was used was called the "cat o' nine tails" with each strand having broken bone and lumps of lead woven into them so as to be able to rip through flesh and muscle. Jesus actually took thirty-nine multiplied by nine lashes, which equals 351 lashes!'

This was news to Tim but not having learned about it, was not in a place to argue against it. He thought to himself that if he was ever interested enough, he would just look it up.

'In Isaiah 50:6 it also says,' continued Mark, who knew that he had to finish up, '"I offered my back to those who beat me, my cheeks to those who pulled out my beard, I did not hide my face from mocking and spitting." Andrew, please read Psalm 22:16–18. This is the last of the three prophecies I requested to mention.'

'"Dogs have surrounded me,"' read Andrew, having speedily found the scripture, '"a band of evil men has encircled me, they have pierced my hands and my feet. I can count all my bones; people stare and gloat over me. They divide my garments among them and cast lots for my clothing."'

'Why would God allow such a thing,' asked Tim contemplatively, having thought for a second after recalling seeing as a child a film about Jesus and the scene at the Cross, which was the visual of what had just been read, 'and why would Jesus go through with it, if He is God and could opt out of it?'

'Good question,' said Mark, who then concluded it all as he went into his final exegesis. 'Many people argue that God is a loving God and would not allow such a terrible thing to happen, particularly not to His Son. Sure, God is a loving God – that's exactly why He allowed it to happen! God is not only a loving God though but also a righteous and a just God. If God hadn't allowed Jesus to be crucified, He wouldn't be a loving God, because we would all be damned to hell. But by allowing Christ Jesus to be a sacrificial offering on our behalf, He showed how loving, righteous and just He is. Firstly, a loving God, as John 3:16 tells us, "For God so loved the world [that is us] that He gave His one and only Son [that is allowed Him to be a sacrifice on our behalf], that whoever believes in Him [Jesus] shall not perish [be damned to hell] but have eternal life [that is be reconciled to God and live with Him forever]." Secondly, a righteous God because His righteous standard could accept no less. God knew that our attempts are feeble and our "righteous acts" are as filthy rags, as Isaiah 64:6 tells us. Therefore, reconciliation to Him would have to come from Him. Even though God knew that because of His righteousness, His Son, the very lifeblood of God the Son, would have to be sacrificed, He was not prepared to lower, change or compromise His righteous standard. Thirdly, a just God because His justice system demands the punishment for sin. God knew that we are incapable of paying the price and, therefore, did not compromise His justice by cancelling the debt or overlooking the offence – He paid the very high price Himself. Isaiah 53:4–6 says, "Surely He took up our infirmities [weaknesses] and carried our sorrows, yet we considered Him stricken by God, smitten by Him, and afflicted. But He was pierced for our transgressions, He was crushed for our iniquities; the punishment that brought us peace was upon Him, and by His wounds we are healed. We all, like sheep, have gone astray, each of us has turned to his own way, and the Lord has laid on Him [Jesus] the iniquity [evil] of us all." Colossians 2:13–15 says, "When you were dead in your sins and in the uncircumcision of your sinful nature, God made you alive with Christ. He forgave us all our sins, having cancelled the written code [Law/Ten Commandments], with its regulations, that was against us and that stood opposed to us; He took it away, nailing it to the cross. And having disarmed the powers and authorities, He made a public spectacle of them, triumphing over them by the cross." In 2 Corinthians 5:21 it continues, "God made Him [Jesus] who had no sin to be sin [or a sin offering] for us, so that in Him [Jesus] we might become the righteousness of God." This is why God allowed Jesus to be crucified and why Jesus was prepared to be sacrificed. Only God's righteousness can overcome our unrighteousness; only He who had no sin could overcome our sin. Remember that in Isaiah 53 it says, "The Lord has laid on Him [Jesus] the iniquity [evil] of us all." On the cross Jesus carried sin; on His shoulders was laid all the sin and evil of this world. But take note, through all this Jesus did not become sinful or sin Himself! That's it in a nutshell.'

Mark let out a quiet but drawn-out sigh as he placed his hands on the table and leaned back against the chair back.

'So what you're saying,' said Andrew, who had been listening intently to this final explanation, 'is that because Jesus paid the price or became the sin offering for us, His righteousness may be given to us. God takes our filthy rags and gives us His own righteousness through Jesus Christ?'

'Exactly!' replied Mark.

'Ah!' said Tim slowly, a look of annoyance written all over his face and still sitting slouched over the side of his chair's backrest.

After momentary silence, Tim suddenly jumped up and grabbed Andrew by the arm!

Chapter 19

The silent trip home

'COME, Andy!' ordered Tim aggressively. 'It's really late; we're out of here!'

'Okay, Tim,' responded Andrew as he got up, his thoughtfulness shaken and a little perplexed at Tim's action, 'but I must first settle the account!'

'Wow!' said Mark, looking at his watch, fully aware of Tim's troubled spirit. 'Look at the time! You guys get going, I'll settle the bill.'

'Much obliged, Mark,' said Andrew gratefully, just managing to give him a thumbs up and grab his Bible and carry bag before being yanked away by Tim. 'Till next time!'

A second later the antiquated doorbells could be heard ringing profusely as the door was wrenched open, Tim and Andrew heading out in a flurry. Mark was left sitting silently by himself, the bistro now nearly empty, with only a few customers dotted here and there.

The evening rain had abated, but threatening clouds remained. The grass was sodden, and the tree branches hung down, looking sad from the weight of the water that was affixed to them. The droplets of water, however, provided a contrasting glitter to the sad façade as light intermingled with them while the branches slightly swayed in the gentle north breeze.

Andrew cautiously avoided the puddles along the way, but Tim, who determinedly led the way towards the car, anxious to get out of there, marched purposefully, taking no heed to where he walked.

'Let's get going,' snapped Tim gruffly, turning to Andrew when he reached Andrew's car.

'Sure,' said Andrew, not wanting to fuel further irritability, 'I'm—'

'Blast!' yelled Tim, interrupting Andrew with a loud moan and clenching his fists next to his sides as he looked up to the heavens, having stepped off the pavement and right into the middle of a large puddle. 'What a horrid night!'

A few people nearby turned their heads at Tim's outburst, but he did not provide enough of a show to solicit their continued interest. Andrew did not comment, he just got on with what he had to do, and they were soon out of Sunny Valley's parking area and on their way to Tim's house.

Tim sat staring out the passenger window at the black night all around him. The street and house lights provided the only glimmer of contrast, as heaven's illuminations continued to remain shut out by the thick cloud cover. Andrew felt the tension but was not sure there was anything he could do about it.

'It looks like a large cold front has rolled in from the north,' commented Andrew in an effort to try and ease the situation a little, having looked up through the front windscreen. 'We may have some more rain later tonight or early tomorrow.'

Andrew shot Tim a quick glance, but there was no response.

He was unmoved and seemed deaf to the world and what it was presenting before him. Andrew thought it best to remain quiet himself, and leave Tim to himself, perceiving that he was either in deep thought or trying to contain a feeling of great irritability and disdain.

Tim folded his arms against his chest, a sour look still heavily fixed on his face. Although he knew he had been a bit arrogant, he had listened to what Mark had said, but there was something other to the whole thing. There was so much religion, so much differing opinions between them and even conflict! Then there was evolution that denied Adam. Who was one to believe, other than one's own self? Tim had been left all his life to make his own way when it came to religious aspects, which he felt he had done pretty well up until then.

Something, however, had challenged him. It had challenged his standpoint, defying his perception and perspective on life and ultimately his religious views. He could not deny it, but hated the very feeling that it created in the pit of his stomach. He hated the note that Mike had written for himself; he hated the fact that he had read it; he hated the challenge that it had brought into his life; he hated that gentle, prodding voice that encouraged him to open his heart to that which he had shut out of his life for so long; and he hated himself for his own preparedness to consider it. Furthermore, he now hated having partaken in the discussion only moments ago, which had left him with concerns and questions that he knew he could not ignore! He did not know why he had allowed himself to be drawn into it in the first place, but could not override its impact.

Tim choked at the thought of it all, now hating Mark too. He felt that if he never saw him again it would be too soon! What was worse, he hated Andrew, his beloved cousin, for calling upon

Mark to join them at Roccocoa's. Tim was not happy, but a caution arose in his spirit. He realised that these circumstances, which he presently so vehemently hated, and which he considered just plain bad luck occurrences and poor decision making, could be considered by those of the Christian faith as being providential. He did not want to consider this option, for he was not even sure there was a God. However, something once again cautioned him about his attitude and opinions. In the cold night, Tim was red with rage, for he now hated the fact that he knew he would fight his own feelings and heed the internal caution.

Andrew soon pulled into Tim's cobble-paved driveway, which widened towards the double garage. Before the car had properly stopped, Tim was already getting out. Andrew felt rebuffed as he watched Tim climb out, slam the car door behind him without saying a word and just walk away. Tim strode purposefully along the pathway, up the three adobe steps and onto his front porch. He quickly unlocked the front door and disappeared behind it, having slammed it shut too. Andrew sat for a few seconds, the car purring quietly as it idled away, and saw the upstairs lights switch on.

'If that's how it's going to be,' said Andrew to himself in total astonishment, 'then that's just how it's going to be – no problem!'

Andrew wasted no further time, realising that it would be to no avail. He backed his car out of Tim's driveway, glancing briefly towards the house before pulling away and heading off towards his home. He was ill at ease and unhappy at what he had just witnessed.

Andrew sat at one of the main intersection traffic lights, a thousand thoughts trying to attack his brain all at once. His mind was so preoccupied that sounds bounced off his eardrums, not even hearing his vehicle's direction indicator ticking away faithfully. He realised that he could not rationally put everything together nor entertain all stabbing thoughts that wanted to lay blame at his door for the uneasiness of the preceding events, but he was troubled nonetheless. The traffic lights turned green and after waiting for oncoming traffic to pass, Andrew turned and headed on his way.

'Dear Lord,' prayed Andrew, quietly lifting a prayer to God as he made his way along the main road. 'I cannot explain the issues just passed nor reason them out properly, but please have mercy on all of us – particularly on Tim. In Jesus' name I ask it, Amen.'

Andrew took a deep breath, breathing out slowly as he leaned across to his console and turned on the radio that was tuned to the classical channel. For the few minutes that it took him to get home, he was able to relax a little and enjoy the broadcast of the Blue Danube.

Andrew pulled quietly into his driveway and parked his car under the beige shade-cloth canopy located at the side of the garages that was for his car. He climbed out slowly and headed inside, lethargy, tiredness and a degree of disheartenment plaguing him.

George and Kelly were still up when Andrew entered the house, sitting in the living room eating freshly baked cheesecake and drinking hot coffee. Andrew always loved the smell of cheesecake and coffee together, but his sensory feelers were dulled, and the smell passed his notice.

'You're quite late!' commented Kelly as she heard Andrew in the entrance hall. 'Is everything alright? I was about to phone you – how was Tim?'

Andrew walked down the steps into the sunken living room, placed his keys on the glass-top table and dropped into one of the couches opposite Kelly.

'We're alright,' replied Andrew, 'but Tim was in an irritable mood!'

'Oh?' responded Kelly with interest.

'Yes,' confirmed Andrew, 'you won't believe what happened!'

Chapter 20

George's synopsis

'TELL us, Andy,' asked Kelly as she nibbled pleasurably on a chunk of cheesecake.

George, as usual, popped his head out around the side of the newspaper, Andrew's comment having caught his attention and interest. It was as though the only time he heard someone speak was when it interested him, a trait often to Kelly's frustration.

'What are you eating?' asked Andrew, suddenly noticing what he thought looked like cheesecake on his mother's side plate.

'It's cheesecake, Andy!' answered Kelly incredulously. 'I'm surprised you didn't comment on the smell when you came in!'

'My mind's been elsewhere,' responded Andrew, a look of tiredness clearly evident on his face. 'I must have been dulled to the smell, but may I have a small piece, please?'

'Certainly you may,' answered Kelly warmly, 'I'll cut you a piece, then tell us what we would *not* believe happened!'

Kelly quickly went off to the kitchen and returned with a nice piece of yellow cheesecake proudly perched on the side plate she was carrying.

'Thanks, Mom,' said Andrew with a smile that made his face a little brighter than it had been for some time. 'This is bigger than expected, but I'm sure I'll manage it!'

'We're all ears,' said Kelly as she flopped down in the soft sofa. 'George, please put the paper down.'

'After the church service,' began Andrew as he dug his spoon into the side of the cheesecake and severed off a piece, 'Tim was not too impressed, so I offered to take him for some coffee.'

'We would have believed that!' remarked George, causing Andrew to stop and look at him for a second.

'Your father's just being funny, Andy,' said Kelly, unimpressed with George's interruption, 'don't mind him. Carry on, we're both listening – and *no* peanut gallery comments please, George!'

'Tim was in a bit of a huff,' said Andrew, continuing after enjoying the piece of smooth cheesecake he had just broken off, 'and complained that he'd given up happy hour at Down and Out's for, as he termed it – "that"! So I offered to take him for coffee.'

Andrew severed off another spoonful of cheesecake and promptly popped it in his mouth.

'Swo,' continued Andrew, inaudible with his mouthful of yummy cheesecake, 'yhoo swhe—'

'Andy!' groused Kelly, quite aghast with his etiquette. 'We know you're good at multi-tasking but please! Finish your mouthful before continuing the story.'

Andrew's eyes widened as he suddenly realised what he was doing, and he calmly ate the rest of his cheesecake.

'I'm not doing too well, am I?' said Andrew a little irritated with himself, as he placed the soiled side plate on the coffee table. 'This was the third time in three days that my table manners have not been what they should!'

'Never mind,' assured Kelly, 'just concentrate. Finish your story.'

'So you see,' said Andrew continuing where he had left off as he sunk back into the plush couch, the cushions enfolding around him, 'Tim accepted the offer of coffee, so I took him to Roccocoa's. There we started talking, and out of the blue, Tim began to challenge me on what Mark had preached this evening. Shortly after we had begun, to my amazement, Mark walked past Roccocoa's on his way to Sunny Valley Supermarket. I jumped up and ran out of the bistro after him, to see if he had some free time and would be in a position to join us. I thought that he may be better able to answer some of the issues Tim was objecting to.'

'That wasn't such a bad idea,' said Kelly, looking at George to see what he felt about it. 'Rather thoughtful if you ask me.'

'Yes, indeed!' agreed George. 'But probably not if you were looking at it from Tim's point of view!'

'I hadn't thought of that when I jumped up,' responded Andrew reflectively.

'So what was Mark's response?' asked Kelly.

'And what was Tim's response?' asked George, who seemed to have insight into how it would all unfold before being told the story. George had this way about him. He would sit quietly and not normally ask too many questions or make many comments but was able to look at the picture like a judge at his bench. The questions he normally asked and the comments he normally made were relevant to the point. Rapidly firing questions and comments was not his game.

'Mark was more than happy and willing to join us,' replied Andrew, 'but as Dad is hinting at, Tim didn't share the same sentiment. He felt that he'd had enough of Mark for a lifetime already and then to have him intrude on his coffee time was not well received.'

'Did Tim respond poorly then?' asked Kelly while George quietly continued to listen.

'You bet!' answered Andrew energetically, having mustered some energy from the chunk of cheesecake. 'I had to ask him not to be so disrespectful, even if he wasn't too pleased.'

'And Mark,' asked Kelly probingly, 'what was his response?'

'He took it in his stride,' replied Andrew, 'almost as though it wasn't unexpected. He laughed, saying that Tim actually had a good sense of humour, but then you know Mark, he's not greatly niggled by such responses. Even the waiter seemed to have been hassled by Tim in some way – it must have been while I was outside talking to Mark.'

'But did Tim give you both the cold shoulder all the time,' quizzed Kelly, totally interested in what had happened, 'or did he settle down, prepared to continue with the objections he had earlier raised?'

'That was another amazing part,' replied Andrew with animation, 'because although Tim was put out by Mark's arrival, he continued straight on from where I had interrupted him – of his own free choice!'

Both George and Kelly listened quietly as Andrew unravelled the evening's happening at Roccocoa's. Kelly interjected with a comment or two and a question here and there, but the floor was mainly Andrew's. He carefully narrated it all, from himself reading the scriptures to Tim literally pushing him out the door.

'The thing that got to me quite a bit,' said Andrew as he drew to a close, 'was when I pulled into Tim's driveway. I hadn't even stopped the car properly, and he was already getting out! Tim didn't say a word or even look at me, he just went inside the house and disappeared. I felt quite horrible!'

'I can imagine,' said Kelly supportively, 'but don't let it get to you.'

'Easier said than done,' said Andrew as he looked at his side plate to double check that he had finished every crumb of his piece of cheesecake. 'You know how fond I am of Tim, and we have great times fishing together, going to ball games, lunch times at university and so on – but this seems to be a blow! He seems to have a real in-depth resistance to the things of God. A lot of what was told to him tonight were aspects he had previously heard from us too!'

'Sometimes people need to hear it from someone else,' mentioned Kelly.

There was silence in the living room for a while as they all seemed to ponder the evening's event, with the only noise coming from the heavy breathing of George as he sat cross-armed, his chin resting on his chest while looking over the top of his reading glasses.

'What are your thoughts on it, Dad?' asked Andrew eventually.

There was more silence as Kelly and Andrew fixed their attention on the head of the home, waiting in anticipation for his response.

'There are a few possibilities,' said George thoughtfully as he pushed with his hands on the sofa's seat and sat upright.

There was silence once again as George gathered his thoughts together so as to be able to present them in the best possible way.

'Firstly,' began George after a moment, 'we need to understand that people today don't want the things of God. They do not want to be accountable to Him and do not want anything that encroaches on their supposed freedom, not realising that they're in fact leading themselves into bondage. Secondly, we're living in an age where the sophistication of knowledge and societal development have tried to rule out God, saying that man no longer needs religion, not realising that our achievements, knowledge and ability do not rule away sin and the need for a saviour. Thirdly, we're also living at a time in which the Bible says in 2 Timothy 4:3 that people will surround themselves with teachers who satisfy what their itching ears want to hear, rather than surround themselves with those who speak the truth. However, one point that may be the issue, is that Tim may have been truly interested in what was said—'

'It didn't seem that way to me!' interrupted Andrew.

'Let me finish, please,' protested George but with a calm tone of voice.

'Sorry, Dad,' apologised Andrew, 'go on.'

'Tim may have been truly interested in what was being said,' continued George, 'he may just not have been showing it. The problem with truth is that it doesn't always jell well with us or go down well, but it's still truth. Remember what the Bible says in Hebrews 4:12, "For the Word of God is living and active. Sharper than any double-edged sword, it penetrates even to dividing soul and spirit, joints and marrow; it judges the thoughts and attitudes of the heart." For Tim this may have been the case, which may not have been pleasant for him. For him, the issue will be whether he accepts what has been shown and explained to him or whether he rejects it!'

'The *man* has wisely spoken!' commented Andrew in a deep monotone voice as George leaned back and rested in the sofa.

'You asked my opinion,' said George with a smile, Kelly

sitting pondering what he had said.

'It's late!' exclaimed Kelly as she jumped up, startling both George and Andrew after her brief moment's contemplation of it all. 'It's definitely an aspect that we need to continually lift to the Lord in our daily prayers, but in the meantime, Andrew you head upstairs to wash up for bed, and I'll clear the dishes. George, if you would help me, I'd be very grateful.'

'Sure thing, dear,' responded George obligingly, 'and we'll continue to keep Tim in our prayers.'

The three of them retreated from the living room, leaving it dark and silent after all the lights had been turned off, not knowing what would soon transpire in that very room!

Chapter 21

The unexpected surprise

'**M**Y precious boy is up,' said Kelly warmly as she watched Andrew come galloping down the old, creaking and moaning mahogany staircase and into the entrance hall area.

'And what do I smell this lovely Saturday morning?' asked Andrew, a knowing look of satisfaction on his face. 'French toast and freshly brewed coffee – only the best!'

Andrew gave Kelly a big one-armed squeeze around her shoulders and went to sit down at the dining room table, Kelly returning to the kitchen to fetch the food.

'Is your father up yet, Andy?' asked Kelly as she sat down at the table, having placed a large platter of French toast at the centre of it. 'I called him a while ago – I hope he hasn't forgotten about the meeting he has this morning about the church's upcoming golf day!'

'He was shaving when I last saw him,' answered Andrew as he slipped a piece of French toast off the platter and onto his plate, 'so he shouldn't be much longer.' Just then they heard the stairs creaking.

'Ah, he doth cometh!' commented Kelly with animation, to the amusement of Andrew. 'And not too soon either!'

'French toast and coffee,' said George cheerfully as he entered the dining room, 'it's what makes weekends real weekends!'

The bright morning sun had raised its head by then and was shining its warm rays boldly through the window upon the family trio, who blissfully began eating their breakfast. They were suddenly startled by a car pulling into the driveway and the doorbell ringing shortly thereafter.

'It's only 08:30,' said George as he answered the look on Kelly's face. 'My first visitor is only due here at nine o'clock, and he's not normally so early, he keeps prompt times.'

'I'll see who it is, Dad,' said Andrew as he got up from the table while wiping his mouth with a napkin.

'Thanks, Andy,' said George gratefully, not wanting to interrupt his breakfast.

'It's Tim!' exclaimed Andrew, absolutely surprised as he looked out the bay window and saw Tim's cream-coloured sedan parked in the driveway.

George and Kelly looked at each other and then at Andrew. They realised that he was not joking as he rushed out of the dining room with eagerness and headed for the front door.

'It's been two weeks since we heard from Tim!' remarked Kelly quietly as she leaned forward over the dining room table, not wanting anyone other than George to hear her.

'Personally,' said George with less caution, 'after listening to Andrew's recount of what took place on the Sunday evening a fortnight ago, I feel that two weeks isn't that long!'

'Oh, go on with you,' responded Kelly with a chuckle as she waved her hand at George, knowing that he was just toying with her. 'You and that philosophical pragmatism of yours!'

Andrew in the meantime had just finished unlocking the front door. He reached for the door handle and yanked the door open as fast as he could.

'Tim!' exclaimed Andrew in an excitedly surprised tone that actually startled Tim. 'We've been worried silly about you! How've you been doing?'

'Gee,' said Tim half recoiling, having not expected to receive such a response from Andrew, 'I'm okay – been busy doing stuff and things, you know.

'Well,' added Tim a little sheepishly after a brief silence, 'are you going to invite me in or not?'

'What!' said Andrew. 'You know you don't need an invitation, not for this house – come right on in!' Andrew promptly stepped out of the way, making room for Tim to enter. 'You never answered my text message,' remarked Andrew as they walked to the dining room, 'or the message that I left on your phone.'

'Morning, Tim,' greeted Kelly cheerfully before Tim could answer Andrew. 'Would you like some French toast and coffee?'

'I wouldn't mind,' replied Tim hesitantly, 'but truly – only if I may, Aunt Kelly?'

'You may with the greatest of pleasure, Timmy boy,' replied Kelly without reserve, 'so sit yourself down.'

Kelly headed off to the kitchen to fetch Tim a plate and mug, a little spring in her step and joy in her heart that Tim had of his own desire arrived at their house.

'It's nice to see you this bright and cheerful morning,' said George while sipping his coffee. 'Any news from the western front?'

'I'm fine thanks, Uncle George,' answered Tim, knowing what his uncle was asking. 'I've just been busy and not wanting to be disturbed – that's all.'

'I see,' said George in a way that indicated that he was sure there was more to it than what Tim was prepared to say.

'I received your messages,' said Tim quickly as he turned to Andrew, wanting to avoid further prodding from his uncle, 'and saw you arrive at my house, but I was busy and didn't want to be disturbed.'

'That's okay,' said Andrew understandingly, not wanting to make Tim feel more out of sorts than he clearly already was. 'It's no problem, as long as you were alright.' Andrew gave Tim a half-smile and helped himself to some French toast while Kelly handed a plate to Tim and poured him some coffee.

Tim seemed a little hungry, which did not seem to surprise his aunt at all. She quickly fried some more toast and had it on the table in minutes.

'Here you are,' said Kelly warmly as she placed the steaming French toast on the platter, 'feel free to tuck in without reserve.'

George finished his breakfast and sat quietly drinking his coffee while Kelly, having already finished eating, cleared the table of what she could and kept herself inconspicuously out of the way, leaving the two boys to eat steadily away. Andrew finished eating before Tim, as he had already begun eating before Tim arrived. He got up and excused himself so that he could run upstairs and quickly wash up.

'Is it already 08:55!' exclaimed George as he looked at his watch. 'You'll have to excuse me too young Tim, I have a meeting at nine o'clock and need to fetch a few things from the garage that I require at the meeting.'

'No problem, Uncle George,' said Tim, continuing to enjoy his food while his uncle stood up. 'Make yourself at home, and do what you need to do.' Tim produced a wry smile.

'Ah, Timmy boy,' said George with a hearty laugh while shifting the dining room chair back into place. 'I'm sure you would make a great politician!'

Tim felt easier as a result of the response he received and just laughed a little as he watched his uncle leave the dining room. He sat quietly eating, a feeling of peace and tranquillity descending on him with every pleasurable bite. His seat of serenity was short lived though as only moments later, having just finished eating, the doorbell rang, interrupting his stillness.

'I'll get it for you, Aunt Kelly,' called Tim as he jumped up, realising that George and Andrew were not in the immediate vicinity. Before Kelly had time to respond to Tim, he was off and at the front door.

Tim opened the front door and stared at the cheerful and smiling face looking directly at him, his eyes narrowing as the seconds ticked by.

'Hello, Tim,' greeted Mark Marsh warmly. 'I didn't expect you to open the front door, but a pleasant surprise nonetheless.'

Tim never said a word and in a rather cool manner just closed the door. A few seconds later the doorbell rang again.

'Are you still here?' asked Tim sarcastically, having jerked the front door open, his feeling of peace and tranquillity having long since disappeared, being replaced with a prickling turmoil inside.

'That's not acceptable, Tim!' reprimanded Kelly sternly, overhearing him as she walked into the entrance hall while busy drying her hands on a dish cloth.

Tim was taken by surprise as he had not known his laidback, bubbly aunt to respond with such a tone, and he just turned and looked at her. Kelly took hold of the door handle and opened the door wide bringing Mark, who was still patiently standing there, into her view.

'Tim,' said Kelly firmly, 'you're more than welcome in this home without reserve, but you're also a guest in this home. Therefore, you'll respect those whom we invite into this home as we respect you – understood?'

'Yes, Aunt Kelly,' answered Tim, not able to manage more in reply as he was a little stunned by the rebuff.

'Come in, Mark,' said Kelly politely. 'You're always welcome in our home. George will join you shortly in the living room.'

'Morning, Kelly,' greeted Mark amiably as he wiped the soles of his shoes on the door mat. 'I'll find my way to the living room.'

'That's fine,' said Kelly, standing to the side so that Mark could enter.

'In spite of my "royal welcome",' commented Mark, turning towards Tim, 'it's a pleasure to see you again.'

'The pleasure's all yours!' retorted Tim derogatorily as he looked at Mark coldly.

'Tim!' snapped Kelly firmly. 'That's not acceptable!'

'I heard that on a film many years ago,' said Mark as he laughed, 'and although rude, I've always seen the funny side to it.'

'Even so,' said Kelly, clearly angry at Tim's behaviour, 'I'll not accept it – not in this house!'

'I have a bone to pick with you,' snarled Tim as he shot Mark a flaming glare.

'Oh?' responded Mark a little innocently but not surprised after their encounter a fortnight ago. 'Join me in the living room, and I'll happily listen to you while I wait for your uncle. Is that okay, Kelly?'

'Sure, no problem,' answered Kelly, giving Tim a glare that informed him that she would not tolerate any more of his disrespectful nonsense. 'Provided Tim conducts himself in a well-behaved manner!'

'Okay,' agreed Tim, 'you have my word.'

'I certainly hope so!' said Kelly, displeasure at Tim's conduct still clearly evident in her voice. 'Have you had enough to eat?'

'Yes, thanks,' replied Tim, gratitude for the tasty meal quickly returning to his thoughts, 'it was delicious.'

'Okay, then,' said Kelly, promptly heading back to the kitchen to prepare tea and coffee, while Tim and Mark headed for the living room, where a bone was about to be picked!

Chapter 22

Tim's defiant challenge

'**S**o, what's up?' enquired Mark as he and Tim sat down and sunk into the soft sofas, the early morning sunlight streaming in through the main window and lighting everything in its path, including the dust particles floating about.

'You made a claim the other night at Roccocoa's,' said Tim bluntly, 'that God gave Adam a command not a choice, and as a result of disobedience to that command, sin entered the world.'

'Yes,' replied Mark just as George entered the room, 'that's correct.'

'Well,' said Tim with definite assurance, 'it cannot be true!'

George, realising that a dialogue was about to transpire before him, took his seat by the window and sat quietly, providing himself with a good view of proceedings.

'You obviously have some definite reasons for your confident statement,' said Mark calmly, 'so let me have them.'

'Firstly,' said Tim, 'it's said that all religions lead to God, but not all religions accept the concept of Adam. Therefore, Adam doesn't play a significant role. Secondly and more importantly, many religions don't accept Creation, with many Christians and Christian churches also following the principle of Theistic Evolution, which implies that creation came from the Big Bang and from that we've all evolved. Evolution is claimed to have been proven; therefore, we couldn't have come from Adam. If we didn't come from Adam, there can be no origin of sin and if no sin, we cannot come under "God's" judgement! How do *you* account for and reconcile that?'

Tim now sat silently, satisfied with his synopsis of two critical points and the fact that he was able to get it off his chest – not to mention the justification it provided him with for the rejection of what had been presented to him at Roccocoa's a fortnight ago.

'I don't account for what isn't true,' began Mark thoughtfully, 'nor reconcile with that which didn't happen.'

'What do you mean?' asked Tim with big, staring eyes, stunned by such a statement and unapologetic viewpoint.

'Who ever told you that all roads lead to Rome,' asked Mark, 'or as you put it – that all religions lead to God?'

'That's the generally accepted norm!' replied Tim, a little flustered at the question.

'The two questions we should rather be asking are these,' responded Mark, 'with the first being: even if the Big Bang and evolution have been claimed to be true and proven, is it really true, is it possible and is it proven? And the second being: was it God Himself who said that all religions lead to God, or has this just been assumed by man because there are many religions, and the "politically correct" view is to accept them all?'

Andrew, who had been leaning against the wall at the entrance to the living room after having recently come back downstairs, decided that this was his opportunity to slip in and find a comfortable seat on the sofa rather than continue standing where he was, particularly if the last encounter at Roccocoa's was anything to go by. He greeted Mark and promptly seated himself next to his father.

'I would firstly like to address your comment on "proven evolution",' said Mark, turning his attention back to Tim, 'and then the point on "many faiths". There are many churches and denominations that have adopted the theory of evolution over the Creation account and have declared that Genesis 1–11 are incorrect. However, this is a fatal flaw because there's so much contained in the rest of the Bible with direct reference to these eleven chapters that it's uncanny. To be more specific, there are over 100 references to Genesis in the New Testament, sixty of which are references to Genesis 1–11. All eleven chapters have been referred to, and Jesus referred sixteen times to Genesis 1–11. If these chapters in Genesis were untrue, then so would be the words of God recorded in Isaiah 44 which says, "I am the LORD, who has made all things, who alone stretched out the heavens, who spread out the earth by myself" [29], as would the words of Jesus recorded in Mark 10 where he says, "But at the beginning of creation, God 'made them male and female'" [30], as would the words of the apostle Paul as recorded in Hebrews 11 where he says, "By faith Noah, when warned about things not yet seen, in holy fear built an ark to save his family." [31] These are just a few examples.

'If God's words and Jesus' words and Paul's words are wrong, then the whole Bible cannot be true or trusted, as you sharply pointed out earlier. It should then be discarded and church doors closed, which is the end goal of the institutions and the atheistic evolutionary proponents. In fact, a well-known atheistic and evolutionary proponent has slammed those churches who have accepted such a compromising stance as Theistic Evolution. He said that if Adam and Eve were only ever symbolic, then Jesus had himself tortured and executed for a symbolic sin by a non-existent individual. He said that those who reached such a verdict would be absolutely mad.[32] What an indictment against the church, but it's true. It's sad, however, that it needs to come from the mouth of an atheist!'

'Yes,' agreed Tim, 'that is an indictment against the church, but that comes about because Christianity is a figment of the imagination and doesn't have fast and hard evidences for its grounding.'

'What you're indirectly getting at in that statement,' said Mark, 'will have reference to multiple religions, which I would like to address after the issue of evolution. Many of the compromises in the church today, however, aren't because Christianity is flawed or has no foundation, but because the people in the church are flawed and have no foundation.'

'Mike will be here shortly,' mentioned George. 'He may be able to answer a few of the questions and shed some light on the issue as well.'

'That would be good,' replied Mark, 'and most certainly helpful. Although I've had to do research into this topic because of the very challenges as presented here by Tim, input from Mike is always appreciated. He's often provided me with answers in the past.'

'Are you referring to Michael Aldenberg?' asked Andrew, looking at his father.

'Yes,' replied George, 'he's due here shortly for the meeting about the golf day.'

'In the meantime,' said Mark, keeping focus, 'let's look at some of the issues and see how we do. You refer to the Big Bang.

Many people will ask what this has got to do with evolution, but it's the basis from which all else stems, and it's the heart of what stands against Creation. In my opinion, if a theory were fundamentally true, it would be fundamentally sound, not fundamentally flawed. In evolution, the very concept of how life began, from the beginning of space to its climatic heights, the humanoid, is flawed. A professor of physics who accepted the Big Bang principle said that from the Big Bang there shouldn't be galaxies out there at all, and that even if there are galaxies, they shouldn't be grouped the way they are, and that the Big Bang can't account for the origin of stars either. He said the problem of explaining the existence of galaxies has proved to be one of the thorniest in cosmology.[33] It has also been mathematically shown that galaxies would not form from the Big Bang.[34] This represents problem number one for evolution – if galaxies could not form from the Big Bang, the earth could not have formed, and if the earth could not have formed, life could not have formed. It's a logical progression.'

'The issue,' countered Tim, 'is that they may not have yet correctly discovered the way it could have. There may be parts still missing that will soon be discovered!'

'I'll get it!' said Andrew as they heard the doorbell ring, interrupting the conversation. Being fleet-footed, he was up and out the living room in seconds.

Chapter 23

The counter reasoning

ANDREW cheerfully opened the front door for Michael and without delay took him through to the living room. Michael greeted everyone as he walked down the two steps.

'I'm glad you could make it,' said George, 'You know my nephew, Tim.' Tim was more good-natured with Mike than he had been at Roccocoa's with Mark, promptly standing up to greet him. 'As you know,' added George, 'Tim has a differing perspective on evolution, and we've been discussing some of the issues once again.'

'More a questioning perspective,' responded Tim, quickly clarifying his stance on the matter. 'I don't just accept a view nor do I just discard a view because of a religious hold.'

Kelly decided it was the perfect time to intrude with her fresh brew of coffee and tea, cookies included. She placed her ornately-engraved silver tray on the centre table as the others found their places and sat down. She began quietly and unobtrusively serving everyone while the conversation continued.

'Let's assume there was a "Big Bang",' said Mark, having

received his hot mug of coffee from Kelly, 'and that all the galaxies came into existence, and that the earth was formed. Let's address a further-down-the-line critical step – the living cell. Maybe you would like to continue on this point?' he asked George, who was once again sitting comfortably listening.

'If you like,' replied George, sitting a little more uprightly, the sun still streaming nicely in through the window and providing a gentle warmth. 'I was actually reading an article yesterday, which claimed that an ancient lake on Mars had been discovered. The article continued to say that the exciting part was that lakes were considered the perfect environment for simple life to develop.[35] I'm not sure if they were referring to the "primordial soup" that was to have apparently sparked off the first living cells, but the point is this: it all seems great, but none of it comes with hard facts or provides the true issues involved. It's like me showing you a rock and saying that from this rock will emerge a motor vehicle because the rock contains iron ore. In the days of Darwin some may have considered this feasible, but it shouldn't be so today. In Darwin's day the cell hadn't yet been discovered, but today we not only know about the cell, but have great in-depth detail about it. We have in-depth knowledge about DNA, including ATP and Kinesin, and I'm sure that we've not yet reached the greatest depths yet! Currently, the ATP synthase enzyme is the tiniest motor known to man, 100 million billion of them could fit into a pinhead.[36] Darwin said the following, "If it could be demonstrated that any complex organ existed which could not possibly have been formed by numerous, successive slight modifications, my theory would absolutely break down."[37] Today, however, his theory is still being held up and hailed by the evolutionary proponents who do not provide the intrinsic criteria, statistics of probability, irreducible complexity or genuine hard-core evidence for what is simply claimed.'

'That can't be true,' objected Tim.

'It is true, Tim,' defended George. 'The complexities of life form, and the amount of perfect matches and degree of information needed to form life is staggering. The more we've found out and learned, the higher the percentage of improbability of chance climbs. As I mentioned about the comparison of the ore to car and the lake to life, you would never consider that a sophisticated automobile with all its moving, interlinked and interdependent parts, could possibly form on its own from a lump of rock containing iron ore, let alone work perfectly! The intensity of complexity within living organisms requiring life to form is even greater than this!'

Tim met George's eye contact, not liking what he had heard but not prepared to comment.

'Let me ask you the following question,' said George after having paused momentarily. 'No, rather let me be fair; let me ask evolutionist professors the question – how did life originate?'

'That's for the biology boffins,' perked up Tim cheekily, knowing that his uncle was a microbiologist and Andrew was studying to become one.

'You see, Tim,' continued George, 'some people, including professors, will try and answer this question. However, they cannot confidently or effectively do so. Two honest evolutionist professors have answered it by saying in simple terms that nobody knows how a mixture of lifeless chemicals spontaneously organized themselves into the first living cell,[38] and we, meaning science and professors, don't really know how life originated on this planet.[39] In Darwin's day it was simple – there was no living cell, and there was no DNA. But now the depth of the simple question can be asked as follows – how did life with hundreds of proteins originate just by chemistry, taking into account that a minimal cell needs several hundred proteins? Even if every atom in the universe were an experiment with all the correct amino acids present for every possible molecular vibration in the supposed evolutionary age of the universe, not even one average-sized functional protein would form.[40] So how was this accomplished by mere chance, without intelligent input?'

Tim kept silent and listened as George continued.

'Let me ask a second question,' said George. 'How did the DNA code originate? The code is a sophisticated language system with letters and words where the meaning of the words are unrelated to the chemical properties of the letters, just as the information on a page is not a product of the chemical properties of the ink. How did the DNA coding system arise without it being created?'[41]

'What about mutations?' asked Tim. 'They account for development and change.'

'Mutations account for change, yes,' replied George, 'but for development, no. You see, this is where evolutionists get the ordinary layman, who doesn't know the real in's and out's about these things, but they are deceptive and not truthful. How could mutations, which are accidental copying mistakes – DNA "letters" exchanged, deleted or added, genes duplicated, chromosome inversions, etc. – create the huge volumes of information in the DNA of living things? How could such errors create 3 billion letters of DNA information to change a microbe into a microbiologist? There is information for how to make proteins but also for controlling their use. This is much like a cookbook containing the ingredients as well as the instructions for how and when to use them. One without the other is useless. Mutations are known for their destructive effects, including over

1,000 human diseases. Rarely are they even helpful. But how can scrambling existing DNA information create a new biochemical pathway or nano-machines with many components, to make "goo-to-you" evolution possible?

'For example, how did a 32-component rotary motor like ATP synthase, which produces the energy currency ATP for all life, or robots like kinesin, which is literally a "postman" delivering parcels inside cells, originate? [42] These are real questions that cannot be answered by random chance or mutations, the issues are too complex. An evolutionary biochemist once wrote that we must concede that there are presently no detailed Darwinian accounts of the evolution of any biochemical or cellular system, only a variety of wishful speculations.[43] My last question is, why do we even consider wishful speculations, let alone accept them as fact?'

'What about the computer "simulations" of evolution,' asked Tim, not merely accepting what was being told to him, 'that have proved that random selection can be achieved in relatively short spaces of time? [44] The computer "simulations" are not assumptions!'

'That's an interesting question, Tim,' responded Andrew, joining in the discussion for the first time. 'I'm very familiar with that as it was used by one of my professors in a lecture to illustrate the speed at which evolution can develop. He told us that in the 1980s a computer program was written that generated phrases randomly while preserving the positions of individual letters that happened to be correctly placed; in effect, selecting phrases more like Hamlet's. On average, the program re-created the phrase in just 336 iterations, less than 90 seconds. Even more amazing, it could reconstruct Shakespeare's entire play in just four and a half days! [44]

'Well, there you have it!' remarked Tim, satisfaction written all over his face.

'That is quite amazing,' said Andrew, 'and it's widely used by atheists and evolutionists as being "simulations" of evolution. However, I did a check into it because it sounded too good to be true.'

'What were your findings?' asked Mark with great interest.

'I found out it's a lot of bluff!' replied Andrew.

'How can you say that!' responded Tim disapprovingly.

'Easily,' replied Andrew, 'let me explain. Such simulations work toward a known goal, so they are far from a parallel to real evolution, which has no foresight. The simulations also use "organisms" with high reproductive rates producing many offspring, high mutation rates, a large probability of a beneficial mutation, and a selection coefficient of one, which is perfect selection, instead of 0.01 or less, which parallels real life more accurately. The "organisms" have tiny "genomes" with minute information content, so they are less prone to error catastrophe, and they are not affected by the chemical and thermodynamic constraints of a real organism.[45] However, the goal is not reached if realistic values are programmed, or it takes so long that it shows that evolution is impossible.[46]

'Also, when it comes to the origin of *first* life, natural selection cannot be invoked, because natural selection is differential reproduction. That is, if it worked at all, it could only work on a living organism that could produce offspring. By its very definition, it could not work on non-living chemicals.[47]

Therefore, chance *alone* must produce the precise sequences needed, so these simulations do not apply. And a further problem with the alleged chemical soup is reversibility, intensifying the difficulty of obtaining the right sequence by chance.' [47]

'What about the fact that believing in Creation still requires a person to have faith,' threw Tim at them, quite annoyed by what he had heard, 'as there's no provable evidence for it?'

'Let me ask you the following two questions,' said Mark. 'A being greater than our ability to fully understanding Him or the vastness of His intelligence, power and might, created the heavens and the earth and all that inhabit it. This you see as requiring faith to believe it, is this correct?'

'Yes,' replied Tim.

'Second question,' continued Mark. 'Total unintelligence, without the ability to think or reason, with no power, with no might and with no purpose formed the heavens and the earth, and this same unintelligence, without the ability to think or reason, with no power, with no might and with no purpose developed a human being from pond scum – the only thing required being time. This you see as not requiring faith to believe it, is this correct?'

Tim looked at Mark for a moment, his dark eyes penetrating the light.

'But there's scientific proof,' said Tim eventually, skirting the question, 'there's evidence!'

'We've just told you,' said George, 'the proof isn't real; the evidence is non-existent. In fact, there is no concrete answer at all for the critical and fundamental issues, and the more we learn and discover, the greater the rift for the possibility of chance becomes, but it is something you will not be told.'

'You seem to use logic,' said Mark politely, 'as was evident by your earlier analysis, so let me present a few points of logic to you.'

Tim looked at Mark once again with penetrating eyes, his

arms folded tightly against his chest.

'The atheist and evolutionist,' said Mark, 'reject certain occurrences in the Bible such as the Flood, virgin birth, and the raising from the dead, based on the assumed fact that it's impossible or highly illogical. Yet on the other hand, they accept aspects in their evolutionary model that are impossible and defy logic. Let me explain. Have you ever seen dead fish sink to the bottom of the sea or lake? No, they float, but evolution requires that they did sink, and that they weren't scavenged. How is it possible that fish fossils have been found on Mt Everest, and certain animals are fossilised standing up? Could animals have stayed standing in the upright position for millions of years, undamaged by time, scavenging or decay while slowly being fossilised as layer upon layer built up? When trees die do they stay standing for millions of years, not falling over or rotting away? Yet the evolutionary model requires that they did. This is not what we see today, yet the evolutionary model uses the principle of uniformitarianism!'

'I explained uniformitarianism to Tim at the hut,' informed Mike, interjecting, 'when we were on the Smoking Gorge trail two weeks ago. Do you remember it, Tim?'

'Yes, I remember,' replied Tim. 'It's the principle that what we observe today is what took place in the past.'

'Then you're all ahead of me,' said Mark with a smile. 'That's good news! The question we have to ask is, why is it all so flexible? This isn't only convenient, it's hypocritical and illogical too! How is it that an evolutionary biochemist can say that they must concede that there are presently no detailed Darwinian accounts of the evolution of any biochemical or cellular system, only a variety of wishful speculations[43] – and evolution is accepted? How can an atheist and evolutionary proponent say that biology is the study of complicated things that have the appearance of having been designed with a purpose,[48] yet not consider that these complicated things are designed by an intelligent designer? How he can further say that evolution has been observed, it just has not been observed while it is happening,[49] is unintelligible. How can a former Harvard palaeontologist say that the maintenance of stability within species must be considered as a major evolutionary problem,[50] and we must happily accept evolution? A further hypocrisy is that intelligent man has turned to "unintelligent creation" to find out how things work and to copy "unintelligent chance" because it works so well!

'This recalls to mind Proverbs 25:2, which says the following, "It is the glory of God to conceal a matter; to search out a matter is the glory of kings." What it reminds me of is that man can discover hidden things such as the living cell, ATP and kinesin. We can discover the hidden universe and the vastness of it as it was hidden from us until we developed machinery and equipment to see into it, but none of it points to the glory of man, it points to the magnitude and glory of God the Creator. Man, however, doesn't want to acknowledge this nor does he want to accept it, because it makes him accountable to a God that on a daily basis becomes greater as we discover more both in the micro and macro worlds!'

'The evolutionary model,' said George, 'is like a puzzle. The starting pieces, which can be described as the Big Bang, have been force fit. This has increased the problem for the subsequent pieces that are to fit around it as they have to force fit even more to get the pieces to fit. In the end you have a fantastic story that is beyond the realms of probability or reason, and provided that you only briefly glance at it from a far off distance, it looks like a credible picture. Get up close and you see the gaps, the forced effort and more importantly, a distorted and warped picture that is not only not trustworthy but one that makes no sense at all! However, you have to make the decisions for yourself, Tim, no-one can make them for you!'

Tim looked at George and let out a sigh but did not say a word!

Chapter 24

God and His signature

'**I** WOULD like to answer your second point that you raised, Tim,' said Mark.

'What point is that may I ask?' enquired Mike.

'Tim mentioned the concept that all roads lead to Rome,' replied George, 'or as he put it, all religions lead to God.'

'I would like to answer your statement in two sections,' continued Mark, realising that the statement was not a simple one, and time was once again going to be a factor in getting the information across before irritability stepped in, or a state of weariness was reached, 'the first section being what the Bible and God say about the way to Him.

'The first of the Ten Commandments that God gave,' began Mark, having first shifted and leaned back in the sofa, 'was recorded in Exodus 20:2 – "You shall have no other gods before me." God continues to say that He is a jealous God and will punish those who disobey His commands. Jesus said in John 14:6, "I am the way the truth and the life. No-one comes to the Father except through me." The apostle Peter said in Acts 4:12,

"Salvation is found in no-one else, for there is no other name under heaven given to men by which we must be saved." Peter was talking about Jesus. The apostle Paul said in 1 Timothy 2:5, "For there is one God and one mediator between God and men, the man Christ Jesus, who gave himself as a ransom for all men – the testimony given in its proper time." As recorded in Acts 17, Paul also spoke to the Athenians about the "unknown God" which he explained was "the God who made the world and everything in it, the Lord of heaven and earth." He called the Athenians "very religious" but told them that they needed to turn from their idols, for as he said in verse thirty, "In the past God overlooked such ignorance, but now he commands all people everywhere to repent." If you remember what was told to you at Roccocoa's, that God gave Adam a command not a choice—'

'Yes,' interjected Tim casually, 'I remember.'

'Of course you remember!' exclaimed Mark quickly, giving himself a tap on his forehead with the palm of his hand. 'That was part of your initial dispute that you raised this morning, wasn't it?'

'Yip,' responded Tim a little cheekily.

'Anyway,' continued Mark, 'Jesus also gave the command for his disciples to "go and make disciples of all nations" [51] and to "teach them to obey everything I have commanded you." [52] Again, here is a command, not a request or a suggestion or a plea. But the issue that I'm getting at is this: why was this the case if many religions lead to God? If God knew that all religions lead to Him, why did He say what He said? As such, religion in its context of current world understanding will not save a man, it only provides him with a false sense of security. With God it's about repentance, restitution and relationship. Salvation cannot be won or bought or forced!'

'Those are rather interesting words,' remarked Tim disrespectfully, 'coming from someone whose livelihood and income depends on the church!'

Mark stopped, briefly having been thrown from his continuing point, and took a moment to catch what Tim had said. The others looked on silently, quite surprised at Tim's impertinence. George nearly rebuked Tim but held his tongue at the last second.

'I do not sell salvation,' responded Mark, maintaining composure so as not to move away from the focus and miss his point, 'I preach the Word of God and minister where needed. My duty is before God, not the church, and it is to speak the truth, not woo the people or tickle their ears. If I stray from that I have no right to stand behind the pulpit, and I would be of no value to the people who sit before me.'

Mark leaned forward and calmly flicked a bug off his knee, Tim staring at him.

'Getting back to the point,' continued Mark steadfastly. 'If God knew that all religions lead to Him, why did He say what He said, why did Jesus say what He said, and why did Peter and Paul say what they said, if it wasn't necessary?'

'I don't know about God,' said Tim suspiciously, 'but maybe Jesus, Peter and Paul wanted followers?'

'I don't think so,' responded George, not liking some of Tim's manner but careful not to reprimand him unnecessarily, 'because if you look at the lives of Jesus, Peter and Paul they were never trying to win friends, gain favours or please the crowd.'

'That's absolutely so,' confirmed Mark. 'The reason was because they knew it was true. There's only one way to God – and God commands that all people repent!'

'That's all good and well,' said Tim, 'but you're overlooking one issue.'

'What's that?' asked Mark.

'The fact that you say this is true,' answered Tim firmly, 'and someone from another religion says differently. Who says that you – or to put it more directly, Jesus or Peter or Paul were right? And who says the Bible holds the authority and that it's credible?'

'A very pertinent observation and question,' responded Mark. 'It's in fact the second point in the answer to your original statement. The Bible makes some substantial claims, and if it is not the Word of God and not credible, why should anyone believe it? For me to accept what it says and to pass on what it claims, I must have reason for it, so let's look into that aspect.'

'Is this going to be another "Roccocoa's"?' asked Tim a little sarcastically, not wanting to repeat what he considered to have been an ordeal.

'I was waiting for that,' replied Mark with a chuckle. 'I'll be as brief as possible, but it's vital that you are given the full perspective as best as possible.'

'I'm listening,' responded Tim, in jest making as though he was yawning, causing the others to laugh.

'Let's start at the beginning,' continued Mark after the light-hearted moment. 'In 2 Timothy 3:16,17 it says, "All Scripture is God-breathed and is useful for teaching, rebuking, correcting and training in righteousness, so that the man of God may be thoroughly equipped for every good work." This means that from the beginning it was God-breathed; that includes Genesis 1:1. An interesting theme that runs through the Bible from Genesis to Revelation is the number seven. It's the number of perfection, and the Bible indicates that the number seven is God's number.'

'Can you explain that in more detail?' asked Andrew, who promptly received a scowl from Tim.

'Certainly I can!' replied Mark enthusiastically before drinking the last of his coffee. 'In Genesis we have Creation which was seven days – six days of creating and on the seventh day God rested.[53] There is Enoch who was taken to God – he was the seventh generation from Adam.[54] Noah was given the rainbow as a sign from God – it has seven colours.[55] In fact, as a slight diversion, music has seven notes and all scales are divided into seven, with the major scales of the same letter equalling seven sharps or flats together. For example, the key signature of C major has no flats and no sharps, but the key signature of C-flat major has seven flats. The key signature of E major has four sharps, while the key signature of E-flat major has three flats, thus always equalling seven in total. Continuing on, Pharaoh's dream, as recorded in Genesis, consisted of seven fat cows and seven thin cows.[56] In Exodus, God called Moses on Mount Sinai on the seventh day.[57] The Sabbath, the seventh day, was instituted and made holy to the Lord.[58] The ordination of Aaron, as recorded in Leviticus, took seven days.[59] They sprinkled oil seven times in the anointing of the tabernacle.[60] The seventh year became the Sabbatical year, a rest to the Lord.[61] The Jubilee year was made up of seven Sabbaths of years, then the Jubilee year.[62] In Deuteronomy it is recorded that debts were cancelled every seventh year.[63] In Joshua, they marched around the walls of Jericho for six days. On the seventh day, seven priests had trumpet horns and they marched seven times around the city.[64] We know what happened after that!'

'If you believe it,' interrupted Tim, a cheeky smirk on his face.

'Yes, Tim,' responded George, giving him a look of

displeasure, 'if you believe it!'

'In Kings,' continued Mark, unfussed by the remark, 'Elijah prayed for rain, and the seventh time he prayed a cloud appeared.[65] Elisha raised a dead boy and the boy sneezed seven times.[66] Naaman had leprosy and was told to go and wash seven times. At the seventh washing he was healed.[67] In the book of Job, God's command for a sacrifice was seven bulls and seven rams.[68] In the book of Daniel, God in judgement consigned Nebuchadnezzar to living like a beast of the field for seven years, and Gabriel's prophecy to Daniel constituted seventy sevens.[69] In the book of Matthew, Jesus declared seven woes.[70] John's gospel strongly emphasises Jesus' deity and points to Jesus in the number seven: seven signs or works done,[71] seven "I AM" statements made[72] and seven witnesses calling Jesus the Son of God.[73] And in Revelation, there are seven churches[74], seven seals[75], seven trumpets[76], seven plagues[77] and the period of tribulation and great trouble is seven years.[78] There are a myriad more instances in which the number seven comes up. These are just some that I recall from Genesis to Revelation.'

'That may just be coincidence,' remarked Tim, happy to down play any possible form of divine association.

'You could look at it that way,' responded Mike. 'However, when taking into account that the Bible was written by forty authors from diversified backgrounds and locations over a period of 1500 years and the authors not having worked together, it's not likely at all.'

'Further to that,' added Mark, 'if you recall, Tim, the sermon when you attended the service, where I spoke about the birth of Jesus and about the plain recorded text of his genealogy – regarding the forty-two generations divided into three groups of fourteen. Was that also coincidence?'

'Maybe yes, maybe no,' replied Tim with a smirk.

'Let's go deeper then,' said Mark with a brief smile. 'There's a further part to the verses in Matthew, and I'll explain it to you shortly, but there's an interesting occurrence regarding the Bible that is unique to it that I want to mention beforehand. The Old Testament was written in Hebrew, with a few parts in Aramaic, while the New Testament was written in Greek. The interesting thing is that both the Hebrew and Greek languages use the letters of their respective alphabets for numbers. The English language along with other languages use separate alphabet and numeric codes, but these two, the Hebrew and the Greek, use them combined. What this means is that each word and each sentence has a numeric value that can be calculated. There was a man by the name of Ivan Panin, a Russian, who was an active nihilist—'

'Do you know what a nihilist is, Tim?' asked George, interjecting.

'Someone who rejects all religious and moral principles,' replied Tim, 'and has a belief that nothing really exists.' Tim produced a big Cheshire grin as he polished his finger nails on his shirt in cheeky self-confidence.

'We have a smart cockerel here,' chipped in Mike with a chuckle.

'Well, Panin was a nihilist,' continued Mark, 'and due to his rebellious plots against the ruling authorities of his country, was exiled. He ended up in the United States, where he studied at Harvard. He converted from agnosticism to Christianity, which actually made headlines in the local newspaper.[79] As a mathematician, Panin said to himself that if God were a mathematician, He should be able to show Himself in such a way. He then discovered the aspects of the Hebrew and Greek alphabets containing numeric values and began analysing them.'

'Didn't he start with the New Testament?' asked George.

'Yes, that's correct,' replied Mark, 'but for our purposes, I would like to start from the beginning with Genesis.'

'If I may butt in quickly,' asked Kelly from the living room entrance. 'Can I bring a fresh pot of tea and coffee and a few more cookies?'

'That would be lovely, dear,' replied George, pleased with the offer. 'I'm sure we all would enjoy that. You should have seen Mark's face when he drank the last of his cold coffee.'

'Not so, not so!' objected Mark as they all began to laugh. 'Kelly, your coffee was enjoyable, even cold.' Mark pulled a face that showed otherwise, and they all just laughed some more.

'You need to drink it while it's hot,' responded Kelly as she gathered the tray from the centre table. 'That's not my fault!'

Kelly turned and headed for the kitchen, knowing they were only joking with her. She had the kettle on and the tea and coffee brewing in no time at all, filling the house with the fresh smell of the delightful brews.

The light-hearted jest was a welcome reprieve from the general intensity of the discussion. Andrew thought to himself that the conversation was a little easier than the one they had had a fortnight ago at Roccocoa's, but that maybe this was due to there being more people involved, and because it was a little more relaxed on the whole. However, the topic of discussion was no less intense and still created a degree of tension in certain camps as it continued!

Chapter 25

God's watermark

'GENESIS 1:1,' said Mark as he returned the attention to the discussion, 'has an interesting part to play. It's the very first verse of the Bible, provides the very first explanation of existence, is the foundation of the principle that we are accountable to God, and is also the very point that evolution stands against, being at the very heart of the continuing feud evolution has with Christianity and Creation. The verse in English reads, "In the beginning God created the heavens and the earth". Do you recall that I mentioned shortly ago that the theme throughout the Bible contains the number seven, and that God's number in the Bible is seven?'

'Yes,' replied Andrew, the others including Tim just nodding their affirmative.

'Here's a breakdown of this verse,' said Mark, 'both in its word structure, and in its numeric structure.'

'This is based on the Hebrew writing,' checked Mike, 'not on the English translation, correct?'

'Correct,' confirmed Mark. 'I gave you the English

translation as it's the language we know, however, the breakdown is based on the Hebrew text. The number of Hebrew words used is seven. The number of Hebrew letters used is twenty-eight, which is a multiple of seven. There are three nouns – God, Heaven and Earth – the letters of which add up to fourteen, which is a multiple of seven. That was the structure and words of the verse, now I'll provide the numeric aspects. The three nouns – God, Heaven and Earth – which have a cumulative fourteen letters have a numeric value of 133, which is a multiple of seven. The first and last letters of all seven words have a numeric value of 1393, which is a multiple of seven. The last letters of the first and last word have a numeric value of 490, which is a multiple of seven. There is only one verb in the sentence – created – and it has a numeric value of 203, which is also a multiple of seven. These are only a few of the dozens of numeric features represented here.' [80]

'What are you actually trying to say?' asked Tim a little offensively.

'What it's showing,' replied Mark, 'is that such structure couldn't very easily have been established by man. More so, it points to God in all its form. The very first piece of the puzzle, as George put it earlier, and the very foundation upon which Scripture starts is centred in and around God in every way.'

Kelly popped her head into the living room again. She saw that she had a small window of opportunity to sneak in with her silver tray bearing the coffee and tea pots and an assortment of colourful cookies that made the sight all the more appealing. Her entry caused the conversation to pause once again as they all watched her.

'Here you go, gentlemen,' said Kelly warmly as she placed the tray on the centre table, steam wafting from the pots' spouts and providing a strong, pleasant aroma in the room that complimented the enticing look of the colourful cookies.

'That looks good,' complimented Mike.

'I'll leave you all to do the serving,' said Kelly as she turned to leave. 'I have a few things I need to attend to.'

'I'll assist,' said George as he got up. 'Thanks very much, dear.'

'No problem,' responded Kelly as she turned and gave him a loving smile. 'Please just drink it while it's still hot!'

George was not quite as skilful with tea or coffee pots as Kelly was, but he managed to do the job adequately and they all received a fresh cup of hot coffee, Andrew being the only one to take tea. There was silence for a while as they enjoyed the delicious cookies and sipped their pleasant hot drinks, thoughtful expressions on their faces. The sun, still beaming in through the window, cut through the air with its rays that now spread out across the room. Its ability to reveal and bring to life the small dust particles that would not ordinarily be seen even in the daylight, caught Andrew's attention as he sat chewing quietly on a tasty cookie.

Tim sat silently. He had been listening, as he wanted answers, but there was something inside that resisted just accepting what he was being told. He knew that he was being influenced by that which had challenged his standpoint and cautioned him about his attitude and opinions. This was the reason he was prepared to sit and listen, even if he was resistant. That gentle, prodding voice that had previously stopped him from overruling that which he did not like was now silent, but its influence was nonetheless present. Tim's thoughts were in a state of unrest, for there had been aspects presented to him that he could not overrule but which beat at the foundation of his understanding. Was he to just abandon his understanding of what life meant, without a fight? What would it do to the rest his beliefs, and where would it leave him? Tim wrestled within himself, for he was not going to be hoodwinked yet felt that in some way he had already been by his current beliefs. However, he thought his life was fine. To change it, he had to be convinced; the reason had to be clear in his understanding!

'What you've just told me doesn't convince me entirely,' remarked Tim firmly, restarting the conversation after having finished his coffee. 'It may convince you, but not me!'

'That's fair comment,' responded Mark calmly, placing his empty coffee mug on the centre table before sitting back in the soft, comfortable sofa. 'I said that I would get back to the verses read in Matthew about the genealogy of Jesus, which was forty-two generations, a multiple of seven and six. Well, another way of looking at it is from Abraham, the father of the chosen people, to the exile when they ceased as an independent people and from the exile to Jesus, the promised Deliverer. This still retains the groupings of seven, just in two thirds and one third – in other words, twenty-eight generations and fourteen generations. If this is done, Matthew 1:1–11 fits the first part, and verses 12–17 fits the second part. For the first division – the number of words in total is forty-nine, the number of words beginning with vowels is twenty-eight, the number of words beginning with consonants is twenty-one, the number of words that end with a vowel is seven, and the number of words that end with a consonant is forty-two. These are all multiples of seven, but it goes further and the following are all multiples of seven as well. The number of letters is 266. Of these 266 letters, 140 are vowels and 126 are consonants, there are thirty-five words occurring more than once, there are fourteen words occurring only once, the number of words occurring in more than one form is seven, and the number of words occurring in only one form is forty-two. Of the forty-nine words, forty-two are nouns and seven are not. There are twenty-eight male proper names and there are seven female proper names. Verses 12–17 also have their own unique forming where numerical value is included. The remaining verses of the chapter have their own unique aspects as well, such as there being 161 words, which is a multiple of seven; it uses a vocabulary of seventy-seven words, of which twenty-eight were spoken by the angel, and their numeric value also being a multiple of seven.[81] This is just a few of the aspects.'

'What you're getting at,' commented Andrew, 'is that this too couldn't have been devised by man.'

'Yes,' said Mark.

'What you're also indirectly saying,' added Mike, 'is that the Bible validates and vindicates itself as true, it doesn't need the testimony of man to uphold it.'

'That is true,' confirmed Mark. 'God requires man to proclaim it and defend it, but He Himself will also defend it and has validated its authenticity and will uphold it.'

Tim just quietly listened and did not respond to the comments.

'You see,' added Mark, 'it's like a monetary bank note. The bank note needs to be signed by the governor of the reserve bank to make it valid, and it's authenticated and proved not to be a fraud by the watermark it contains. The Word of God is no different. The number seven is God's signature throughout the Bible, and the numerical aspects are His watermark, which no human could duplicate.'

'You don't think that this could have been done over time?' asked Tim sceptically and rather sarcastically. 'I mean, you did say that it was written over a period of 1500 years!'

'Yes, Tim,' replied Mark confidently, 'it was written over a period of 1500 years. However, it wasn't "worked on" over a period of 1500 years. There's another aspect that I would like to show you, one that Ivan Panin produced that demonstrates the impossibility for this phenomenon to be created by the hands of men even over time. The same way that the evidential statistics show that evolution couldn't have happened over time is the same way it can be shown that this wonder within the Bible, which is real, couldn't have been created by chance or over time. There's design in Creation and there's design in the Word of the Creator!'

Chapter 26

True validity

'**I**'M hearing you,' said Tim with a wry smile, 'but I don't know if I'm listening.'

'I'm not sure if I'll get the following all right,' said Mark, 'as it also contains a number of points, but I'll try my best.'

'Are you perhaps going to be referring to the numerical connection that the New Testament books have with each other?' asked George, taking a guess at what Mark would likely mention next.

'Yes,' replied Mark, looking at him quizzically, 'I am.'

'Hang on a second,' responded George as he slowly got up from the sofa. 'I have that in my office. I once cut and pasted the main facts and then printed it. You can read it.'

'That will be great!' exclaimed Mark enthusiastically. 'I was able to memorise the first numerical aspects, but for some reason I've not been able to master this section yet – although the numbers aren't unbearably large or the information too difficult to retain, seemingly anyway!'

'There's no need to wrack your brain this early on in the

morning,' said George with a chuckle as he disappeared round the corner on his way to his study. He was back in a moment and stretched out his hand to give his folder containing the printout to Mark.

'You read it, George,' said Mark.

'Are you sure?' questioned George.

'Of course,' replied Mark as he chuckled softly. 'You're more familiar with your font than I am.'

'Putting it that way,' said George, laughing lightly at the silly joke, 'how can I refuse!'

George sat down again in no hurry and made himself comfortable.

'Shall I start with the second chapter of Matthew,' asked George after clearing his throat, 'seeing that you've already mentioned chapter one?'

'Absolutely fine,' replied Mark.

'"The second chapter of Matthew,"' began George, reading loud and clear, '"tells of the childhood of Jesus. The number of words is 161, there are 896 letters, these letters represent 238 forms, these are all multiples of seven. The numeric value of the vocabulary is 123, 529; the numeric value of the forms is 166, 985, and these are multiples of seven. This continues through the pages. This chapter has at least four logical divisions, and each division shows alone the same phenomena found in the chapter as a whole. There are speeches made by Herod, the Magi and the Angel, but the numeric phenomena remains pronounced despite this, such that it represents aspects within aspects. Each is perfect in itself, though forms only part of the rest and makes sense as a whole. Every paragraph in Matthew is constructed in exactly the same manner, the only aspect changing being the degree of difficulty of construction increasing in geometrical progression. The reason being is that Matthew writes numeric relations to what has been before and to what goes after. In his last chapter, he uses seven words not used by himself before. Furthermore, in his first section, the genealogy—"'

'The genealogy was mentioned earlier,' inserted Mark.

"'the words found nowhere else in the New Testament occur forty-two times and have 126 letters,'" continued George after Mark's quick insertion. "'These are a few numeric features of these words, and they contain multiples of not only sevens, but 6 sevens. This you will recognise as a feature further on. The question asked here being – how did Matthew know that such words would not be used by the other seven writers of the New Testament, the formation of which consists of twenty-seven books. This could have only happened if Matthew had the entire New Testament before him when compiling his book, however, we know this was not possible as the New Testament was only put together in the fourth century. The Gospel of Mark shows the very same phenomena. The last twelve verses of Mark presents some sixty features of sevens. A few of them being: it has 175 words, a vocabulary of ninety-eight words, there are 553 letters, and these letters have 133 forms. All are multiples of seven, and so it goes on in great detail. Furthermore, it can also be shown that Mark would have had to have had the whole of the New Testament before him when writing his Gospel, because he uses one word found nowhere else in the New Testament. This word represents seven features of sevens, the numerical value of it is 581, which is a multiple of seven, in the vocabulary it is preceded by forty-two words, in the passage itself, by 126 words, both of which are multiples not only of seven, but of six as well.

"'The Gospel of Luke presents the same phenomena, and so

does the rest of the New Testament books written by John, Paul, James, Peter and Jude. All eight writers present the same mathematical aspects, and all must have had the complete New Testament in order to write their book containing such phenomena. But considering that four of the eight wrote two books or more, it makes it more perplexing to try and find out how each book was written last, John having written five books and Paul having written fourteen.'" [82] George stopped reading and looked up, silence filling the room. He got up and walked across to the centre table, cheekily stretching out and tapping Tim on his head with the folder.

'Yes, yes,' groused Tim as he watched George place his folder on the glass-top table, rather unimpressed with his uncle's antics, but his thoughtful, yet determined look quickly returned.

Andrew gave Tim a glance and from the look on his face was glad that Tim was not relying on him for a lift home.

'It's amazing,' said Mike, breaking the silence, 'how the connection of the numerics fits. It reminds me of 2 Timothy 3:16,17, which you mentioned earlier, Mark, which says, "All Scripture is God-breathed and is useful for teaching, rebuking, correcting and training in righteousness, so that the man of God may be thoroughly equipped for every good work."'

'It is amazing how it all fits,' agreed Mark, 'and the verses in Timothy are certainly applicable. Unless Tim has further questions or issues, I would like to conclude the point regarding the authenticity, credulity and authority of the Bible with a few final aspects.

'No questions,' responded Tim, 'you may happily finish off!'

Andrew was not sure if Tim was being agreeable or sarcastic but knew it would not touch sides with Mark if it was meant as sarcasm.

'No-one ever questions the accuracy of current prints of writers such as Aristotle or Plato,' said Mark as he began to conclude, 'but between them there are only fifty-six manuscripts which have a time gap of 1200–1400 years from the time of the writer to the earliest manuscript held. However, the Bible is placed under question, saying it has changed and couldn't be the same as the original writings, yet there are over 24,000 manuscripts, some with a time gap of only twenty-five years.[83] The transmission standards used in those days were so high that no jot was omitted as the scroll would have been rejected and redone. Sadly, today some of the *new* translations coming off the press are corrupt, but this isn't because the publishers don't have sound texts to work from, it's because they have chosen to produce the translations with a slanted, prejudiced, even purposed perspective or agenda, and one needs to be selective.

'Predictive prophecy is another part that plays a major role and is the most powerful way to demonstrate that the Bible came from God and had to come from God. There are over 300 prophecies, to the minutest detail, about the birth of the coming Messiah, all of which are fulfilled in Jesus. Using the science of probability, the chance of any one man fulfilling just eight of these prophecies is 1×10^{17}. To make this a visual understanding of the chance of probability take silver coins, fill the state of Texas 2-feet deep, mark one coin, blindfold a man and let him try to pick the marked coin first try.[84] The chance of fulfilling just forty-eight of the over 300 prophecies is 1×10^{157}. To explain this in size of selection, the estimated number of electrons in the whole universe is only 1×10^{79}. [85] There are a number of confirming factors, including archaeology and science. A former director of an institute of archaeology said he knew of no finding in archaeology that had been properly confirmed, which was in opposition to the Scriptures and that the Bible was the most accurate history textbook the world had ever seen.[86] One of the earliest books of the Bible that was written was Leviticus, and it says that the life is in the blood.[87] This was something that took a long time to discover, yet it was written in the Bible millennia before. In fact, the first American president, George Washington, died in AD1799 as a result of the medical practise of bloodletting, whereby a doctor would bleed a person to remove impurities or sickness. What they didn't realise was that they were removing his life not his sickness, but had they known what Leviticus says, it may have been different. The sceptic is normally the one who won't look at the facts but will make arrogant assumptions based on ignorance!'

'But what you've mentioned,' objected Tim, 'was all relevant to times more than two millennia ago! All the prophecies you mentioned were more than two millennia ago and apparently fulfilled more than two millennia ago! That seems rather convenient to me, being spoken today.'

'That's true,' affirmed Mark, 'from a history point of view but not from a relevance point of view. Are you familiar with the history of Israel?'

'What I do know,' replied Tim, 'is that in AD70 the Temple was destroyed, the Jews were expelled, and as a nation they no longer existed until AD1948 when the current Israel was established.'

'That's good enough for the moment,' said Mark with a smile. 'Now listen to the following, keeping in mind the history that you've just mentioned.'

Mark paused for a second while he scratched his neck.

'You've heard me mention the prophet Isaiah who lived more than 2600 years ago,' said Mark, continuing on. 'Well there were also the prophets Ezekiel and Zechariah who lived around 2500–2600 years ago. These three prophets also prophesied concerning the second coming of Jesus, not just for his first coming that took place 2000 years ago. Some of these prophecies were concerning the nation of Israel and here are a few: they'd return to the land again, Isaiah 43; they'd become a nation again, Isaiah 11; they'd become a nation again in one day, Isaiah 66; they'd become a united nation – in other words no longer the two tribes of Israel and Judah, Ezekiel 37; they'd have a powerful military and become a source of world conflict, Zechariah 12; their currency would become the Shekel, Ezekiel 45; they'd blossom as a rose in the desert, Isaiah 35. These are a few Old Testament prophecies made more than 2500 years ago, and we've seen them fulfilled in our day!

'One interesting New Testament prophecy comes from Revelation 11, saying that they would rebuild the Temple. In fact, they have all the pieces they need ready and are just waiting for the right time to erect it.[88] Jesus Himself said the following in Matthew 24 after being asked about the dawning of the end of the age, "You will hear of wars and rumours of wars, but see to it that you are not alarmed. Such things must happen, but the end is still to come. Nation will rise against nation, and kingdom against kingdom. There will be famines and earthquakes in various places. All these are the beginning of birth-pains." Just look at the world over the past 110 years. The Bible is relevant today!'

'Absolutely so!' affirmed George.

'There's no doubting the validity of the Bible based on the evidences,' said Mark after a brief pause, looking directly at Tim. 'The issue is whether or not you're prepared to recognise and accept them and do something about it!'

Chapter 27

Miniature golf at Munchkins

'THANK you all for that,' said Tim fairly calmly but with a strained look on his face. 'The only thing I'll accept at the moment though is that the time is getting on. The morning is nearly over, and I came here to see if Andrew wanted to join me for a game of miniature golf before my afternoon's study session.' Tim looked at Andrew questioningly as he stood up.

'Uh, sure, why not,' said Andrew as he also stood up, a little surprised but wanting to have done something that morning anyway. 'Let me just fetch my cap and wallet.'

'Please also tell your mother where you're going,' requested George.

'Many thanks to you both,' said Andrew to Mark and Mike as he headed across the living room, Tim in front of him on his way out. 'I certainly appreciated it and learned from it too!'

'Anytime,' said Mark with a smile, happy to see Andrew's enthusiasm and commitment to all aspects relating to God and his walk with the Lord.

Andrew quickly headed upstairs but was back down again in

a moment with his cap and wallet in hand.

'I'm going with Tim to play miniature golf, Mom,' informed Andrew as he passed the dining room where Kelly was sitting at the dining room table reading her gardening magazine and sipping coffee.

'That's fine, Andy,' responded Kelly as she looked up, just in time to see Andrew and Tim disappear past the entrance. 'Please just remember that you have studying to do today.'

'I won't forget it,' assured Andrew. 'That's a priority; I won't be late!'

'Let's get going!' said Tim anxiously, eager to be on his way and away from any further discussion about the Bible and related topics. Although he had wanted to play miniature golf, he now felt that it had also provided him with a legitimate escape from continuing that which was tearing into his soul and making him feel uneasy.

The two lads were out the house in a flash, leaving Kelly to her quiet self and the three gentlemen in the living room to discuss the details surrounding the church's upcoming golf day.

The sun continued to beam down as Tim and Andrew drove leisurely into town, the early morning having given way to a hotter late morning as the temperature slowly pushed up the mercury on the thermometer. Cirrus clouds were painted sporadically across the sky, providing a pleasant contrast and softening the deep-blue above. Tim manoeuvred his way in and around all the vehicle and pedestrian traffic, the town's folk having by this time fully risen from the dawn of the day and were about their business.

'Nearly there,' said Andrew as he saw the distant landmark palm trees of the theme park appear on the horizon. The theme park was adjacent to Sunny Valley shopping mall and was bordered on the street side by mature palm trees.

'Ready for some fun?' asked Tim with a smile as he flicked on the indicator and simultaneously slowed his car.

'Definitely!' responded Andrew enthusiastically, scouting as much of the park as he could as Tim drove past a portion of it, the large hoisted signboard of Munchkins Theme Park casting a huge shadow across the road.

Tim entered slowly between the entrance's stone pillars and into the narrow yet long parking area that was already two-thirds full.

'We have just on two hours,' said Andrew, looking at his watch, 'then I must be back. That should be enough for two rounds easily. Are you game, Tim?'

'Yip,' replied Tim, switching off his car and pulling up the handbrake. 'I was actually keen to play two rounds. Loser of the first round buys sodas between rounds!'

'You're on!' responded Andrew with a fiery facial expression, warming to the challenge.

The theme park was quite large, with a number of attractions that included waterslides, two smallish roller coasters and three miniature 18-hole golf courses. The landscaping was exquisitely done, with palms presenting themselves ubiquitously throughout the park and standing like majestic grandfathers in watch on the proceedings below. Water features with exotic fish and seasonal flowers provided a colourful variance of moving and still beauty that always caught the attention of visitors. In winter time, the theme park was closed, and its appearance matched that of the weather, dull and dreary. However, spring time brought it to life, and its vibrancy matched that of nature. Although it was not the case in reality, Andrew always got the impression at the start of spring that it was like one of the old eighteenth-century English mansions in the countryside that awoke after winter when the menservants and maidservants entered the home, threw off the table and furniture drapes, opened the shutters, lit the fires and the pongs of damp and miff were replaced by the fresh aromas of wood, baked bread, cooking stews and fragrances of all kinds, thus presenting itself a great invitation for the arrival of its masters.

'Look!' exclaimed Tim, touching Andrew on his shoulder as they walked towards the theme park building. 'There sit the Harris twins!'

'That's neat,' said Andrew lively, his eyes lighting up at the site of June and July, having noted where Tim was looking. 'I wonder how long they've been here?'

'If they're still going to play,' suggested Tim, 'do you want to make it doubles?'

'Oh, dear me!' responded Andrew despairingly. 'Have you ever seen June play miniature golf? She plays as though she has two left hands!'

'You don't like her that much then, do you?' remarked Tim as he began to laugh.

'I'm greatly fond of June,' affirmed Andrew, 'and find her most pleasant. I certainly wouldn't give up the opportunity for us to play together in teams – her being on my side. It was the sodas I saw myself having to buy that was the issue!' Andrew hung his head in defeat and began to laugh as well.

'If I had known,' said Tim, seeing the amusing side of it as he patted Andrew softly on the back, 'I would have raised the stakes!'

'Trust you!' exclaimed Andrew, not minding the light-hearted jest. A moment later he and Tim walked up to the double features.

The two sisters were sitting on one of the wooden benches to the side of the main building. Large outdoor umbrellas shielded them from the hot sun, with a number of large trees extending their green leafy branches over them as well.

'It's nice to see you both,' said Andrew cordially. 'Are you playing, leaving or just visiting?' The girls greeted him.

'We've played one round already,' answered July, who was sipping crème soda through a bright, luminous orange straw, 'and going to play one more round. Hello, Tim,' added July with a bright and lively smile. 'I hope you're well and enjoying the warm weather?'

'Hello,' replied Tim softly as he stood with his arms behind his back while stubbing his shoe against one of the rock features. 'I am or wanting to at least – that's why we're here.' Tim was rather coy, remembering that the last time he had seen them he had not been very polite. He felt a little embarrassed.

'I like your French plait, June,' remarked Andrew. 'I don't often see you wearing your hair like that.'

'You always like the way June has her hair done,' chirped July cheekily. 'How do you like my pig tails?'

'They look really nice,' said Andrew thoughtfully as he made her turn her head, 'rather becoming of you – kind of pig like!'

'You brat!' scolded July as the others laughed, and she puffed her cheeks and pursed her lips. 'Typical you – I shouldn't have expected less!'

'Would you like to join us for a game,' asked Andrew as he sat down on the bench under the shade of the umbrella, 'we can play teams if you like? Afterwards I'm buying sodas.' Andrew gave Tim a knowing look.

'Okay,' agreed June, not waiting for July to turn down the invitation in retaliation to Andrew's jest.

'Happy, happy!' exclaimed Andrew. 'You and I can team up against Tim and July – is that alright?'

'I don't think July will team up with you now!' replied June with a wry smile, first glancing at July. 'No laughing though,' added June quickly as she gave Andrew a friendly yet stern look. 'I know what you think of my playing!'

'Much the same as he thinks of my hair!' joked July, a bright but cheeky look on her face.

'Andy thinks I play with two left hands, Tim,' informed June, not knowing that Andrew had already told him what he thought.

'Honest engines,' replied Andrew with a deadpan look, 'this is serious stuff – we're playing for sodas!'

'Ah!' exclaimed June, her quick mind not letting her down. 'That's why you said you were buying because you knew you would likely team up with me. I know you, Andy!' Andrew and the other two began to laugh, June joining in as well, fully aware that miniature golf was not one of her skilled pastimes but not fussed about it.

'Andy,' said Tim as he looked around, the light-hearted banter having subsided, 'why don't you and I quickly go to purchase our rounds while June and July finish up here? There isn't much of a queue at the ticket booth at the moment.'

'We'll see you girls now-now,' said Andrew, heeding Tim's advice, and the two of them headed off to the ticket booth that was located between the miniature golf courses and the waterslides.

In less than three minutes the lads were back, each having purchased two rounds of miniature golf.

'We're set,' commented Andrew to the twins, holding up his tickets.

'Good,' said June as she stood up. 'We're done here and ready for the next round.'

'And I'm ready to give you a whipping!' remarked July, pretending to still be a tad irritated and sulky after Andrew's earlier remark.

'Looks like you had better play really well, Tim old boy,' said Andrew, 'otherwise you'll be in the pig pen like me!'

'You mean the dog box, stupid!' responded July.

'No,' said Andrew. 'In your case I meant the pig pen.'

'You brute!' moaned July, having pursed her lips again and puffed her cheeks after catching on. 'You really are an ogre today!'

'Come on you three,' said June, noticing the activity around them. 'The courses are getting quite busy, so let's get into the line, shall we?'

Chapter 28

The twins' expositions – part 1

THE unanimous decision was to play course two, as the two girls had already played course one. All three courses presented their challenges, but course two seemed to have the most varying of circumstances. There were more easy holes yet also more difficult ones than the other two courses, for there weren't many holes of average difficulty. The main pleasure of the course, however, was that it threaded its way underneath a number of leafy trees and past a water feature.

'Oh!' exclaimed Andrew, turning to June as the four were waiting for the group in front of them to move onto the second hole so that they could start. 'We had an interesting morning!'

'What was so interesting?' asked June with a degree of surprise.

'Mark Marsh and Michael Aldenberg arrived at our house to have a meeting with my father about the church's golf day,' replied Andrew enthusiastically, 'and as a result of a question Tim asked – or should I rather say as a result of a challenge Tim made, Mark went through some major points on certain Bible aspects.'

'Like what?' asked July with interest.

'It was a mixed participation really,' replied Andrew, maintaining his enthusiasm, 'but the majority was given by Mark on aspects regarding the authenticity of the Bible and the numerical structure.'

The group in front cleared the first hole, so the youthful foursome immediately began to play, intent not to hold up the group waiting behind them.

'I know a little about the authenticity of the Bible and Bible numerics,' remarked June after missing her putt on the second hole, causing her and Andrew to go two down to Tim and July, 'but it's always fascinating to listen to.'

'I find it the same,' said Andrew. 'I always learn something new during such discussions.'

'Did you find it interesting, Tim?' asked July as they arrived at the third hole, Tim to play first.

'Yes, very interesting,' replied Tim, having first carefully placed his ball on the green, rubber starting matt before looking up at July. 'Who doesn't find those topics interesting? However, I always hear people say, "Jesus is the answer, you must turn to Jesus", and I'm not quick to just "*buy*" into that!'

Tim then set up to make his play, his words having silenced the other three, and promptly sunk his putt in one after the ball moved first left, then right, then left again over the undulating surface before navigating the slight dip and into the hole. The answer to July's question was temporarily forgotten as the others congratulated a smiling Tim, whose effort bolstered him and July to three up on the other pair.

Andrew and June managed to stem the tide a little as July missed a small putt on the fourth, and her ball lipped the cup on the fifth, enabling them to claw two back.

'You know, Tim,' said July after the two pairs had levelled at the sixth and were on their way to the tricky seventh. 'You said that you always hear people say that Jesus is the answer, and you were not, as you put it, quick to just "*buy*" into that.'

'Yes, that's correct,' responded Tim.

'However,' continued July, 'Jesus *is* the answer, but He's also the problem.'

'What!' exclaimed Tim in disbelief, stopping and turning to face July. 'Say that again, please?'

Andrew and June also looked at July a little surprised and wondered what she meant or was getting at.

'Jesus *is* the answer,' repeated July, 'but He's also the problem.'

'That's a good one and news to me,' remarked Tim as he moved onto the tricky seventh hole and stood aside as it was June's turn to play first, a cynical look on his face. 'I would like to understand how that one works!'

'Sis,' said June as she placed her bright-green ball on the starting matt, not bothering to specifically select a spot, 'you must have some reason for saying what you've just said, so could you explain?'

June proceeded to hit her ball, which hopped off a mound and ended up out of bounds in the bright array of flowers located at the right side of the hole, causing her to end the hole taking maximum score.

July politely waited for the others to play before responding to her sister's question, not fussed about talking while she played.

'The counter remark generally often made,' said July, 'is that Jesus is the easy way out, and that He's for those who "need a support". However, Jesus is the answer because we need a Saviour, not because we need a crutch. Furthermore, the moment you become a Christian you accept the ways of God and the teaching of the Bible, which is likely to conflict in certain areas of your life. If you don't accept this, then don't become a Christian, because all you'll become is a hypocrite, for Jesus says in John 14:15, "If you love me, you will obey what I command."' July continued to talk as they moved on, her and Tim having won yet another hole thanks to June's bad score. 'You now introduce a standard that you never had to try and hold to before,' said July, 'or principles that you never had to live by before. This isn't punishment, it's because God knows what's right and what He wants in us. You will now have friends that may not like your perspectives and viewpoints. In fact, peer pressure, the thought of "what will my friends say, or what will my family say?" is probably somewhere at the top of the list as to why people don't take the step, not because it's a cop-out. You'll have to start asking yourself certain questions and will have to question some of your activities, something which you never had to do before. As I said, you will have friends who no longer appreciate your stance or viewpoint. There'll be those who will be offended by the fact that you no longer want to hang out and indulge with them in certain activities. They will put pressure on you at first to continue to join in, and if you hold out they will then look with disdain upon you.'

Tim just stared at July with a bland facial expression, not a sound coming from him as she spoke.

'This doesn't mean that it will be like this, of course,' continued July steadily, 'but depending on the person's life that was lived up until then, it could be like this. You see, Romans 12:2 tells us not to conform any longer to the pattern of this world, but to be transformed by the renewing of our minds. Ephesians 4:23,24 also tells us to be made new in the attitude of our minds, and to put on the new self, created to be like God in true righteousness and holiness. You would ask yourself if getting drunk on New Year's Eve with your friends and bearing the effects of intoxication the following day is something God is happy with, even though it may be a tradition with some. You would ask yourself – and God – about your attitudes, behaviours, character disposition, etc. if you were serious, and where they were shown up poorly in the light of Scripture it would be a task to change them, something you wouldn't have considered doing before.

'Remember, churches are not the standard, the Word of God is. If you didn't do this and, sadly, many Christians don't, you would be like the third point in the parable Jesus gave, as recorded in Luke 8, about the sower. It tells us that the seed that fell among thorns stands for those who hear, but as they go on their way they are choked by life's worries, riches and pleasures, and they do not mature. Before one becomes a Christian, self-indulgence and self-focus are normally what rules and reigns; in other words – what I want, and what I want to do, but they have no place in God's kingdom. I do not mean that Christians should become inwardly focused, but Christianity is a journey of being prepared to listen, being humble and teachable and growing in the ways of God, which sometimes can be difficult to do. This would be like the fourth point in the sower parable, which tells us that the seed on good soil stands for those with a noble and good heart, who hear the Word, retain it and by persevering produce a crop. This doesn't mean that life has to be dull, but it needs to fit in with God's ways. The Christian walk is no cakewalk!' July took a deep breath and let out a loud sigh.

Tim continued to look at July but did not utter a word. He eventually placed his ball on the starting matt, played out the hole and moved on, either being unable to provide a comment or considering what had just been said.

'I think I can give a little description of what July was saying,' said Andrew as they all left the following hole having tied it. 'If you take golfers for instance, there are amateur golfers and pro golfers. Many amateur golfers will just play week after week, year after year, without improvement or thought to their games. However, the pro golfer will analyse his game in all areas – driving, approach shots, short game, putting and even his course management. This doesn't mean that he sits continually having self-introspection, but he checks these areas on a regular basis, almost always with a coach, because they impact on his daily game. Under normal circumstances, if not kept in check and improved upon with effort and perseverance where necessary, he will be no better than many amateur golfers who just indulge their established way, habits and attitudes every time they play! In the true Christian walk, the Holy Spirit is our "coach", pointing out the areas that we need to work on, and then He encourages us and helps us to do so.'

Nothing more was said on the topic for the remainder of the round. The youthful foursome just enjoyed the opportunity to get outdoors after the winter and spend some time soaking up the sun and having fun at the same time. It was clearly evident who would win, but Andrew never stopped trying right to the last, hoping to make the inevitable loss at least respectable.

'I know I'm buying sodas!' said Andrew as they headed from the last hole and along the red-brick path towards the canteen area. 'The question is, how bad was the loss, and what are the individual scores?'

Chapter 29

The twins' expositions – part 2

'AT least wait until we sit down at the table,' said June, who had been keeping the score card.

'Dear me!' joked Andrew. 'Is it that bad?'

'Shame on you, Andy!' responded July, laughing lightly. 'We all know exactly what you mean!'

Andrew and June walked side by side along the pathway quietly chatting. Tim and July followed behind them, equally cheerful. July was particularly so as she could light-heartedly harass Andrew with her and Tim's victory.

'June and I will fetch the sodas,' said Andrew, turning to face the two behind him, having neared the outdoor eating area. 'You two can pick a table in the meantime.'

'Okay,' said Tim, 'but are you happy to buy?'

'Absolutely yes!' answered Andrew with a smile. 'I sold my old pair of ice skates this past week, so I'm happy to oblige. The usual for you both – cola and crème soda?'

Andrew received a thumbs up from both Tim and July, so he turned and, along with June, promptly took the pathway that led up a small embankment. The canteen area opened up before them like a tropical jungle scene as they moved past the last of the pathway-lined trees.

The canteen matched the park's landscaping theme, with its thatched roof and palm-leaf-shaped shutters on the windows. Inside, overhead ceiling fans attached to the beams twirled away constantly, providing a cool breeze mixed with a warm reed smell.

Andrew happily made his purchase, and after June had taken four individually-wrapped straws from the straw holder, they returned to Tim and July. Tim had managed to find an open table at the outskirts of the area. It was underneath a shady tree that was being constantly fed small amounts of water from the fun-seekers splashing water over the side as they slide round the waterslide's turn that was just before it. June sat down next to July, and Andrew sat next to Tim.

'So what are the scores?' asked Andrew impatiently, his interest getting the better of him. He leaned forward across the table as June began poking the score card with the pencil at every written score, her left hand moving slowly down the column as she tallied up.

'Wait, my dear fellow!' objected June, stopping her count and holding the pencil against her last added score while she looked at Andrew. 'Patience, please.'

'Sorry,' apologised Andrew, sitting back. 'I'm just curious, that's all.'

While June totalled up the scores, the others sat quietly and sipped their sodas.

'Tim and July won by four holes,' informed June after scribbling the last total. 'Tim was one better than Andrew, who was five better than July, and I was trailing her.'

'How many shots were you trailing her by?' asked Andrew, knowing that June had purposely not told them.

'It's not important,' replied June coyly, pulling the card away.

'Of course it isn't,' said Andrew, chuckling, 'so long as we all enjoyed playing.'

'I was eight behind July,' mentioned June, 'but for me that isn't too bad at all! But it was bad enough to cost you four sodas!' added June as she began to laugh.

'No fuss,' said Andrew, maintaining a cheerful spirit. 'I lost to Tim anyway.'

The four young adults sat quietly enjoying the comfort of the shaded area, shielded from the bright sun proudly looking down from on high while the cirrus clouds, in the form of painted white brush strokes, slowly changed shape and pattern as the late morning wore on. The noise from the surrounding activities remained constant, rising every now and again as thrill-seekers whizzed past on the nearby roller coasters or down the waterslides. The water in the slide that ran past them produced a constant swishing noise as it followed the curves and headed for the pool below, the four always knowing when someone was coming down.

'Here comes someone big,' informed Tim, seeing a huge man flop down into the waterslide at the start, causing the structure to shake with the impact. A moment later came the familiar sound just above them as the rider slid round the curve. The waterslide shook, and water sprayed up and over the side. Almost instantly, July let out a loud shriek, startling the other three and causing others to turn and look. She froze in her position, with closed eyes and her face screwed up.

'What's the matter, July?' asked June, rather surprised and

concerned.

'Water from the slide landed on my neck and ran down my back,' replied July hurriedly, suddenly bursting out with laugher, the others joining in.

Normality and calm eventually returned amongst the four, but the peripheral activities kept up their energetic intensity.

'I heard what you had to say earlier,' said Tim out of the blue as he sat stirring the ice in his glass with his straw, 'and I'm still not buying it, but answer me the following: I'm a good sort of guy – at least I think so, so does that not count for something? I've also heard people say that they were wealthy, so didn't need religion or Christianity. What about them?'

'Give me a second to think about what you've just asked,' requested Andrew, a little startled once again by Tim's unexpected questions. He put his half-finished glass of cola on the table, the ice inside it now looking like little pebbles, with a few condensed droplets still clinging bravely to the outside of the glass.

'The world's full of "good guys",' said Andrew eventually, shifting a little so that it would be easier for him to speak directly to Tim, 'according to our definition of the word. However, in Mark 10:17,18, Jesus was addressed by a young man as "good teacher". Jesus replied by saying, "Why do you call me good? No-one is good – except God alone." Jesus, nonetheless, knew that He was also God. So you see, from God's perspective He doesn't see us as "good guys", it's the world that does! A further problem is that God doesn't only want so-called "good guys", He wants righteous guys, but as Isaiah 64:6 says, "All of us have become like one who is unclean, and all our righteous acts are like filthy rags." The issue is that we can't be made righteous by our own efforts as Romans 3:10 says, "There is no-one righteous, not even one." So to answer your first question: yes, being a good sort of guy does count but not when it comes to the ways of God and the issues of sin because "good guys" are also sinners. Sin cannot be atoned for by good deeds or by being a good guy, it can only be atoned for by the blood of Jesus Christ, the one who was sinless!'

The fizzy green liquid drained from June's straw back into her glass as she released the straw from her mouth.

'I think I can answer the second of Tim's questions,' said June as she sat upright.

'I'm sure you can,' responded Andrew confidently. 'Give it your best.'

'Sadly,' said June, beginning after wiping her mouth with a tissue, 'the issues of money have been exploited by all throughout the ages, and the so-called Christian church has been no exception. Today it's often used by the evangelical pulpits as a draw for blessing, and it was used by the Catholic clergy for the purchase of penance and salvation. People, both today and in the past, have been kept in ignorance as to the truth about this aspect in order to aid the personal gains of some individuals but at great danger to multitudes. There are, however, those who don't want to hear and who have their ears stuffed with bank notes, but may their ears and hearts be opened before it's too late!'

Tim looked at June and quietly listened, having been surprised by the composure with which she had begun to speak.

'What we need to understand,' continued June, 'is that we enter this world without money, even if we stand in line for an inheritance, and we leave this world without it. Before God, man is equal in his naked state, even if he's not equal in circumstance or abilities. Furthermore, the power and price of the cross cannot be purchased with pennies. Ephesians 2:8 tells us that salvation is a gift from God; it is for all who will receive it. All the money in the world could not purchase the soul of a single person! Wait a second, I have a small Psalms and New Testament Bible,' mumbled June, having suddenly looked down between her and July and begun scratching in her handbag. 'I carry it with me in my bag.'

The others watched as she scratch in her handbag like a squirrel digging for a nut.

'Here we are,' said June, a pleased look on her face as she righted herself after pulling out the small midnight-blue-covered book. 'Let me read a Psalm that couldn't address the issue more directly or appropriately.'

June paged with light fingers through the thin and delicate pages, the others affording her the time and sitting patiently, including Tim.

'Psalm 49,' said June eventually and promptly began reading. '"Hear this, all you peoples; listen, all who live in this world, both low and high, rich and poor alike: My mouth will speak words of wisdom; the utterance from my heart will give understanding. I will turn my ear to a proverb; with the harp I will expound my riddle: Why should I fear when evil days come, when wicked deceivers surround me – those who trust in their wealth and boast of their great riches? No man can redeem the life of another or give to God a ransom for him – the ransom for a life is costly, no payment is ever enough – that he should live on for ever and not see decay. For all can see that wise men die; the foolish and the senseless alike perish and leave their wealth to others. Their tombs will remain their houses for ever, their dwellings for endless generations, though they had named lands after themselves. But man, despite his riches, does not endure; he is like the beasts that perish. This is the fate of those who trust in themselves, and of their followers, who approve their sayings.

Like sheep they are destined for the grave, and death will feed on them. The upright will rule over them in the morning; their forms will decay in the grave, far from their princely mansions. But God will redeem my life from the grave; He will surely take me to Himself. Do not be overawed when a man grows rich, when the splendour of his house increases; for he will take nothing with him when he dies, his splendour will not descend with him. Though while he lived he counted himself blessed – and men praise you when you prosper – he will join the generation of his fathers, who will never see the light [of life]. A man who has riches without understanding is like the beasts that perish.'" June snapped the small Bible shut between her palms and looked up. 'You see, Tim,' said June warmly, 'for Him who created the heavens and the earth and all that is within them money is not an issue, nor when it comes to salvation is He a respecter of persons!'

There was silence once again!

Chapter 30

A heart's desire

JUNE returned to sipping her soda, Andrew looking at her for a moment.

'What?' said June without uttering a sound as she looked at Andrew quizzically.

Andrew did not want to say anything or draw attention, so he winked at her to indicate that he had appreciated her answer to Tim's second question. June, however, looked at him with big eyes and raised eyebrows, then suddenly looked down and sipped the last of her soda as she began to blush.

'It's time we were on our way,' said July, looking at her watch. 'Thank you guys for an enjoyable round of mini golf and for the soda, Andy.'

'An absolute pleasure,' said Andrew amiably. 'Your presence and contribution was greatly appreciated too.'

'Come on, Sis,' said July, tugging on her sister's sleeve as she stood up after giving Andrew a polite smile. 'We must go now.'

June put her little Bible back in her handbag and shifted out from the bench.

'It was most enjoyable,' said June coyly as she half glanced at Andrew, still a little flustered from his wink. 'Thank you Andy, Tim.'

'Tim, old boy,' said Andrew, looking at his watch, 'I know your heart's desire is to play another round, but I don't think we'll make it comfortably and still get back on time.'

'Do you want to call it quits for today?' asked Tim.

'I think so,' replied Andrew. 'We can always use the tickets on another day. I really don't want to be late getting home.'

'That's fine by me,' said Tim as he got up, 'I also have a lot of work to do.'

'Maybe we could arrange another doubles game sometime?' suggested Andrew, looking from one twin to the other.

'That would be nice,' responded July, who looked at June for confirmation. 'I'm sure June would enjoy that too. You can then compliment her again on her hair do,' added July quickly and began her rapid machinegun-fire laughter.

'That's enough of that!' objected June, gently slapping July on the forearm with the back of her hand before shyly looking at Andrew. 'Yes, that would be nice indeed. You can give us a call sometime.'

'Done and dusted then,' said Andrew, pleased. 'It's quits for today, but we have something to look forward to in the future.'

The sun continued to shine brightly from above as they all departed the theme park, the cirrus clouds now having been gently erased from the firmament as a southerly wind began to make its presence felt. Andrew waved to the twins as the two cars parted company and headed in opposite directions, the study schedules of the four young adults their next main priority.

'You don't think that all of what was presented today in respect to God, sin and the issue of salvation is one big pretence and a little over dramatized and emphasised?' asked Tim as they passed by the arched entrance to Ailensbury Medi-Clinic on their way to the main intersection, Tim wanting to quickly pop into Renbro's Hardware Store in the heart of town to purchase some materials he needed for a project.

'Definitely not!' replied Andrew. 'There's a story I read in a bicycle magazine that I'll never forget, which is a perfect illustration of the issue. A subscriber wrote in to the magazine and told them that he'd been a big consumer of beer and had enjoyed a regular barbeque. Although not very old, he was vastly overweight. He went to a doctor because of some complaint, and that was the turning point for him.'

'Why,' asked Tim with interest, 'what happened?'

'The doctor examined the man,' replied Andrew, 'and with frankness told him that if he continued to do what he was doing and live the way he was living, he would soon be dead from a heart attack or other related issue. The man had a choice – either he could heed the doctor's warning or pass it off as fanatical or over-dramatized nonsense. Of his own decision, the man heeded the warning. He went out and purchased a stationary exercise bicycle and changed his diet. The man said it was terrible for the first few weeks, and he felt horrible, yet he persevered and slowly lost weight, gained in fitness and started to feel much better. At the time of writing the letter to the magazine, the man had progressed to the stage where he was lean and fit and was participating in long distance cycle rides.'

'What's the point of the story?' asked Tim a little sarcastically.

'The point is twofold,' replied Andrew. 'Firstly, had the doctor been humanistic and just told the man that what he was doing was not quite the best thing, and that he should consider changing his ways, it wouldn't have provided the man with the reality of what was before him. Most likely, it wouldn't have sparked a response, as the man wouldn't have understood the seriousness of what the doctor could see. That's the same as what has been presented to you today with respect to the spiritual aspects, which also have an outworking in the physical. It's not over dramatization or over emphasis, it's reality, and it is truth!

'Secondly, the man had a choice to make. He was given the true facts but had to decide what he wanted to do. Thankfully he chose the right option, even if it was the harder option, and it created a lot of struggle and difficulty in his life before he came right. This parallels what July so vividly and fittingly described are, or can be, the issues that face a new Christian who truly seeks to do what is right. You've been told the issues that you are facing and have been given the facts – it's no pretence. Now it's up to you to decide the course of your life!'

Tim stopped briefly at Renbro's, made his purchase, and then they were off again. He remained silent for the remainder of the short trip to Andrew's house, the happenings of the morning pulsating through his brain. He had seen their visit to Munchkins Theme Park as an escape from further exposure to Christian influence, only to walk right into it again moments after they had arrived. Was it just bad fortune once again or providence as some may suggest? Tim again balked at the thought of the latter, but he could not deny the possibility if God was real. That small voice at Roccocoa's that had told him he did not know all things, which had cautioned his spirit on the way home from there about his attitude and opinions and which had been a gentle, prodding voice of encouragement to open his heart to that which he had shut out of his life for so long was not presently speaking, but its influence was nonetheless operating.

He could not comprehend it but wondered at his preparedness to listen. Was it foolishness or wisdom to do so? He dared not consider it for fear that the answer may be wisdom, in which case he would then have no leverage to stand against it. Maybe it was just inquisitiveness? This was an option Tim liked, as he felt it sat between foolishness and wisdom, giving him room to investigate and manoeuvre without being threatened.

Tim was baffled though, for twice in one day he had had no intention, at this point in time anyway, to bring up such issues, but the circumstances had presented themselves amenably, and he had seized upon them. Neither of them though had produced the results he would have liked or expected. Apart from Mark and George, he had been given a mouthful from July and received an earful from June, both whose words were clear and seemed to make sense. Tim recoiled, realising the impact upon his life that it would have if he felt that it made perfect sense, for he would then be compelled to act and be a fool if he did not! Nevertheless, there was something amiss to him, something that just did not fit – the application of it all. This was not only a mystery but a problem to him, one which he was not prepared to ignore or overrule. Was it faith he did not have? Was it a lack of understanding? Was it certain unanswered questions or outstanding explanations? Or was it perhaps wisdom acting intuitively and sparing him from trouble, the very thing he had always seen Christianity and religion as being?

Tim's thoughts wrestled, and he took a deep, silent breath, exhaling slowly. He had already opened himself up to a degree that concerned him, for he was not only listening to but even asking questions about that which he had until then shut out of his life! He could not, he would not give in to it, not unless he was convinced, and at present, he was not! A lot had been revealed to him over the past two weeks, including a lot that both stirred his spirit and troubled it. If it was real, how did it all piece together? Tim mused. If God was real, He would have to disclose something further; and if God was real, he wanted Him to as well. Otherwise, he would never be able to accept it, how could he? For if it was truth, truth is not mindless, and he should be able to comprehend that which is truth, provided he allowed his heart to be receptive to it in the first place! Being rebellious would not cut it. Tim was adamant in his conclusion, and it was his heart's desire. There was no further question, nothing further to discuss. He would not budge unless that which was missing, if there was indeed something missing, was clearly shown to him!

Tim shut off his thoughts and seconds later pulled into the Renshaws driveway.

'Thanks, Tim,' said Andrew as he hopped out of Tim's car. 'I truly was glad to see you this morning, and I had fun at mini golf.'

'Loved it myself,' responded Tim good-naturedly. 'The next two weeks are going to be hectic, but maybe after that we can go fishing again. No promises though. I'll give you a call if that suits you?'

'That would suit my schedule too,' replied Andrew, giving Tim the thumbs up. 'I'll wait for your call.'

Andrew turned and headed for the house, hurdling the flowers instead of following the path, and was on the porch in seconds waving farewell to Tim as he drove off down the road. Andrew quietly went inside, shutting the door behind himself. He put his hands behind his back and leaned back against the door, bouncing himself repetitively with his hands. For a minute he silently dwelt on the conversations that had taken place at Munchkins – the very direct exposition of July's and then the equally apt and sharp explanation of June's. Andrew then contemplated why June had looked at him with big eyes and raised eyebrows and blushed when he indicated that he had appreciated her answer.

'I wonder why June looked at me that way?' said Andrew quietly to himself, stopping his bouncing and leaning still against the door.

For a moment he gazed at the painting on the wall opposite him, then his eyes grew big with realisation, a big grin quickly forming on his face.

'Oh, *dear!*' exclaimed Andrew as he bolted from the door and up the staircase. 'Is it possible?' He was now a little flustered and flushed himself as he entered his bedroom, partly from his dash up the stairs and partly from the comprehension of what had just crossed his mind.

Andrew dropped his cap and wallet onto the old rustic side table. He hastily removed the study book he wanted from his shelf, pulled out his typist chair from under his oak study desk and sat down. He paged quickly in his book to the location where he wanted to start from but could not help himself, a grin quickly developing again as the comprehension about June returned to his mind.

Andrew suddenly found himself staring at the pages, not registering anything at all. This would not do, for he had to focus now, it was time for him to make great effort in his studies. He quickly lost his grin, directing his attention to his learning but had to fight hard to keep focus, his heart's desire wanting to dwell elsewhere!

Chapter 31

Off fishing again

KELLY looked up at the wall clock, steam rising from her cooking and the French toast sizzling away as she stood working over the stove. She sighed, wiped her hands on her bright flowery apron and headed for the kitchen door.

'Andrew!' shouted Kelly in the direction of the stairs. 'Where are you? I would have thought that after more than a month of you and Tim not having gone fishing you would be "up and at 'em". Tim will be here any minute to fetch you!'

Kelly stood for a second and took a deep breath after forcing all that from her lungs in virtually one loud bellow.

'Coming, Mom,' called Andrew from upstairs, already halfway out his bedroom.

He shut his bedroom door, made the few steps along the lush carpeted passage it took him to reach the staircase and descended in his signature manner. The entire staircase, with its old mahogany handrail and ornately turned balustrade spindles, not failing to boisterously protest. Across the hall he sped towards the kitchen.

'I warned you!' half-scolded Kelly as she took Andrew's plate of French toast from the oven's warming drawer. 'Here's Tim now, pulling into the driveway!'

Andrew could see the customary silhouette of Tim's cream sedan grow larger as he glanced out through the dining room window.

'There's no fuss, Mom,' assured Andrew, quickly grabbing three pieces of French toast and putting them in an open plastic container. 'I'll eat these on the way. One piece for Tim,' said Andrew with a smile, quickly grabbing a forth piece and dropping it on top of the others.

Andrew kissed Kelly on her cheek, turned and swiftly headed for the front door, his fishing tackle and equipment already there waiting, having been prepared and packed the previous evening.

'Don't be late, please,' called Kelly as Andrew picked up his possessions.

'I have no intention of being late, Mom,' called back Andrew and promptly exited the house.

"Honk, honk, honk-honk-honk," went Tim's car's hooter as he gave Andrew a welcome blast, joyfully showing his approval at Andrew's appearance.

'Do you mind!' groused Kelly from the dining room window. 'We have neighbours you know, and it's still early in the morning!'

Tim could not resist the opportunity to respond, so he acknowledged Kelly too. "Honk-honk," went his car's hooter again, and he gave Kelly a double thumbs up, smiling cheekily.

'Be gone with you!' moaned Kelly, waving her hand at Tim, but she could not help laughing at his antics.

Andrew placed his fishing tackle and equipment in the trunk of Tim's car without delay, the bright morning sun already beating down upon him, which he could feel burning on his bare arms. He jumped in Tim's car so hastily that he bounced on the passenger seat.

'Gently does it, old boy!' objected Tim quickly. 'Just because we couldn't make it as previously planned, doesn't mean you have to be over enthusiastic now!'

'Morning, Tim,' greeted Andrew cheerfully, eager to be underway. 'The sun's already cooking. I could feel it on my arms while just placing my stuff in your trunk!'

'I know,' affirmed Tim, 'but we'll be in the cool of the overshadowing trees, remember?'

'Not when we make the fish barbeque,' replied Andrew. 'We're not permitted to make that in the wooded area, it must be in the clearing!'

'I had remembered that too,' responded Tim. 'Have you got your sunblock?'

'Yip,' replied Andrew.

'Hat?' asked Tim also.

'Yip,' replied Andrew again.

'Then there's nothing to worry about,' assured Tim with a smile as he looked over his shoulder and backed his car out of the Renshaws driveway.

In seconds they were heading off, with the approximately 10-minute pleasant drive to their destination, Ailen Oak Lake, ahead of them.

The more densely populated suburb gave way to thinned out housing with interspersed fields as they travelled happily along. Andrew again watched the scenery flash by, but this time, the cool, fresh spring breeze had yielded to a warm breeze as spring was now long since established and the days had become hotter. The flora was in full bloom and radiating its glory while basking in the sunlight. Butterflies and birds still flittered here and there, and the back and forth flapping of cows' tails remained a feature, but now it was amongst a palette of colours to behold and a melody of angelic sounds. The songs of the birds could not be heard above the hum of Tim's car, but Andrew knew them from the times spent on the balcony at Misty's up on the hillside.

Tim's car suddenly slowed, breaking Andrew's contemplations, for just up ahead was the old rusty turnoff signpost with its faded and peeling brown lettering indicating Ailen Oak Lake. They were soon on the familiar gravel road that wound its way into the distance.

'What a contrast from when we went on the Smoking Gorge trail,' noted Andrew quite energetically as they wound their way up the gravel road. 'The mist was quite heavy amongst the trees that day, but now it's clear and open. The trees seem able to breathe!'

The densely populated pinnate trees had given up their hold of the past season to the strength of the sun, which now penetrated their inmost places with its warmth and life.

Tim navigated the last bend and onto the straight section, the light in the distance, indicating the opening to the lake area, faithfully appearing before them. Tim's cream sedan was again spat from the trees into the clearing like a pea from a pea shooter as it emerged into the open.

'Ailen Oak Lake,' said Andrew satisfyingly, 'and fishing!'

'And barbequing!' added Tim energetically.

'You hope!' said Andrew, beginning to chuckle. 'We still have to catch the fish! Anything like last time and we'll be back at Misty's!'

'That wouldn't be a bad alternative, Andy boy,' joked Tim as the two lads laughed heartily, 'if it wasn't for the fact that

Ailensbury Fair is on tonight, and those of your particular interest are busy in preparation for it.'

'Good point there, cousin,' replied Andrew, having enjoyed the banter. 'We had better catch some fish!'

Tim pulled up slowly to the edge of the gravel parking area, stopping with the nose of his car just over the start of the grassed section. The lads hopped out and for a few seconds took in the scenery before them as they usually did.

'Ah, fresh air,' said Andrew enthusiastically. 'Smell the fresh air!'

'Come on!' responded Tim. 'I want to smell the fish barbeque!'

Andrew, not hastened by Tim, first wanted to finish his habitual stretch with his hands extended to the sky.

'Come on,' urged Tim, this time protesting, 'we don't have all day!'

'Okay, I'm moving,' mumbled Andrew as he relaxed all his muscles, and his hands dropped to his sides. 'Where do you want to fish from?' asked Andrew as he opened the trunk of Tim's car. 'The same place as last time or a little further round?'

'The same place as last time will do, Andy,' replied Tim from inside his car as he was busy pulling out a basket. 'There are folks 100 paces further round, and I don't want to encroach upon them, it won't be necessary.'

Andrew looked in that direction and saw four people already settled, sitting comfortably with their line floats already bobbing lightly in the water.

'I didn't see the other folks there,' mentioned Andrew as he bent down to lift his fishing tackle and equipment from the trunk of Tim's car. 'The same place as last time it is then.'

Tim made his way to the fishing spot with his lot, while

Andrew decided to split his load and make two trips. He had no desire to stagger like a drunken sailor nor fancied the prospect of dropping some of it, for he would be carrying the barbeque equipment this time. Andrew flung what he could over one shoulder and carried the rest, following on after Tim.

'There are just a few things left for me to fetch,' said Andrew as he drew near to Tim, 'mostly the barbeque equipment. It won't take me long to get, but I'll set up here first.'

'While you set up here and fetch the rest of the stuff,' said Tim, who was a master at setting up quickly and had already put everything of his in place, just not his fishing line, 'I'll go and gather kindling for the fire. At least then we don't have to worry about it later on.'

'Whatever you want to do,' responded Andrew, not actually paying too much attention to Tim as he began organising the stuff he had just brought.

Tim headed off for the nearby woodland across the way from the clearing.

Andrew returned to Tim's car to fetch the remaining few things and barbeque equipment just after Tim entered the forest.

Tim searched for a minute or two, winding his way through the relatively dense vegetation. He spotted a cluster of twigs about fifteen paces away from him that he thought would do quite nicely for what they wanted.

'No need to go further than that!' said Tim to himself, quite pleased with the quick find and for not having to break branches.

Tim was so taken by the find that his thoughts focused on it, narrowing his attention to the exclusion of his surrounds. He moved swiftly forward, not sensing or noticing the danger that lay just ahead, off to the side. Tim stretched out his arms as he bent down to gather the kindling and "Wham"!

Chapter 32

The unexpected shock

A BROWN, camouflaged object with black spots lying restfully to the right of Tim sprang to life with great power and force.

'Owh!' yelled Tim as he recoiled, the snake fixed to his forearm, having sunk its fangs deep into his flesh. It released its grip and disappeared into the underbrush when Tim waved his arm.

Andrew looked up, as did the fellow fishermen, startled by the blood curdling cry that came from the forest across the clearing.

'Tim!' shouted Andrew, a cold shiver running down his spine as he looked in that direction.

Tim looked at his arm, the white fang punctures filling with red blood almost instantly, and his arm began to burn. He was not sure if it was the bite or the shock of what had just happened, but he suddenly felt nauseous and slightly giddy. He retraced his steps immediately.

Andrew dropped what was in his hands back into the trunk of Tim's car and started running in the direction Tim had headed. Two of the fellow fishermen did the same, but Andrew had more than 150 paces start on them and an athletic advantage. He was halfway there when Tim came staggering out of the woodland clutching his right forearm, looking pale and bewildered.

'What happened, Tim?' yelled Andrew as he came running up to him.

Tim did not need to answer as Andrew caught sight of his pussy and swollen arm.

'A snake!' exclaimed Andrew as he felt the claws of a vulture dig into the depths of his gut and squeeze tight.

Tim just nodded the affirmative.

'Do you know what it was, did you see it?' asked Andrew in as composed a manner as possible, trying not to make matters worse through panicky conduct, realising that Tim needed to be kept calm.

Tim was doddery, and as Andrew began walking him back to the car, he just nodded and then shook his head.

'I'm not sure, I didn't see it next to the kindling,' said Tim eventually. 'It looked like it was brown with black spots, that's all I can say.'

The fellow fishermen ran up to them panting and seeing Tim's arm, also did not need to ask any questions about what had happened.

'My name's Tom,' said the more senior member of the two, a little out of breath. 'Is there anything we can do to help?'

He was an elderly gentleman of pleasant and friendly features, wearing blue dungarees and a multi-coloured checker shirt. His well-worn, yellow, straw sombrero, which he now placed back on his head, was harpooned with various types of fishing hooks all over it. His fishing companion, who was wearing similar clothing to him, just stared at Tim's arm.

As they all walked back to the carpark, Andrew supporting Tim, Tom tied a tourniquet around Tim's arm.

'Do you know of a type of snake that is brown with black spots on it?' asked Andrew.

'I know nothing about snakes,' replied Tom, 'other than to stay away from them!'

Tom's friend started to laugh but promptly received a swift backhand in his gut from Tom, who also gave him a sharp glare.

'What I do need to do,' said Andrew thoughtfully, 'is get him into the car quickly and carefully and get him to the hospital as fast as possible.'

Tim was starting to feel substantially dizzy as they approached his car.

'I'll phone ahead for you if you like?' offered Tom, trying to be as helpful as possible, not knowing the severity of the situation but realising that it did not look good.

'That would be a great help,' replied Andrew hastily. 'Ailensbury Medi-Clinic should be the quickest to get to, provided the traffic in town hasn't become too heavy yet.'

'There's also the lake's boating club emergencies,' mentioned Tom, it coming to mind, 'which is just on the other side of the lake.'

'I know about them,' said Andrew quickly, 'but I'm not sure if they'll be able to help or just be an undue delay!'

He mulled it over for a second while they helped Tim into the car and strapped him in.

'Phone Ailensbury Medi-Clinic, I'm headed there!' requested Andrew as he rushed round the back of Tim's car and slammed the trunk shut. 'Give them as much detail as you can.'

'Will do,' replied Tom as Andrew jumped in the driver's seat, 'and don't worry about your stuff, we'll watch it for you.'

Andrew had not even considered his and Tim's fishing equipment patiently waiting for their masters to return. He gave Tom the thumbs up and hastily backed Tim's car from the fringe of the grassed area. As Andrew shoved the car into gear he gave Tim a quick glance, his blood nearly curdling inside him. Tim was as white as a sheet, with sweat beads beginning to form on his brow.

'Hang in there, Tim!' encouraged Andrew courageously, not knowing if his words were idle or not. 'We're on our way.'

Andrew pressed his foot against the accelerator pedal with force and spun the car around, spraying gravel in an arc and creating a dust cloud that caused Tom and his friend to jump and run. He headed for the gap in the trees as fast as he thought was reasonable, knowing that Tim did not need a bad and bumpy ride but also knowing it would not be the wisest thing to dawdle.

The cream automobile with Andrew at the wheel penetrated the mass of trees with purpose, leaving a large dust cloud as the only trace of their recent presence. Andrew had to momentarily slow down, being unable to clearly see what was before him as a result of the change from light to dark. He was soon back up to speed though, having adjusted quickly to the change, and raced along the gravel road, reaching the first bend in no time at all. Andrew braked slightly, then accelerated again, spitting gravel out from under the front tyres and assaulting the pristine trees lining the road, which stood firm against the onslaught.

'Hang on, Tim!' encouraged Andrew once again as he negotiated the final two bends and approached the main road. 'We're at the main road now and headed for Ailensbury Medi-Clinic.'

Andrew slowed, checked that the coast was clear, then flawed the accelerator causing the car to bounce and jerk a little, the tyres screeching from the transition from gravel to asphalt.

'Aw,' groaned Tim in protest, but Andrew had to keep going.

The motor's revs climbed quickly, the speedometer keeping pace with it. The surrounding serene and tranquil countryside was oblivious to what was happening and seemed to stand momentary motionless as Tim's sedan shot past with intense momentum.

Andrew's palms were now sweaty, and he was gripping the steering wheel so tightly that the blood receded out of his fingers, leaving them white. His heart was pounding and his mind processing thoughts at a prolific pace as he tried to contemplate what to do up ahead. He fought to maintain composure, for he realised it would not help anyone if he lost his nerve just then.

Andrew maintained his high speed for as long as he could, but as they neared town, he had to back off as traffic became more of an issue.

'This is not what we need!' complained Andrew quietly to himself, not really wanting Tim to hear.

The traffic had begun to thicken as people were up earlier than usual due to the Ailensbury Fair taking place later that day, and there was much to be done by many in preparation for it.

Andrew, who had engaged the vehicle's emergency flashers and switched on the headlights to bright when they had turned onto the main road, weaved through the traffic. Some of the people noticed in their rear view mirrors that something was wrong and pulled out of the way, but others, too focused on their own interests, frustrated his cause, and he had to use the hooter for assistance.

Tim now seemed to lie motionless in the passenger seat, only moving as a result of the car shifting. Andrew gave him one last glance as he headed for the central area of town, the hospital just beyond that. He saw the handkerchief Tom had tied around Tim's upper arm to make a tourniquet and wondered if it had been the correct thing to do. Then again, had he made the right decision rushing Tim directly to the hospital instead of first taking him to the boating club's emergency unit? He could not stop to consider nor could he worry about it nor would it help to glance at Tim! He had to keep his focus on what was before him and just keep going and hope!

After navigating a left and then a right bend, Andrew approached the main intersection knowing that a bad break could be detrimental. With sweat now forming on his own brow, he pulled up quickly behind an old couple, who were too fixated on their own cause and the shop they were looking for to be aware of what was going on behind them. Andrew's heart continued pounding inside him, and he felt as though it was lodged in the uppermost part of his chest.

'Come on, come on!' shouted Andrew as he honked the hooter, not worrying now if Tim heard him. 'Get a move on or out of the way!'

Just then the traffic lights unexpectedly turned orange, and to Andrew's shock and horror, the rear brake lights of the elderly couple's coupe lit up!

Chapter 33

A race against time

IN a fraction of a second Andrew had glanced in his mirrors and made a decision. He jammed the accelerator to the floor of the car so hard that his leg muscles tensed as though doing a leg press and his foot hurt. At the same time, he yanked the steering wheel to the left, causing the car's body work to roll to the right. The engine roared and the tyres screeched as he pulled out from behind the old couple's coupe and shot across the front of the car to his left, which was also slowing down for the traffic lights. Andrew yanked the steering wheel back again and pressed the hooter as the car slewed back.

'Come on!' shouted Andrew as they sped through the intersection, trying also to keep a lookout around him, for the traffic lights had just turned red. The continuous "honk" of the hooter turned many heads, but they made it through a fraction after the opposite traffic lights had turned green.

Andrew glanced at the time display on the dashboard. It had only advanced a few minutes since they had left Ailen Oak Lake, but for him it felt like an eternity as he continued to race against time. He quickly gathered his thoughts and focused again, Ailensbury Medi-Clinic not far up ahead.

Several blocks later Andrew entered through the large arched gateway reading "Ailensbury Medi-Clinic". He headed for the emergency trauma unit and as he drew near, a doctor and three nurses wheeling a hospital bed emerged through the extra wide double doors. Andrew swung Tim's car around the curb and pillars supporting the extended entrance roof overhang so that they could deal with Tim without having to come around the car. He stopped the car with a short skid and jumped out.

'Did you receive a phone call about a snakebite victim?' asked Andrew with laboured breathing, directing his question to the nurse nearest to him.

'Yes,' she replied as he ran around to the passenger side, the doctor already having begun checking Tim over.

'Do you know how much he weighs?' asked the doctor, not interested in cordiality.

'About 75 kilograms,' answered Andrew swiftly, his heart still pounding heavily from the ordeal.

Andrew glanced at Tim and had to catch himself. He had not looked at him since approaching the main part of town, and for the first time, Tim really looked deathly. His face, eyes and chest were puffed, and he sat there with his mouth slightly open, saliva drooling out.

'His pulse is too low,' informed the doctor, looking up at the nurse standing with him, 'I'll have to give it direct. Hand me both code one-five-three's – one at level five, the other at level four.'

Andrew did not understand a word of what had been said, but the nurse quickly turned, took hold of two ready prepared syringes and gave one of them to the doctor. She adjusted the dose of the other one before making it available to him.

While the nurse was adjusting the dosage of the second syringe, the doctor inserted the needle of the first one into Tim's jugular vein and proceeded to force in the antidote. He worked skilfully and speedily. Without hesitation he did the same with the second syringe. The doctor then placed his stethoscope on Tim's chest again and fingers on his wrist.

'I want him on a drip before we move him,' said the doctor purposefully, a serious and solemn look on his face. 'This could only have been caused by one type of serpent that may be resident to the surrounding wildlands – I hope the one-five-three's take effect!'

The nurses responded immediately, and again the doctor worked deftly and swiftly as he proceeded to connect the drip to Tim. The needle went effortlessly into Tim's arm, Tim not even aware of what was going on. It was taped down and the release valve opened. Fluid began flowing along the feed tube, and little droplets began falling into the small cylindrical reservoir just below the bag.

One of the nurses held the drip bag while the doctor and the two other nurses carefully lifted the corpse-like figure out of the passenger seat, his arms hanging limply down and his head hanging to one side.

'Slowly,' said the doctor as he manoeuvred Tim out of the car.

'The bed is secure, doctor,' mentioned one of the nurses, seeing him glance over his shoulder. 'He can be lifted on to it.'

'Carefully now,' said the doctor as they lifted Tim onto the bed, the nurses in their clinically clean, white outfits with matching nurses' caps following the doctor's every request and command without question.

The medical personnel proceeded with extreme care and caution, nevertheless, had Tim on the bed in no time at all. They kept him sitting upright, and a nurse pulled up the cover sheet and blanket, tucking them loosely under Tim's chin. An oxygen mask was fitted over his mouth and nose and the drip bag latched to the side hook that was purposely fitted to the bed. With one nurse holding Tim's head up, they wheeled him over the black rubber entrance mats, straight to ward C4 – I.C.U.

Andrew watched as they wheeled Tim off through the extra wide double doors, disappearing as the doors closed behind them. The reality of what had just happened suddenly hit him with extreme force, as up until then he had had no time to think about it at all, and adrenalin had been flowing strongly.

Andrew felt as though the blood started to drain from his head and began to feel queasy. He sat down against one of the supporting pillars, shielded from the blistering sun by the overhanging rooftop. He pulled his legs up almost to his chest, folded his arms on his knees and let out a heavy and drawn-out sigh as he hung his head.

Emotion welled up from the depths of Andrew's soul and overwhelmed his ability to suppress it. Tears began to trickle down his cheeks as he sat there and soon found himself weeping softly. The surrounding colourful array of pansies in the plant boxes that would normally detract one's attention slightly from the solemn building were of no comfort to him at all.

Andrew heard the emergency doors whiz open and the light footsteps of a person come towards him, but he did not respond or look up. He felt the presence of a person next to him, then a hand gently touch him on the arm. Andrew slowly raised his head and looking through bleary eyes, saw the warm smile of one of the nurses who had now bent down next to him.

'Here you are, young man,' said the nurse with a kind and understanding tone of voice as she handed Andrew a tall glass of cola. 'Drink this up, it will help a little.' The nurse smiled again at Andrew and patiently waited for him to take the glass from her. 'It's a race against time, but all has been done that can be done,' added the nurse compassionately, 'we now just have to wait. In the meantime, we need you strong so that you can move your car and come and assist us with some paperwork that's required.'

Andrew had completely forgotten about Tim's car that was parked next to him, the doors still standing wide open. He realised that he needed to move it from the emergency entrance right away, having been grateful that the entrance had not been blocked when they had rushed in.

'Thanks,' said Andrew gratefully, giving the nurse a clipped smile as he took the glass of cola from her, promptly wiping his eyes and nose with the back of his other hand. 'I'll move the car now and come inside shortly.'

'Ward C, reception,' said the nurse as she squeezed Andrew's forearm gently and gave him a warm smile once more. 'Take the second passage to your right, then the third door on the left.'

'Got it,' responded Andrew. The nurse stood up and promptly returned inside.

The nurse's warm smile and her words – *"It's a race against time, but all has been done that can be done, we now just have to wait."* – lingered in Andrew's mind for a few seconds. He quickly got up, downed the cola, not realising how dry his mouth and throat had become, and attended to Tim's car.

Andrew managed to find a parking bay that still had some shade before the afternoon sun would come and slowly peel it away. He was soon making his way back up the gradual incline towards the hospital but suddenly reached down, clasping the side pocket of his faded, blue baggy short pants!

Chapter 34

Andrew's hope

'MOM!' thought Andrew as he felt the familiar shape of his mobile phone and recollected. 'I haven't contacted Mom or Dad – and they need to contact Aunt Gloria!'

Gloria, Tim's mother, was away again handling an important business conference taking place on the other side of the country.

Andrew hastily removed his phone from his side pocket, pleased to see both the battery charge and reception signal showing maximum. He wasted no time, fervently dialling home, hoping there would be no delay in getting through. As Andrew walked up to the emergency entrance, he was relieved to hear the call connect.

Upon entering, the blistering heat outside immediately gave way to pleasantly cool air-conditioned air. The solemn white walls of the façade of the building also gave way to a softer and peaceful tone. The floors and side walls were carpeted with light-green carpet tiles up to about waist height, and the remainder of the wall was a dark-cream colour. Framed pictures, simple in nature but with beautiful colours, lined the walls at measured spacing.

Andrew walked down the corridor breaking the news of Tim's incident to Kelly as quickly as he could. He entered ward C just after ending the call and promptly found himself in the midst of hectic I.C.U. activity.

Andrew glanced through the first doorway as he walked past on his way to the reception desk but did not see Tim there. He peeked in at the second ward on the right, having noticed activity going on there, and his heart sank.

Tim was at the far end of the ward, by the window, still propped up on the bed. His puffy eyes were closed. The oxygen mask was still fitted over his mouth and nose, with the drip feeding him steadily. A doctor was standing next to him and two nurses at the foot of the bed. The only sign of life from him was the very slow and constant "beep —— beep" coming from the heart monitoring machine as the line peaked slightly with every heartbeat.

'Excuse me, Sir,' quietly called one of the nurses manning the reception counter, stirring Andrew from his sorrowful gaze. 'Please come over here.'

Andrew responded immediately.

'Are you associated with the young man just admitted for being bitten by a snake?' asked the nurse.

'Yes,' replied Andrew gravely, 'that's correct.'

'Please will you fill in all the details on this form,' asked the nurse as she handed Andrew a clipboard with the form attached, 'including at the allocated section on the reverse side a summary of what happened?'

'Certainly,' replied Andrew steadfastly, but deep inside he felt sick and limp, particularly not wanting to provide a narrative of the whole ordeal.

Andrew sat down on one of the cushioned side benches and filled out the form, hoping that by a miracle and God's mercy the end would not also be a sad tale. On his way to return it to the nurse, George and Kelly entered the ward. He was greatly relieved to see them.

'We got here as soon as we could,' informed Kelly, approaching Andrew with her arms out to hug him. 'Where's Tim?'

'He's in ward four,' replied Andrew, giving Kelly a gentle hug and pointing in the direction. 'It's the one over there.'

'How is he?' asked George, who was less tense and shaky than Kelly.

'I don't actually know,' answered Andrew dejectedly. 'The only thing that I've been told thus far by one of the nurses is that it's a race against time, but that all has been done that can be done, we now just have to wait.'

'Oh, my goodness!' exclaimed Kelly nervously, fearful concern visible in her eyes.

'The best thing we can do,' said George as he put his arm around Kelly, 'is just sit patiently and pray for him and wait for further news.'

Kelly nodded in acknowledgement, and they headed for the cushioned side benches.

'Are you alright, Andy?' asked George as they sat down.

'Sort of, Dad,' replied Andrew, 'just shaken I guess.'

George gave Andrew a warm smile and a pat on the shoulder.

'Did you get hold of Aunt Gloria?' asked Andrew after a while as he sat leaning forward, his hands firmly clasped between his knees.

'Yes, I did!' answered Kelly after a few seconds, looking a little distant, her mind occupied. 'Gloria said she would get here as quickly as possible.' Kelly quickly returned to her thoughtful and serious manner.

Half an hour passed as the three of them sat there silently, looking very uncomfortable and gloomy. The nurses and doctors continued moving in and out of the wards, but there was no word forthcoming about Tim. Andrew kept looking at his watch every five minutes, and to him it felt as though a large rock had been tied to the minute hand. He tried to relax as best as he could and made a conscious effort to breathe deeply and slowly, but it did not work as well as he had hoped.

Just short of an hour of anxious waiting in strode the twins, dressed in identical outfits and looking beautiful but with worried looks upon their faces. Andrew did not notice them even though they came right up to him.

'Andy,' said June, alerting him to the fact that they were there.

'June! July!' exclaimed Andrew with a high-pitched tone of voice, a little surprised and hoping that nothing was wrong with them. 'What brings you here?'

'I informed June about Tim, Andy,' said Kelly. 'She phoned me after you spoke to me, to check if it was okay to fetch the boxes they need for tonight.'

'How's Tim?' asked July with great concern.

'We don't yet know,' replied Andrew.

'But we haven't received bad news,' said George, 'so we can still hope and pray.'

The two young ladies, realising that it was not the time to discuss what had happened, sat down quietly beside Andrew. Within another 15 minutes, the doctor who had attended to Tim from the start emerged from Tim's ward. He headed towards them sombrely and with intent. Andrew, realising his purpose, stood up, fearing the worst.

The doctor was a tall slender man, clean shaven, with short, grey hair and in his middle to late fifties.

'I presume you are all of the same party?' asked the doctor as he looked at Andrew and then at the rest.

'Yes,' replied George as he stood up, quickly introducing himself and the rest.

'I'm Doctor Jenkins,' informed the doctor and without hesitation got straight to the point. 'Young man,' he said, turning to Andrew, who was looking at him apprehensively, 'I take my hat off to you for getting Timothy here without delay. Had you been a few minutes later, I don't think I would be standing here about to tell you what I'm going to!'

Andrew's heartbeat doubled almost instantly, and July clutched the arm of her sister while the others looked on with bated breath.

'Timothy is past the worst,' continued Doctor Jenkins, instant relief clearly evident on the faces of his listeners, 'although he's not through it yet! His condition was critical enough that I wasn't sure if the antidote would work, and at times I thought we were losing him, but he rallied and it worked. He's still critical but presently stable.'

Andrew gave a small smile, then quickly turned away from the doctor as a second wave of emotion, similar to when he was outside siting against the pillar, welled up inside. His eyes filled with tears, but after taking a deep breath he managed to catch himself and maintain composure.

'You may all go in to see him if you would like to,' added the doctor, 'but do not speak, touch or disturb him in any way, he must be kept quiet.'

'We'll wait here for you, Andy,' said June in answer to

Andrew's questioning look at her and July.

Without further ado, Doctor Jenkins turned and led the three Renshaws quietly into the ward. Andrew had at least seen Tim in this condition, but for Kelly it was a total shock. Tim was lying as still as could be, unconscious, his face puffy and deathly pale.

Kelly placed her fingers over her mouth as her lips began to quiver. She turned and hurriedly retreated from the ward as she could not contain her emotion, bursting into tears as she exited, causing July's eyes to well up with tears when she saw her.

George placed his hand on Andrew's shoulder and motioned with his head that they too should leave. He gave a nod of appreciation to Doctor Jenkins, who gave George a closed-lip smile and saw the two of them out of the ward.

'He's past the worst,' reassured Doctor Jenkins when they were out of the ward, but it was little comfort to Kelly who was sobbing.

'Thank you, Doctor,' said George, unsure of what to do with Kelly other than to get her out of there.

'When can we come and see him?' asked Andrew, who was managing to maintain composure but still very peaky.

'You can pop in tomorrow if you like,' replied Doctor Jenkins warmly, 'but he'll not be in a condition to talk and needs to be kept as quiet as possible. If it all goes well, in three days' time he should be up to receiving familiar faces and a friendly visit.'

Doctor Jenkins politely excused himself and headed off into one of the other wards.

'It was just such a shock to me,' said Kelly, pulling herself together and drying her eyes with a tissue. 'I didn't expect it!'

'That's okay, dear,' comforted George as he put his arm around her. 'There's no need to explain, we understand. Let's get going though, no need to be here any longer.'

The five of them headed out the ward, along the picture-lined corridors and out the air-conditioned building into the heat and blazing sunshine.

'George,' said Kelly, 'you go with Andy to Ailen Oak Lake to fetch their fishing equipment, I'm fine now.'

'We'll see Mrs Renshaw home,' said July reassuringly.

'We still need to fetch the boxes,' added June quickly, 'so need to go there anyway.'

'Oh, yes!' exclaimed Kelly. 'I had completely forgotten about that!'

'I had completely forgotten about tonight!' remarked Andrew.

'I'll go with Andrew,' agreed George, 'and we'll see you later.'

'Will *we* see you later, Andy?' asked June questioningly, hoping in her heart that she would.

'I don't think so,' replied Andrew, feeling quite drained and deflated just then. 'It's been quite a day thus far.'

'We'll see later on, June,' said Kelly, giving her a gentle smile and nod of approval as she thought it may be good for Andrew to get out rather than sit at home contemplating the events of the day.

They dispersed and headed to their cars.

Andrew and George were soon on their way back to Ailen Oak Lake where the troubles of the day had first begun. Andrew quietly thanked God for His mercy and hoped that He would somehow use this incident for His purposes and glory and bring Tim through – and through to salvation!

Chapter 35

A grave concern

FOR the first time since leaving the lake in the mad rush to get Tim to the hospital, Andrew was concerned about their fishing tackle and equipment. He would never have questioned his actions, and in respect to Tim's life, they were worth nothing but nonetheless, he did not want to have to replace the stuff if it could be helped. He did not know the man at all who said he would look after their stuff nor if he and his fishing companions would have stayed there until this time, possibly having other commitments that would require them to leave; what then?

Andrew wanted to rush back, but tiredness suddenly overpowered him, and he knew that he could not. He lifted it to the Lord and left it at that, his mind quickly picking up on the rest of the day's events.

Andrew retraced his path back to the lake but in a much more leisurely manner. When they passed through the centre of town, he was grateful that it had not been such a hive of activity and as heavily congested a few hour ago when he had had to get through in a hurry. The scene raced through his mind as they passed through and out onto the open road towards Ailen Oak Lake. Andrew's thoughts made the trip extra quick for him, almost as though he was not able to focus properly on his driving, with the whole episode of Tim's incident replaying vividly in his mind.

The four fishermen were still fishing when Tim's car emerged from the trees into the clearing. They immediately recognised it, so Tom and his friend who had accompanied him secured their fishing lines and made their way towards the parking area.

Andrew brought Tim's car to a stop almost exactly where it had earlier been parked, and he and George climbed out. Andrew looked at the grass in front of him, a little bewildered by all the gravel that was spewed across it, and his eyes suddenly grew large as it dawned on him what had caused it.

'What peasant did this?' asked George with disgust as he pointed to the gravel spread across the grass.

'That must have been me when I pulled away,' replied Andrew sheepishly. 'I just flawed the pedal, not even thinking about it!'

'You rascal,' responded George with a grin.

'I must have pelted those gentlemen something silly,' said Andrew with a brief chuckle. 'I hope I didn't hurt them! At least Tom still made the urgent phone call.'

George and Andrew headed towards the water's edge and were met half way by Tom and his fishing companion.

'How's the young man?' asked Tom immediately upon reaching Andrew and George.

'He's critical at the moment,' replied Andrew soberly, 'but stable.'

'That's at least good news,' said Tom, lifting his harpooned sombrero and wiping the sweat from his brow with his frayed handkerchief. 'We were quite fearful for him.'

There was silence amongst the four men as the reality of what had happened momentary dug deep into their thoughts.

'Good day to you, Sir,' suddenly said Tom sociably, stretching out his hand to George. 'My name is Tom and this is my friend, Herman.'

'I'm George Renshaw,' said George, who politely shook both men's hands. 'I'm Andrew's father.'

'We were here when the whole incident happened,' informed Tom, his old yellow sombrero still perched upon his head, shading his eyes and nose.

'Andrew informed me that he was assisted by two kindly gentlemen,' said George.

'I telephoned Ailensbury Medi-Clinic for you,' mentioned Tom, looking at Andrew, 'as soon as we got back to our fishing spot where my mobile phone was. I was put through to the emergency section – were they waiting for you when you arrived?'

'Yes,' replied Andrew. 'A doctor and three nurses were ready and waiting at Emergencies. They attended to my cousin immediately. I'm very grateful to you for doing that, it was a major help. The doctor said it was a very close call!'

'Awh,' responded Tom, 'don't mention it, it was no trouble at all. Thank God for hospitals and doctors!' added Tom enthusiastically.

'I fully agree,' said George as he put his hand on Andrew's shoulder, 'but I also simply say – thank God!'

'I suppose you can say that too,' considered Tom thoughtfully, gently scratching the side of his face. 'Anyway, what's the young man's name?'

'Timothy Nicholls,' replied Andrew.

'Please give him our best wishes when he has recovered,' requested Tom, 'will you?'

'I sure will,' replied Andrew, happy to be obliging to Tom's request.

'Your fishing equipment and camping gear is still all there,' informed Tom.

'Unless, of course,' piped up Herman, 'a fish swam away with one of your rods.' He began to laugh heartily but suddenly ceased as a back-hand blow to his belly from Tom encouraged him to stop.

'Sorry if I pelted you with gravel earlier,' apologised Andrew, the back-hand blow to Herman's gut reminding him of it.

'No worries there, young man,' said Tom warmly but quite loudly, having jumped in quickly to suppress Herman's desire to respond and giving the man a serious look. 'No harm was done. We just played jitterbugs for a second or two.'

They all had a light chuckle, Herman first checking that the coast was clear before joining in.

After some further dialogue they parted company. Tom and Herman headed back to their fishing while George and Andrew headed off and gathered the belongings that had been left behind.

They were soon back at the car, Andrew just wanting to get out of there. For a moment, however, he just stood staring across the clearing to the spot where Tim had emerged after being bitten. He suddenly felt emotionally drained and requested George to drive home.

On the way home Andrew withdrew within himself. He sat silently staring out the passenger window, his eyes filled with tears and a faint trickle running slowly down the sides of his cheeks as emotion overcame him.

'Are you okay, Andy?' asked George with concern as they neared town.

'Yes, I'm okay,' reassured Andrew. 'It's just that some of the happenings keep coming to mind, and I'm not doing too well in holding them off.'

'How about the fair this evening?' asked George. 'I could see from your mother's response in the hospital parking lot that she was concerned for you and felt that it would be good for you to go. I feel the same way.'

'Maybe you're right,' responded Andrew, 'but I don't know. I'll see later on how I feel and decide then.'

George pulled into their driveway a few minutes later. He and Andrew cleared the car of all the contents they had gone to fetch.

'Tim's car can stay here for the night,' said George, 'we'll sort things out tomorrow. Are you hungry, Andy?'

'No,' replied Andrew.

'Then go upstairs and have a wash and a rest,' said George warmly. 'I'll pack all the equipment neatly in the garage.'

Andrew headed upstairs, silently entering his bedroom. The familiar security of its surrounds provided great comfort to him, and he flopped face down on his bed, letting out a heavy sigh. He roused himself after a few minutes and headed off to the shower.

As Andrew began washing, his thoughts once again returned to Tim and the incident at Ailen Oak Lake. He stopped and under the flowing water stood still in contemplation. How close it had been to fatal, even now Tim was not completely out of the woods so to speak. He was over the worst but still had to recover. What would happen if he had a relapse? He was so young, just twenty-one. He had a full life ahead of him, yet in an instant he could have no life at all! How short-sighted man can be in light of eternity, so often shrugging off its sobering reality and covering it with rose petals to ease one's conscience. Does man really think that by not being able to accept the truth of heaven and hell that it removes it from one's life? Can man not recognise God's mercy and His merciful provision, His desiring that none should perish? Is man's heart so cold that he will reject such a great salvation, and for what? Many times, however, the issue was not that people could not see as much as it was that they did not want to see!

Andrew was troubled at the thought of it all, and a great concern rose in his heart for Tim. He had heard the truth, and life was no game. The sobering reality of it had been told to him, even on the way home from Munchkins Theme Park, just more than a month back. Would he not listen? If he makes it through this, would he not now see how fleeting life is, for some more so than for others? Would he not see how quickly it can turn, sometimes not even giving one a chance to respond? Would he not see that the consideration of man's soul and the destiny of eternity was no trifling matter to be pushed aside for the sake of selfish wants and convenience? Would he not see it or was it that at present he just could not see it?

Andrew silently wept. His tears ran down his cheeks, intermingling with the water cascading off his head and face and plummeting down in a mix of droplets and streams.

'Enable his eyes to see,' petitioned Andrew with an anguished heart, 'his mind to perceive and his heart to receive, O Lord, the glory of the risen Christ and the salvation that comes through no other!'

Andrew began washing again, lifting all his thoughts and concerns to the Lord while being revitalised by the soothing, cleansing effects of the soap and water.

Before climbing out the shower, Andrew turned the hot tap three quarters off, allowing the cold water to dominate. He just stood there momentarily under the refreshingly cooler water. It dawned on him that there was nothing he could do for Tim other than to pray for him, then rest, hope and wait.

Andrew felt a lot better as he headed back to his bedroom, where he quickly dressed into some cool clothes and managed a two hour siesta, having first lifted his grave concern for Tim once again to the Lord.

Chapter 36

Ailensbury Fair

'ANDY? Andy, are you awake?' called Kelly softly as she stood peering round his bedroom door.

'I am now,' replied Andrew as he turned over and sat up.

'Oh, sorry,' apologised Kelly.

'I was actually awake and about to get up,' said Andrew, 'so don't worry.'

'I think it would be good for you to go to the fair tonight,' encouraged Kelly. 'The cool fresh air and a few fun activities may not be a bad idea.'

'I don't know, Mom,' said Andrew, a little disinterested. 'It's been a rough day.'

'Come on,' responded Kelly a little more forcefully, 'up you get. June said she would pick you up and bring you back. Your father also thinks you could do with some cool evening air and activity. We'll be there a little later on.'

'Why not?' said Andrew, not needing much more encouragement than June accompanying him. 'What time did June say she would fetch me?'

'Five o'clock,' replied Kelly with a smile. 'I'll see you downstairs, and I'll fix you a bite to eat if you would like.'

Kelly slipped away and disappeared, leaving Andrew to properly rise and groom himself in preparation for the fair. Half an hour later he was downstairs.

'I'd be grateful for that bite to eat, Mom,' said Andrew as he entered the kitchen, 'if you don't mind.'

'I'm here, Andy,' called Kelly from behind him as she emerged from the living room. 'Wow! Look at you!' she remarked with amazement. 'Where are you going?'

'What's wow?' responded Andrew as he looked at himself. 'Jeans and sneakers – that's all!'

'But so neat and matching!' replied Kelly with animated expression. 'One would think that you were going out with a really beautiful girl!'

Andrew, who was wearing black jeans, matching black sneakers, a white golf shirt and black sleeveless jersey, looked at Kelly for a moment before realising from her facial expression that she was teasing him.

'What would you like?' asked Kelly as she walked past Andrew and into the kitchen, a cheeky grin on her face.

'Just something light,' replied Andrew. 'I'm not that hungry – cheese and crackers would do just fine if we have.'

'We have,' said Kelly. 'Sit yourself down at the table, and I'll bring it for you.'

Andrew ate quietly and contentedly on the provision Kelly had given him until he felt that he had had enough.

'Please clear the table for me, will you, Mom?' asked Andrew as he left the dining room. 'I still need to brush my teeth and hair before June arrives.'

'Okay, Andy,' replied Kelly, who was back in the living room sitting comfortably reading her garden magazine and drinking tea, 'but you owe me a big hug as fair payment.'

'That's fair payment,' agreed Andrew, and he shot up the stairs in his customary fashion, heading straight for the bathroom.

'I'll get it, Mom,' called Andrew, dropping his hairbrush onto his old rustic side table and hastening out his bedroom, having heard the doorbell ring twice. 'It must be June!'

George, who was also sitting in the living room, seemed to anticipate that someone other than himself would feel privileged to attend the front door, as he did not stir from reading the weekend paper.

Andrew was at the door in flash.

'I'll be with you in a second,' said Andrew, June's bright smile and sparkling blue eyes pleasing him as always. 'I just want to say goodbye to the folks.'

'No need for that,' responded Kelly as she walked up behind Andrew and opened the front door wider so that she could see June. 'You can say goodbye to me here – and remember, you owe me a big hug!'

'Oh, yes – that's right,' said Andrew, first looking at Kelly and then at June. 'Demanded payment for clearing the table for me.'

'At least it made you ready on time,' said June with a light chuckle. 'Well worth it, I would say!'

'Enjoy yourselves,' said Kelly. 'George and I will see you both later on.'

'I just have to help July and my mom for about half an hour,' informed June delightedly, 'and then they've given me the rest of the night off to spend with Andy!'

'Get Andy to give you a hand,' suggested Kelly, giving Andrew a soft nudge and a glancing look, 'and maybe it won't even take half an hour!'

'The sooner we get going,' said Andrew, 'the sooner we can get started.'

Andrew gave his mom her hug, called to his father and then disappeared down the pathway with June.

Ailensbury University, which was located on the outskirts of town, was playing host to the fair, with the university's two football fields that lay side by side presenting a perfect venue.

Andrew and June soon arrived, the university rooftops providing a scenic backdrop behind which the sun was now making a slow descent after a hard day's work.

All kinds of vending stalls were present and stationed neatly around the perimeter of the fields, with entrance and exit openings in the centre of two of the sides. All the games, amusement and funfair activity were placed on the inside.

Mrs Harris was running the popcorn and candyfloss stall on behalf of Bright Kids, one of the church affiliated charity organisations she assisted that was involved in child welfare in Ailensbury and the surrounding districts. Final set up still had to be completed before the fair officially opened at 6 p.m.

Millie Harris was a lady of average height and build and just into her fifties. She could still mix it with the best of them when it came to effort and hard work. Her light-brown, long curly hair was youthfully thick and healthy, but she could not hide her few wrinkles that had come with age. She was a pleasant lady, with a warm and drawing personality. She had a heart for others and was always ready to assist if she could, where a need was evident.

'Any more news on your cousin?' asked Mrs Harris after they had all exchanged greetings, sincerely concerned and interested.

'Not since we left the hospital,' replied Andrew, 'but my mom said she would phone the hospital before coming here.'

'After June told me what had happened,' said Mrs Harris, 'I telephoned all my close church friends and asked for prayer for Tim.'

'Thanks, Mrs Harris,' said Andrew, giving her a clipped smile.

'Come, Andy,' said June, seeing that at present the subject of Tim was not the best thing for him, 'help me fetch the rest of the supplies from my mom's car.'

Andrew's face brightened again, his gloomy look being erased by June's naturally warm smile.

After receiving her mother's car keys, June and Andrew made their way back to the parking lot. They made four trips, fetching the coloured sugar and popcorn that was to be the supply for the night, the boxes that June had obtained from Kelly coming in very handy for this purpose.

While placing the finishing touches to the stall, a deep masculine voice greeted them all from behind; it was Mr Harris. June turned joyously and gave him a squeeze.

Mr Harris was a shortish man in his middle fifties, with grey hair and balding on the top. Andrew had to look down at the general manager for the Ailensbury branch of Ottenger's, the multi-national department store, but Mr Harris had a strong character and was well respected by all who knew him.

'How's Tim doing?' asked Mr Harris as he shook Andrew's hand.

'Daddy!' exclaimed June. 'I don't think that's what Andy really wants to talk about right now!'

'Don't worry, June,' responded Andrew calmly. 'I realise that I can't shy away from the question.' Andrew promptly brought Mr Harris up to date.

'Such happenings are never pleasant,' said Mr Harris

sympathetically, 'they wrench the depths of the soul.'

Andrew clearly understood this and felt the situation trying to dig into his gut once again.

'Our prayer though,' added Mr Harris, 'is that the Lord will not let it have been for nothing, but that in some way He will use it to bring Tim to an understanding of His truth and His ways.'

'That's my very prayer,' said Andrew, recalling his thoughts and prayer earlier on in the shower.

Mr Harris gave Andrew a warm smile and a soft tap on the side of his arm as if to say, "we are all with you". Andrew, although quietly choking on his emotion, appreciated it.

The fair was officially opened shortly thereafter, and people from the town and surrounding villages began filling the fields and milling around, looking at the various offerings. Mrs Harris and July were set for trading, the popcorn and candyfloss stand always being a favourite stop-off amongst the kids.

'We're off,' said June buoyantly just as the first visit for the evening was made to their stand by a group of enthusiastic young boys. 'We'll stop by, just to check that everything's okay and running smoothly.'

'Enjoy the rides, you two,' shouted July as they walked off. 'I wish I could do the same.'

Andrew and June headed for the swings on the other side of the field, the sun now on its final leg of descent and about to lay its head low and rest for the night.

The night steadily moved on and darkness set in, but the bright lights of the fair dulled its effects. The fair was packed with people, some milling round and the young running around. Shrieks of laughter and fright filled the air as fairgoers continually filled the rides. Stalls were buzzing with trade, the popcorn and candyfloss stall also in amongst the mix.

'I don't know if you've noticed, June,' said Andrew as they were browsing the stalls, 'but your mom and July must be really busy. It looks as though every second or third kid has either a box of popcorn or a stick of candyfloss!'

'It looks that way,' responded June, looking about her. 'Would you mind if we checked on them now? I would also like to relieve July for a while, and let her have a chance to go on some of the rides.'

'No problem,' replied Andrew, 'I'll help you.'

Andrew and June made their way back to the stall, the tangle of people and darting kids making it more like a journey along a narrow and twisting English country lane.

'Having fun?' asked July as Andrew and June approached.

'Yes,' replied June, 'but now it's your turn.' July looked surprised. 'Off you go,' said June in a friendly manner. 'Lily and Becky are at the Ferris wheel if you would like to go and join them. Andrew and I will take your place for a while.'

'Would I like to go!' exclaimed July with big, bright eyes and a beaming smile. After receiving an approving nod from Mrs Harris, she disappeared into the crowd.

'What will it be for you, Sir?' asked Andrew jokingly, George and Kelly arriving some time later. 'I can definitely recommend the popcorn, and for the lovely lady, the sweet taste of finger-sticking candyfloss!'

'Have all that sticky stuff in my make-up!' objected Kelly, she and George laughing at Andrew's joke. 'No thank you very much!'

'How's Tim, Mom?' asked Andrew anxiously. 'Did you phone the hospital?'

'He's still critical,' replied Kelly seriously, 'but at present, stable.'

'How are you managing, Andy?' asked George.

'I'm okay,' replied Andrew, a little downcast. 'June has kept me well occupied, but Tim's still in the back of my mind.'

'He's on all of our minds,' said George.

'I guess,' said Andrew. 'I realised this afternoon that the only thing I could do for him was pray and then rest, hope and wait – but it's not always that easy.'

'Hey everybody,' called July as she came ambling up to them.

'Back so soon!' remarked June, looking at her watch.

'I've had four rides already,' replied July, 'and Becky wanted to try her hand at throwing the hoops. You know what I'm like at that!' July produced a facial expression that explained it all. 'Besides,' continued July, 'it was nice of you two to give me the opportunity, which I thoroughly enjoyed, but now off you go and I'll finish the night with Mom. Go on, shoo, shoo!'

They all laughed at July's antics as she pretended to chase them away. June quickly confirmed that she and Andrew would assist with the packing up after the fair, to Mrs Harris' appreciation, and they disappeared into the crowd.

The fair continued unceasing, and time almost seemed to stand still as people milled round or revelled in the excitement on offer. Andrew particularly enjoyed the Ferris wheel, for the cool evening spring air was most enjoyable from up high, and the Ferris wheel provided an incredible view.

'How awesome,' remarked Andrew, staring up at the great expanse above him as they reached the highpoint on the Ferris wheel, its immeasurable beauty drawing his attention.

'The only thing more awesome,' said June, also looking up, 'is that the very Creator of all that we can see was the very One who also bought us with His blood. No-one else could have!'

'It's hard to fathom such an aspect,' said Andrew, quickly

glancing at June before looking up again, 'but the work on the Cross of Calvary is the power of God and the glory of God. That's why I find it hard to understand why people are so resistant to Him.'

'It's not God,' said June, 'it's people. People don't want to be accountable to God. They want to do their own thing, little realising that it's to their own bondage and cost!'

'That's the sad truth,' agreed Andrew. 'It boggles my mind to think how many people don't even realise that they're balancing on the edge of a precipice with the wind swirling around them just waiting to hit them unexpectedly and send them over into a bottomless pit! We've just seen how quickly things can happen and circumstances change. For many it seems that life's merry-go-round has made them delirious, and the world's carnival ambience has desensitised them to the realities of the life hereafter! May people wake up before it's too late!'

As twelve o'clock struck, time suddenly seemed to be released from its chains. People began rapidly exiting as rides were closed and stalls began to shut down, the frivolous ambience giving way to a more purposeful atmosphere.

Mrs Harris' stall had had a booming trade going, so there was not much left over when Andrew and June returned. They cleared everything quite quickly, with the machinery to be picked up the next day by other charity members. They exited the fair while many others were still busy packing their things together. June was well-pleased for she was rather tired but did not want to admit it, particularly not to Andrew. Upon parting company, Mrs Harris kindly reminded Andrew that their prayers for Tim would continue.

'Are you going to see Tim tomorrow?' asked June as she pulled into Andrew's driveway.

'I thought I would go tomorrow afternoon,' replied Andrew, 'just to see him. Remember the doctor said I could, but that Tim was not to be disturbed.'

'Yes,' responded June with feeling, 'I remember.'

'Send me a text message,' asked Andrew as he climbed out June's car, 'just to say that you're home safe, will you?'

'Sure, Andy,' replied June, happy to oblige his thoughtfulness.

Andrew unlocked the front door while June backed out of the driveway. He waved to her, headed inside and made his way upstairs to the pleasant quietness of his bedroom, which was in great contrast to that evening's fair. He quickly prepared for bed, finishing up just as June's message came through, which produced a smile – "Thanks, Andy ☺, I am at home♡" it read. Andrew jumped into bed, pulling the covers up over the side of his face, the end to one heck of a day!

Chapter 37

The requested visit

'GOOD afternoon, nurse,' greeted Andrew a little apprehensively at ward C's reception counter, having not heard further news about Tim. 'I would like to enquire about Timothy Nicholls, please?'

'He's still critical,' answered the tall, slender nurse warmly, 'but stable and improving.'

'May I pop in to see him quickly?' asked Andrew.

'You may for one minute,' replied the nurse, 'but please don't disturb him, he's to be kept quiet.'

'I understand,' responded Andrew, 'thanks.'

Andrew turned and headed for ward four where just more than twenty-four hours earlier Tim had been placed in a desperate race against time to save his life. He thought to himself that it must be tough for nurses and doctors to work in such an environment and at the same time keep their spirits up and still present a calm, warm and welcoming face to visitors.

Andrew entered ward four and there, in the corner bed nearest the window, lay Tim, motionless. From first observances nothing seemed to have changed. Tim was still being fed by a drip, an oxygen mask remained firmly placed over his mouth and nose and the heart monitor was thankfully still beeping steadily.

As Andrew neared, his stomach feeling hollow, he suddenly realised that the heart monitor was registering a little more strongly than it had the day before, and this coupled with the nurse's words encouraged his own heart.

'O Lord God,' prayed Andrew quietly, standing at the foot of Tim's bed, 'please continue to have mercy on my cousin!' He stood silently for a moment, just looking at him.

Just as he was about to turn and leave, Tim slowly opened his eyes just enough to see through the slits. The heart monitor started to beat a little faster, which alarmed Andrew as this was not meant to happen.

'Be still, Tim,' said Andrew quickly yet softly, 'and just rest. You're in good hands. We can talk about things later.'

Tim closed his eyes again, and the heart monitor slowly returned to beeping at steady intervals. Andrew quickly turned and left, mixed emotions tumbling inside of him as he was encouraged by Tim's response but concerned because Tim was not meant to be disturbed. He decided that it would be best to wait until Tim was up before paying him another visit and would phone in to check on him.

Tim's improvement was slow but steady. Andrew phoned the hospital each day for a progress report, desperately wanting to visit but not prepared to cause Tim anxiety. As the Wednesday after the incident was a public holiday, Andrew was able to phone the hospital in the morning rather than in the afternoon after varsity classes.

'Mom! Dad!' shouted Andrew as he bounded down the bemoaning staircase, having just spoken to a nurse at ward C.

'What's the matter?' called Kelly, emerging from the kitchen, the smell of fresh scones following her.

'Tim has properly woken up,' exclaimed Andrew excitedly, 'and was able to sit up this morning! That's good news!'

'Yes, indeed!' responded Kelly happily. 'Your father is out back, go and tell him, he'll be glad to hear this too.'

'Tell me what?' questioned George from behind Kelly as he entered the house via the back door. 'What will I be glad to hear?'

'Tim's fully conscious!' answered Andrew enthusiastically.

'I *am* glad to hear that!' said George. 'Do remember though, he'll still be very weak and needs to build his strength again.'

'No doubt,' agreed Andrew.

'But he's a toughie that one,' remarked Kelly. 'I doubt it will take him long.'

'Visiting hours are in an hour,' mentioned Andrew. 'Do you want to visit Tim with me?'

'You go and see Tim,' replied George. 'Your mother and I shall go this afternoon. Remember Gloria is coming round this evening, and we have a few things we're in the middle of doing at the moment.'

'No problem,' said Andrew. 'I'll give June a call, for she wanted to go and see Tim when he woke up.'

'That's fine, dear,' said Kelly as Andrew sped back up the creaking staircase.

Forty-five minutes later Andrew fetched June, and they headed to Ailensbury Medi-Clinic.

The hospital's main entrance's automatic sliding doors opened the moment Andrew and June neared them, the warm outside air stepping aside as the cool air-conditioned air from inside pushed out and welcomed them in. The reception area, with its green indoor plants and calming trickle coming from the water feature, provided a tranquil ambience that almost drew one away from the reality of what lay beyond it.

Andrew and June quickly made their way to ward C4, with Andrew being a little more chatty and joyous than he had been on the two previous occasions at the hospital. He and June entered ward C looking forward to seeing Tim, but as they entered ward C4, Andrew immediately stopped in his tracks, putting his arm out to stop June. June instantaneously halted, bewildered at the sudden happening, but when she looked at Andrew to enquire as to his actions, she caught herself as his facial expression had turned to shock.

Andrew stood staring for a few seconds, his face ashen white and heart pounding. June looked to see what had stunned Andrew, dreading what she might see. Tim was not there, and his bed had been freshly made up in preparation for another patient should it be required. The oxygen facility and heart monitor had also been removed.

'What's happened to Tim?' cried Andrew frantically as he looked at June. He turned hastily before she could even comment and headed for the reception counter, June following closely behind him.

'What's happened to Timothy Nicholls?' asked Andrew with great anxiety as he approached the ward's reception counter. The nurse on duty was startled but quickly regained her composure, realising the issue.

'Don't worry, young man,' replied the nurse. 'Timothy Nicholls has been moved from I.C.U to the general ward, ward B4 in the annex to the right of us.'

'I got such a fright,' confessed Andrew with a sigh of relief, looking at June and then back at the nurse, 'I thought—'

'No need to fear,' interrupted the nurse, 'he's in the next

annex and should be eating a light breakfast by now.'

The nurse just smiled warmly at Andrew while he tried to regain composure and slow down his rapid heart rate. Andrew and June quickly exited ward C and headed for ward B4, the paleness on both of their faces easing the further on they walked.

Tim was busy eating a light breakfast consisting of smooth wheat porridge and toast with strawberry jam when Andrew and June entered his ward. He looked up and saw their two bright faces beaming big smiles at him.

'Hi, you two,' greeted Tim in a somewhat subdued manner. 'It's nice to see you both.'

'It's nice to see *you*, Tim!' exclaimed Andrew with heart-felt gratitude to God. 'We – or at least I – got a shock when we entered C4 and found you missing!'

'*We* got a shock,' perked up June. 'Andrew's shock rubbed off on me.' June briefly chuckled as she looked at Andrew.

'Has much been happening these past few days?' asked Tim, wanting to divert the attention away from himself. His hospital pyjamas were all crinkled around his chest and a drip was still connected to his forearm. He was still very peaky, his hair could have done with being brushed and it was clearly evident that he had lost a fair amount of weight as a result of what had taken place.

'No, not much,' replied Andrew, 'just the general goings on, apart from you.'

'Andrew brought you some fishing magazines, Tim,' said June as she stepped forward and handed them to him.

'Thanks, Andy,' said Tim gratefully as he looked at the various ones. 'These are much appreciated and will come in handy here. There's not that much to do other than rest.' Tim produced a facial expression that let them know he was already bored.

'At this time,' said Andrew, 'rest is not such a bad thing for you to be doing!'

'Yes, Doc,' objected Tim disapprovingly, 'but I've been here for four days already. Anyway, the doctor thinks I should be out of here by Saturday at the latest. Then we can go fishing again!'

'Whoa!' exclaimed Andrew. 'Not so fast, pal. We have exams this coming month remember but in five weeks' time – absolutely yes!'

Tim gave Andrew a thumbs up as he leaned back on the bed and shut his eyes for a few seconds, a little light-headed.

'You missed my mom,' commented Tim after his short rest. 'Did you perhaps see her on your way in?'

'No,' replied Andrew, 'but we first went to ward C4 before coming here.'

'She had to come early,' informed Tim, 'because she has an important meeting this afternoon that she has to attend. It's a pity you missed her though, she would have liked to have heard from you.'

'No loss, Tim,' said Andrew warmly. 'Your mom's coming round to our house for dinner this evening, so we'll have plenty of time to chat then.'

'Oh, yes!' said Tim, recalling. 'She actually mentioned it to me, but I forgot.'

Tim took a bite out of his toast with strawberry jam and after swallowing, lay back again. Andrew realised that Tim needed to rest but knew that he would not admit it or ask them to leave. He gave June a look and nodded that they should be on their way. June, who had been standing back while the two lads chatted, was happy to oblige and follow Andrew's lead.

'Well, Tim,' said Andrew with an upbeat tone of voice, 'it was really good to chat to you, but we must be going. My mom still needs some shopping to be done, and I still have some studying to do, so we'll be seeing you.'

'I was really glad that I could come along,' said June, 'and am so happy to see you on the mend.'

'Okay,' responded Tim. 'Thanks for stopping by.'

'Anytime,' said Andrew, who gave Tim a small wave before he and June turned to head out.

'Hey, Andy!' called Tim, somewhat softly.

'Yes,' said Andrew, turning round to see what Tim wanted.

'Tell your mom,' requested Tim, hesitating for a second, 'that I know she has been praying for me, and whether prayer works or not I don't know, but I'm grateful anyway.'

'Will do,' replied Andrew giving Tim a quick smile. 'Now get some rest and read your magazines when you're up to it.'

Andrew and June glanced at each other in respect to what Tim had said and promptly headed out the ward.

'O Lord, visit Tim,' prayed Andrew as he and June walked down the corridor. 'Let him be able to understand and come to know that you are the Living God!'

'I'll say amen to that,' agreed June, her heart going out to Tim as she echoed the prayer.

Tim's recovery was slow and steady but enough for him to be discharged from Ailensbury Medi-Clinic on the Sunday, eight days after he had been rushed into emergencies. Once out of hospital, he regained his strength and stamina and also managed to sit his exams – his diligent work ethic and effort throughout the year standing him in good stead.

Chapter 38

Return to Ailen Oak Lake

ANDREW awoke a few minutes before his alarm was set to go off, the sun beaming in through his bedroom window and its warmth being felt through his brightly-coloured eiderdown. Outside the melodious tweets were clear as bells, as the birdlife had arisen with the dawn and gone about their business with purpose and vigour.

'Who needs an alarm clock?' thought Andrew as he opened his eyes, laughing to himself. He knew what day it was, and although he was a little concerned, was not about to forget.

Andrew turned over and switched off the alarm the moment it rang. Without delay he threw back the eiderdown, sprang out of bed and joyously opened his bedroom window, instantly increasing the volume of melodic sounds he heard outside. He peered out for a few minutes, which was his customary pleasure, and watched nature's life at work in the garden and trees. Mindful of his intentions for the morning, he did not linger long and in minutes his multicoloured, striped pyjamas lay crumpled on his bed, and he had morphed from a sleepyhead into a man on a mission.

'Just made it!' said Andrew to himself as he looked at the time on his alarm clock, having tidied his room and prepped for the morning. He grabbed his cap and wallet, and was out his bedroom in a flash, skipping down the stairs.

'You're up early this morning?' mentioned Kelly, popping her head out from behind the kitchen door, a quizzical look on her face. 'What's the big occasion?'

'Mom!' exclaimed Andrew in amazement, half-stopping in his tracks. 'Have you forgotten?'

'Forgotten what, Andy?' asked Kelly innocently.

'Exams are over,' said Andrew with great expression, 'and I'm going fishing with Tim – that's what!'

'Oh, of course!' responded Kelly with animation. 'Silly me! I just can't believe the month has flown by so quickly.'

'If you were the one writing the exams,' objected Andrew, giving Kelly a disapproving look, 'you wouldn't have thought it went by so quickly!'

'Of course not, dear,' agreed Kelly warmly. 'Go on, be gone with you. Tim's just pulling into the driveway now.'

Andrew started to head for the front door, his fishing tackle and bag having already been placed there in preparation for the day.

'Wait!' called Kelly. 'Where's my kiss?'

'Sorry, Mom,' replied Andrew, quickly backtracking. 'I just forgot.'

'You also forgot your French toast,' added Kelly with a big smile as she produced a plate of French toast and lifted up a picnic basket, 'and your additional yum-yum for your tum-tum.'

'So you didn't forget after all!' remarked Andrew with big, gleaming eyes as he came and gave Kelly a kiss on her cheek.

'Of course not, dear,' replied Kelly with a chuckle. 'I wouldn't forget such an event!'

'For myself and Tim,' said Andrew joyously, grabbing a number of pieces of French toast and dumping them in the plastic container that lay on the dining room table. 'Thanks, Mom! Hold your horses, Tim old boy!' protested Andrew, Tim suddenly starting to honk his car's hooter. 'I'm on my way.'

With Kelly's help, Andrew was out the door in seconds.

'Morning, Tim,' greeted Andrew cheerfully as he approached Tim's car. 'Are you excited or apprehensive?'

'Both I guess,' answered Tim after a brief deliberation, his car purring quietly as it idled patiently.

'Please just remember,' said Kelly, pleased to see Tim in lively spirits, 'you can make a fish barbeque here!'

'Would you like some French toast?' asked Andrew, having put his fishing tackle down so that he could open the car door.

'I'd love some,' replied Tim with a bright face, and he helped himself to two pieces.

Without further ceremony, Andrew packed his things into Tim's car and they were ready to go in a moment.

'Thanks, Mom,' said Andrew as they began pulling out of the driveway, the sun shining off the car and making Kelly squint a little. 'We'll see you later.'

'Be careful,' said Kelly, 'and have a good time.' She waved to the lads as they slowly pulled away, headed for Ailen Oak Lake.

As the lads headed for the urban edge of town along the main road, Tim was quite cheerful and chatty, but he did not mention one word about the incident that had taken place five weeks earlier. However, as the concentration of houses started giving way to the familiar scenery of lush, tranquil fields and farmlands, Tim's mannerism changed. He became quieter and quieter the closer they came to the Ailen Oak Lake turn off, a serious look appearing on his face. Andrew knew exactly what Tim was dwelling on because it was the same thing on his mind.

A number of cars were already present in the parking area when they pulled up and parked. Andrew quickly hopped out of Tim's car and begun his customary stretch, but Tim was not so hasty. He climbed out slowly and scanned the area intently.

'I don't blame you, Tim,' said Andrew as he watched him. 'It was the very thought on my mind.'

'Just checking,' said Tim, turning to Andrew. 'You know the old saying – once bitten, twice shy.'

'Ah, cousin,' responded Andrew, amused, 'you've still got your sense of humour I see!'

'Never lost it, Andy,' said Tim, chuckling at the sharpness of his own remark, 'never lost it.'

Tim stood momentarily, gathering his thoughts. He let out a deep breath as he took in the scenery, the sunlight shimmering on the water and producing golden ripples as the sail boats passed by. Tim seemed fixed in thought but snapped out of it the moment Andrew spoke to him.

'I forgot to tell you,' said Andrew, lifting up the picnic basket that Kelly had given him, 'that my mom packed us a surprise brunch. She felt that you would prefer it to making a fish barbeque!'

'That's grand!' said Tim, well pleased. 'Aunt Kelly, the star dust of all fallen stars – I wonder how she knew?'

The two lads chuckled, finished unpacking their fishing tackle and gear, made the short trip across the lush, green grass into the shade of the towering trees and through to their desired spot at the water's edge.

'It's about time we caught some decent fish,' remarked

Andrew while they baited their fishing hooks. 'Otherwise, what's the point of bringing fishing tackle?'

'The fishing tackle makes our loafing respectable,' replied Tim with a laugh, 'didn't you know that? How else do you think we could come here? Everyone would frown upon us if we told them we were coming here to sit by the lake and sleep!'

'But we do come here to fish,' said Andrew, sitting up, 'even if *you* sit and sleep at times while fishing!'

'Of course, silly,' responded Tim. 'It was just a tease.'

'Ah, I get you,' said Andrew, settling back in his camping chair and continuing his baiting, 'but let's show them anyway. Let's hope we have a good haul today!'

Andrew was first to cast off but hooked his line in the overhead branches.

'Blast!' groaned Andrew, looking up at the branches. 'I'm sure they weren't here when I stood up to cast out.'

'Of course they weren't,' joked Tim, amused at the incident. 'They snuck up on you!'

Andrew had further embarrassment when the folks a little way down from them started laughing when they saw him and realised what had happened.

'Ha-ha, very funny,' groused Andrew quietly, tugging at his line to see if he could get it loose. 'Wait till it's your turn!'

'Relax, Andy boy,' said Tim, who was fighting off his own laughter. 'Just cut the line and leave the tree with its first Christmas decoration.'

Andrew had no alternative but to do what Tim suggested. He put the issue aside and started again. Tim cast off, his reel whizzing as the hook, float and sinker disappeared into the distance with the line trailing behind it. It was not long before Andrew had fixed up his line and had his red and white float bobbing in the water alongside Tim's.

'I'm now respectably able to sit back and relax,' said Tim as he tipped his hat forward to cover his eyes and leaned back in his chair, a big grin on his face.

Tim sat laid-back in his light-brown camping chair, not too fussed about the world around him, except for the few bugs that irritated him from time to time.

Andrew on the other hand seemed more determined on catching a fish. He worked his reel, cast out multiple times and watched his float closely. Seeing the red and white float being pulled down as the fish nibbled at the bait made him excited as he watched and hoped, but nothing was forthcoming. After an hour of trying, Andrew too decided to adopt Tim's perspective of things and followed his example for about half an hour.

The shimmering water with its steady ripples calmly beating against the bank encouraged the opportunity for a snooze while the sun's rays, filtering between the branches, provided a pleasant warmth. The lads rested comfortably, just enjoying their return to Ailen Oak Lake.

Chapter 39

The surprise response

'ARE you hungry, Tim?' asked Andrew, eventually sitting up. 'Would you like some of my mom's goodies?'

'I'll have later, thanks,' replied Tim lazily to Andrew's great surprise, for Tim never passed up an offer.

Andrew eagerly opened the picnic basket, not knowing what he would find.

'This will do nicely,' said Andrew with satisfaction as he pulled out a toasted cheese, tomato and onion sandwich. 'Who wants fish when you can eat this!'

Andrew promptly began eating away at his sandwich while reeling in his line again, watching his float closely. He suddenly became serious and stiffened. He started reeling in his line slowly, looking intently at his float.

'Whoa!' exclaimed Andrew excitedly. 'I've got one!'

'Another ten buck winner I suppose?' chirped Tim as he sat up, lifting his hat back onto his head.

'This is a fish!' replied Andrew excitedly. 'A real fish!'

Andrew reeled the fish in with finesse, not wanting to lose

the catch, and was well pleased when he pulled it out of the water.

'Not bad, I must admit,' complimented Tim as he nodded his head approvingly. 'Definitely a ten buck winner that one!'

'How about a fish barbeque?' joked Andrew as he removed the hook from the fish's mouth.

'Not a chance!' responded Tim giving Andrew a scowl but knowing that he was jesting.

'Okay, Timmy boy,' said Andrew. 'How about we barbeque the fish at my place this evening, and afterwards I'll take you to Misty's for ice-cream?'

'Is June perhaps working this evening?' asked Tim.

'Why, yes,' replied Andrew innocently. 'How'd you guess?'

'Just a hunch,' answered Tim with a wry smile as he gave Andrew a friendly shove on his shoulder. 'I don't mind playing along, but I want a double of whatever it is we're having!'

'Absolutely fine,' confirmed Andrew cheerfully. 'We cannot sit there all night for no reason!'

Tim and Andrew enjoyed the rest of the morning at the lake. The sun continued its faithful supply of warmth, with the day getting hotter as midday approached. The shelter of the trees, however, provided a haven from a roasting, and the gentle breeze blowing across the lake kept them cool. Kelly's toasted cheese, tomato and onion sandwiches were devoured by Andrew and Tim, including the pack of cookies they found underneath the lot in the picnic basket.

'Are you ready, Tim?' asked Andrew as he gathered his things together, his catch of three fish, wrapped in newspaper and neatly bound, already in Tim's cooler box, the two lads having finished for the day.

'I just want to finish my ginger ale,' replied Tim, having

already packed up and attended to his equal catch of three fish, 'and then we can be off.'

'How about joining me tomorrow evening,' asked Andrew out of the blue, 'and come along to the evening church service? Afterwards I'm buying coffee.'

There was silence.

'What for?' asked Tim gruffly, eventually speaking after finishing his ginger ale. 'The last time you asked me, I said only that once!'

'I remember what you said,' responded Andrew, 'but at the same time I also know what's transpired since then! I personally believe—'

'I don't see the need for church,' interjected Tim, 'because I don't see the need for a saviour!'

'Tim!' exclaimed Andrew. 'You were teetering on the precipice of death! How fine a line do you want to walk on the edge? I personally believe that God has been speaking to you in many ways, trying to get you to listen! What more does He need to say?'

'There's something amiss in the whole thing,' said Tim abruptly, 'and I'm not budging! Besides, one of the issues that's troubled me is the presentation of God's wrath and judgement. It's almost used as a scare tactic to manipulate people!'

'Presenting the truth cannot ever be used as a means of manipulation!' replied Andrew. What is real, is real, Tim! People shove it aside because they don't want it to bother their conscience, but that never removes the reality of it. Jesus told the people that when the Holy Spirit would come, He – that is the Holy Spirit – would convict the world of sin, and of righteousness, and of judgement.[89] If Jesus mentioned judgement it was because it's a reality. Why would the Holy

Spirit convict of judgement if there was no judgement to follow?'

'Beats me!' returned Tim sarcastically.

'Both Peter and Paul spoke strongly about judgement,' said Andrew, ignoring Tim's sarcasm and quickly scrolling through his phone, 'and both spoke about it in respect to the true, born again Christian and the non-Christian! Listen to the following recorded in Scripture: Peter says, "For the time is come that judgement must begin at the house of God: and if it first begin at us, what shall the end be of them that obey not the gospel of God? And if the righteous scarcely be saved, where shall the ungodly and the sinner appear?" [90] He goes on, "For if God spared not the angels that sinned, but cast them down to hell, and delivered them into chains of darkness, to be reserved unto judgement; and spared not the old world, but saved Noah the eighth person, a preacher of righteousness, bringing in the flood upon the world of the ungodly; and turning the cities of Sodom and Gomorrah into ashes condemned them with an overthrow, making them an example unto those that after should live ungodly; and delivered just (righteous) Lot, vexed with the filthy conversation (conduct) of the wicked; the Lord knoweth how to deliver the godly out of temptations, and to reserve the unjust unto the day of judgement to be punished." [91] Peter goes even further, "But the heavens and the earth, which are now, by the same word (which brought the Flood) are kept in store, reserved unto fire against the day of judgement and perdition (damnation and hell) of ungodly men." [92] This doesn't paint a pleasant picture does it?'

Tim just stared at Andrew, not saying a word, his mind trying to process what he was hearing and his own thoughts at the same time.

'Paul was no different as mentioned,' continued Andrew, scrolling further on his phone. 'Listen to what he says, "For we must all appear before the judgement seat of Christ; that every one may receive the things done in his body, according to that he hath done, whether it be good or bad. Knowing therefore the terror of the Lord, we persuade men." [93] Paul has written this for the believers, the true born again Christians! When Paul considers the judgement of the Christian, he fears! And as Peter said, if judgement first begins with the Christian, what will the end be of the non-Christian! The writer of Hebrews goes on to say, "For our God is a consuming fire." [94] Paul says that it's because of the judgement that he speaks! And we should not speak of judgement? God may be a God of love, but He's also a righteous judge! Jesus said, "Whosoever shall fall upon that stone (the stone the builders rejected that has become the cornerstone, which is Himself) shall be broken; but on whomsoever it shall fall, it will grind him to powder." [95] This is reality, Tim!

'If God is real,' said Tim offhandedly, 'He will have to explain it to me, it's that simple! I do not see it, and I'm not going to church with you!'

'If you don't want to go,' responded Andrew putting his phone in his pocket, 'then don't go. I just want to say the following: not only do we need Jesus as our saviour, but there's one further aspect beyond this. It's the sweet fellowship with the Lord, through the Holy Spirit. It's only achieved through repentance and acceptance of Him as Lord and Saviour and as we then walk with Him and get to know Him. He who has the Son truly has life, Tim!'

Tim baulked, the remembrance of the verse at the administration office jumping at him. He quietly picked up his stuff and headed for his car. Andrew sighed and quietly did the same.

As they crossed the section of lush, green grass, Tim was deep in thought. That challenging verse had once again sprung to life, vividly displayed in his mind as if he was standing in the administration office reading it. It had also brought with it other recollections that had for a while lain dormant in the back of his mind. If there was a real God, had He actually been speaking through all of what had transpired? This was a shocking consideration for Tim, for if it was true, what had he missed, what had he not heard and what had he not been prepared to listen to?

Mike had pulled him back to prevent him from stepping right into the path of a snake, for he had not been watching or alert to his surrounds. Even though that snake was apparently not harmful, was it a warning? Was he not seeing what others were seeing, who had tried to keep him from harm? Was he not alert to it? He had made that same mistake, which nearly cost him his life! He could not deny that there was some good fortune or providence in surviving that ordeal. Which it was he was not sure, but if it was providence— Tim shivered.

That gentle voice that had spoken to him previously now pierced his conscience once more, reminding him that he did not know all things. He could not ignore it, he could not overrule the truth of it, and worst of all, he could not deny that when he had heeded it, much had been revealed to him that he had never comprehended nor considered!

If God was real though, what was it that was missing? What was it that he still could not understand, or what was not fitting together in his understanding? Was it that he was not actually giving God, if He was real, a chance to show Himself and reveal this aspect that may bring it all together for him? Tim wondered. He had been concerned that he had already opened himself up to it, but had he opened his heart enough to receive it should it be revealed, or was he fooling himself by just telling himself that he had? Then again, in his deliberations on the way back from Munchkins Theme Park, he had concluded that if God was real, he wanted Him to disclose something further, that something that would piece it all together for him. He had heard what Andrew had just said but was as adamant now as he was then that should this not happen, he would not budge. However, he was also still adamant that should it all be true, he wanted it revealed! But if this was his interest, his resolve, how could it be revealed if he shut off the channels through which he may receive it? Tim considered it.

As they neared the parking area, Tim looked across at the forested expanse where he had entered five weeks before.

'Don't even look there, Tim,' cautioned Andrew, noticing him, but Tim ignored him, still buried deep in his thoughts.

The lads were soon at Tim's car, packing their belongings in the trunk in absolute silence.

'Fetch me on your way to church tomorrow evening, Andy,' requested Tim as they finished putting their stuff in the trunk. 'I'll come!'

'Certainly, Tim,' agreed Andrew, surprised at his response, 'but why the sudden change—'

'Don't ask questions,' interrupted Tim, shutting the trunk and heading round to the driver's side. 'I at least owe it to the church to pay my respects anyway, as I heard that some of the congregants prayed for me when I was in hospital – let's leave it at that! Just fetch me!'

Chapter 40

A timely word

'**A**RE you off to fetch Tim?' called George from the living room when he saw Andrew pass by on his way to the kitchen.

'Yes,' replied Andrew. 'Do you know where Mom is?'

'She's out back watering her chrysanthemums,' called back George.

Andrew placed his keys on the kitchen counter as he walked through on his way to the backyard, his new pair of black moccasins squeaking slightly as he went. He could hear the familiar sound of water spraying from a rose sprayer as he neared the back door, which lead down two steps into the back garden.

Kelly was happily moving the hand-held sprayer to and fro, allowing the water to drop softly on her delicate pride and joy – the beautiful mix of green, white, yellow and purple chrysanthemums, which all huddled together and bobbed slightly as they gladly received their liquid refreshment after a long, hot day. Kelly turned, having seen Andrew out the corner of her eye. She gave him a welcoming smile and put her arm out, inviting an embrace.

'Are you on your way already?' asked Kelly as she put her arm around Andrew's waist.

'Yes,' answered Andrew. 'I don't want the same occurrence to take place as last time, where Tim was hesitant and nearly made us late.'

'At least he knows what to expect,' responded Kelly, continuing to gently shower her plants. 'I don't think he'll do the same as last time.'

'You may be right,' said Andrew thoughtfully, 'but we'll soon find out. I'm a little apprehensive after last time!'

'Trust God to work His works,' said Kelly, 'and rest in Him. He knows His job, what He needs to do and how He needs to do it! Leave Tim to God!'

'That's an apt word for me at this time,' said Andrew, easing a little. 'Thanks, Mom, I'll take it to heart as best I can!'

'We'll see you at church then,' said Kelly, giving Andrew a reassuring smile and squeezing him lightly before letting go.

'Okay, Mom,' said Andrew. 'Keep our seats next to you, please.'

'Of course, Andy dear,' confirmed Kelly warmly as Andrew headed back to the house.

A few minutes later Andrew had backed his car out from under the beige shade-cloth canopy and was on his way to fetch Tim. He let out a deep sigh at the thought of what had happened on the previous occasion when he had fetched Tim but quickly shoved it aside, reaching down and switching on the radio to listen to some calming classics.

Andrew tried not to think about any of it, but when he entered Tim's street, he could not help wondering how long he would have to wait for Tim this time. He glanced at the house before pulling into the driveway and, to his absolute surprise, saw the beautifully hand-carved wooden front door with picturesque inlays standing partly open. There was movement to the side of the porch – it was Tim.

'I don't believe it!' exclaimed Andrew loudly as he brought his car to a stop in the driveway. He did not hoot but stared with big eyes as Tim swiftly made for the front door and disappeared inside the house. 'This time he's not even going to come to the car!' thought Andrew, annoyed by what he saw.

To Andrew's amazement, however, Tim reappeared a few seconds later, shut and locked the door and came purposefully down the pathway neatly dressed in the same casual clothing he had worn to the service two months previously – black jeans and sneakers, with long-sleeve, checker-pattern collared shirt, the sleeves rolled up to his elbows. The only difference this time was that he was not carrying a jersey with him. Andrew just looked on, not knowing what to think.

'What's the matter, Andy?' asked Tim, having climbed in and begun buckling up.

'Nothing's the matter,' replied Andrew. 'I'm just surprised by your attitude – no hesitation or objection!'

'I know what I'm in for,' responded Tim, 'so when I agreed to go I accepted that.'

'That's what my mom said your response would be,' mentioned Andrew as he backed his car out the cobble-paved driveway, 'but I wasn't too sure after last time.'

'I told you yesterday that I owe it to the church,' said Tim, 'so this is what I'm doing – paying my dues, that's all. There's no need for me to be off about it because then it wouldn't be of value.'

'Do remember,' informed Andrew, 'that you cannot "pay" for

such things.'

'I know,' replied Tim as they started off down the street, in no hurry to have to get to the church. 'I remember what was told to me by all of you. Call it paying my respects then, not dues. There's just one condition about going to Roccocoa's afterwards,' added Tim.

'What's that?' asked Andrew curiously.

'The minister's already made his dog food purchases at Sunny Valley Mall!' replied Tim with a cheeky smile. 'I don't want any surprise arrivals!'

'You know the saying, Tim,' managed Andrew, having burst out laughing. 'Lightning never strikes twice—'

'Yes, I know,' interrupted Tim. 'Lightning's one thing, you guys are another!'

There was a marked contrast from the last time Tim had gone with Andrew to church two months previously. The spring season was awakening then but had now fully matured and was knocking at summer's door. The darkness of the evenings two months ago had now given way to the brightness of the early evening sun. Although giving signs of wanting to retire for the day, the sun still hung relatively high in the sky above the horizon, with only a few clouds about trying fruitlessly at times to conceal it from the world.

Andrew turned off his radio, and he and Tim chatted about the previous day's fishing at Ailen Oak Lake. The two lads had a good chuckle as they recounted Andrew's left behind "Christmas decoration". Tim admitted that he had been quite apprehensive about going fishing, although he had tried not to show it.

'In the end,' said Tim as they approached the church, 'I settled quite quickly and really enjoyed the day.'

Andrew turned left round the small but neat signboard

indicating Ailensbury Christian Fellowship and pulled into the cobbled parking area that belonged to the church.

'I say,' said Tim, being alert and observant, 'the flowerbeds bordering the parking area are very neatly presented. I don't recall noticing them being like that before.'

'To your credit, Tim,' responded Andrew, 'it was dark outside then, we were late and you were in a big huff. I'm not sure if you took notice of anything!' Tim did not respond.

Andrew was able to find a parking bay quite close to the main entrance.

'Hey,' said Andrew enthusiastically as he switched off his car, 'there's the Harris family!'

The Harris' had arrived a minute before Andrew and Tim and had parked further up in a parking bay against the walkway. June and July had spotted Andrew's car pulling into the parking area and had stopped along the pathway, leaving their parents to continue on while they waited for him.

'Tim's with Andrew!' exclaimed July quietly as they saw the two lads climb out the car. 'I wonder why he's with him?'

'I'm always glad to see the two of you,' said Andrew good-naturedly as he walked up to June and July, Tim remaining a little further back, 'but then you should know that by now.'

'Especially glad to see June, aren't you, Andy?' teased July with great animation and promptly received a gentle poke in the ribs from her sister.

The two girls were radiant as ever, this time wearing open sandals and three-quarter length, cool summer dresses that not only suited the weather but also matched the season as the dresses sported bright floral prints. Andrew *was* especially happy to see June and thought she looked lovely with her hair plaited and tied in a bun. July was again content to wear her hair in pigtails, but Andrew did not think it the time or place for jest.

'Tim decided to come with me this evening,' mentioned Andrew, quickly turning and giving Tim a glance.

'We see,' responded July.

'Hello, Tim,' greeted June warmly. 'It's nice to see you here again.'

'Hello June, July,' greeted Tim with a nod of the head.

June looked at Andrew a little puzzled, not sure of the reason for Tim's attendance, with no mention made while chatting together the night before at Misty's.

'Tim decided that he needed to pay his respects to the church,' said Andrew, seeing June's questioning look, 'for the fact that some of the congregants prayed for him when he was in hospital.'

'Although I'm not sure if prayer works,' mentioned Tim, 'it was the thought that counts in my mind. I thought it was the least I could do to show my gratitude.'

'Oh!' said June, a little surprised at Tim's reason. 'That's nice of you, Tim.' She looked at Andrew but did not say another word about it.

'Shall we go inside?' asked July after they had chatted a little while longer. 'I don't want to have to sit at the back.'

'You know that Mommy and Daddy always keep places for us,' said June with a chuckle.

'Okay then,' confessed July, 'I just want to go inside now.'

The four of them headed inside, the car park filling up quite quickly as congregants arrived and began filtering into the church.

The transition from the outside to the inside was much less harsh at this time of year, for although the sun was slowly beginning to fix its gaze upon the horizon, it was still beaming its pleasant rays across the now idling town of Ailensbury.

Andrew entered the church and was immediately able to pick out his parents, who had arrived after he and Tim but had entered the church before them as a result of the little chit-chat the lads had had with the twins on the sidewalk.

The faithfulness of certain of the congregants was again evident as the freshly picked flowers placed at the sides of the church bore testimony to their efforts and added colour and brightness to the surrounds in a very neat yet discreet way.

'Will you be able to join us afterwards for a cup of tea?' whispered June in Andrew's ear as they walked down the aisle and past the rows of wooden pews already filling up.

'I don't know,' whispered Andrew back. 'I'd love to, but I promised Tim that I'd take him for coffee afterwards, so we'll have to see.'

'I hope you'll be able to,' said June with a warm smile, her eyes sparkling as she glanced at Andrew before the two parted company.

'My, my!' said Kelly jokingly, looking at her watch and then at Andrew in surprise as he moved in next to her. 'Look here, George – they're not late at all!'

'So I see!' said George, playing along and nodding his head approvingly, knowing that Andrew and Tim had arrived before them. Andrew chuckled lightly.

'Tell the truth, Tim,' said Kelly with great expression. 'Did you perhaps think you were going fishing or to Misty's?'

'Evening Aunt Kelly, Uncle George,' greeted Tim as he sat down next to Andrew. 'Andrew just decided to be ready on time, that's all.' Kelly just laughed and Tim could not help chuckling as well.

'The service is about to start,' warned George after further conversation had taken place between the four of them. They quickly quietened and looked forward, little knowing that the message Mark was about to deliver would be a timely word indeed!

Chapter 41

The Light of life

MARK Marsh stepped up and took his place behind the bland, box-shaped pulpit, the sun still streaming in through the windows and lighting on the lives sitting in the pews. He welcomed everyone and announced the programme for the evening before stepping aside for the praise and worship to begin.

For the next 20 minutes, praise and worship took place. Tim remained silent, not participating in it at all. However, he spent most of the time reading the words of the songs and trying to understand what they were all about. The music and singing was again joyous yet reverend, as had been evident to Tim on his previous visit, but he was glad nonetheless when it came to a close.

'I politely pay my respects to the church,' thought Tim as the people sat back down and Mark returned to the pulpit, 'and then that's that!'

'Good evening again,' greeted Mark, flipping through his notes, which brought the congregants quickly to complete silence, the only noise now coming from the crickets chirping in the shrubs outside. 'I'm going to talk this evening on the same points of discussion I had a number of weeks back with two young men in a bistro one Sunday evening after the church service. Annabelle needed me to purchase some dog food for our pooch, Machie, so hence, after the church service I stopped by Sunny Valley Mall, where the situation arose. Consequent to that, some trying times took place for the concerned parties. I would like to put it all together to give you a full understanding of God's law and grace and provide you with a perfect metaphorical example of why we need Jesus and need to embrace His offering.'

Tim put his hand on his brow and sunk into the pew as the bright, teardrop-shaped hanging lights illuminated the congregation, including himself, providing no shadow in which to hide.

'It looks like lightning's on its way,' whispered Andrew in Tim's ear, nudging him in the arm, 'as it seems the minister's wife ran out of dog food again.'

'Oh, brother!' snorted Tim, still with his hand on his brow.

Mark went systematically through the points of the discussion held with Tim and Andrew on that stormy night two months before at Roccocoa's. Tim seemed to settle as Mark got further into his sermon, removing his hand from his brow and sitting up a little more. Although he was listening, his mind drifted and replayed the events of that evening as the message was given. He recalled vividly what had taken place and had to catch himself when he began to smile as he remembered what he had said to the waiter.

The brightness from outside faded fast, its infiltration through the windows diming with every minute. Tim looked at his watch, having noticed the fade-out, but quickly put his arm down again.

'I owe them my respectful dues,' thought Tim, reminding himself, and then had to cover his mouth with his hand as he produced a long, gaping yawn.

Silence reigned supreme, the congregants sitting drawn to Mark's words as he continued progressively.

'As we read in Isaiah 53,' boomed Mark, which seemed to stir Tim, '"the Lord [that is God] has laid on Him [that is Jesus] the iniquity [that is evil] of us all." In 2 Corinthians 5:21 it continues, "God made Him [that is Jesus] who had no sin to be sin [or a sin offering] for us, so that in Him [that is in Jesus] we might become the righteousness of God." Only God's righteousness can overcome our unrighteousness, only He who had no sin could overcome our sin.'

Tim remembered this quite clearly from the discussion but did not fully understand its application. There was still something missing, but he could not figure it out.

'As one of the young men said during the discussion on this issue,' continued Mark, '"Because Jesus paid the price, or became the sin offering for us, His righteousness may be given to us. God takes our filthy rags and gives us His own righteousness through Jesus Christ."'

Mark's direct mention of Andrew's comment hit Tim hard in the stomach as he recalled his actions thereafter of jumping up, abruptly ending their conversation right there and then and storming out of Roccocoa's, literally dragging Andrew with him.

'Romans 4:3,' said Mark after opening his Bible at the next marker, 'and verses 23–25 explains how this phenomenon works when it says, "What does the Scripture say?" It is with reference to the Old Testament, and it says the following: "Abraham believed God and it was credited to him as righteousness. The words – it was credited to him – were written not for him alone, but also for us, to whom God will credit righteousness – for us who believe in Him who raised Jesus our Lord from the dead. He [that is Jesus] was delivered over to death for our sins and was raised to life for our justification [that is for us to be made just as if we had never sinned].'"

The lights above now took on a more spotlight effect, beaming down upon the colourful congregants below as dusk had completely given way to the night. The earlier comforting natural light that had penetrated through the church windows had completely faded away, leaving the church looking like a beacon of light in the darkness as its light now shone out.

Mark took a moment to gather his thoughts and take a breath, the congregation continuing to sit silently and afford him the courtesy of their attention. He looked up and quickly scanned from one side of the church to the other, looking directly at Tim as he did so but continued on. He looked down again to continue his message but suddenly looked up, aiming his line of vision directly at Tim. Mark gazed at Tim for a split second, not long enough for most people to notice that he had specifically picked out someone but long enough for him to confirm for himself whom he had seen.

'Give me a moment,' said Mark as he looked down again, a half-smile developing on his face, not having known that Tim would be at the church service that evening.

Andrew gave Tim a subtle glance having realised the connection. July, who was sitting in the pews on the other side of the aisle, a few rows forward of the Renshaws and Tim, also picked up the connection. She surreptitiously turned and gave Tim a quick smile, her bright cheeks puffing at the sides as she did so and illuminating her expression as it always did. Tim noticed her, but as she was in front of him this time he could not turn abruptly away from her amiable glance.

'How *do* we receive this then, you might ask?' said Mark with strong emphasis as he resumed. 'Many acknowledge the events, but few accept the purpose and importance of it.'

Mark let out a quiet sigh, now knowing that what he was about to tell the congregants had had a direct impact on the one he was surprised yet pleased to see sitting before him that very evening.

'Let me explain it to you using the following story,' continued Mark resolutely. 'Recently, one of the young men with whom I had had the discussion in the bistro that Sunday evening was bitten by a very poisonous snake.'

There was a muffled gasp from some of the congregants who were not familiar with the events that had taken place. Tim sat absolutely still and listened with great interest.

'He was rushed to hospital,' said Mark, 'where an antidote to overcome the poison was injected into his bloodstream. Firstly, what would the poison have done to this young man's life? It would have killed him. The severity and destructiveness of the poison would have wiped him out if it hadn't been dealt with quickly enough.'

Mark paused for a moment and looked up again, briefly directing his gaze directly at Tim.

'Secondly,' said Mark calmly, 'why did the young man need an antidote? Because his blood wasn't strong enough to overcome the destructiveness of the poison and therefore needed that which was capable of overcoming it. An antidote that could match the poison in strength wouldn't have worked, it had to be stronger; it had to *overcome* the poison.

'Colossians 2:15 tells us,' continued Mark, having paged to its location, 'that this is what Jesus did on the cross to the poison of the power and authority of the evil one – the serpent, Satan. It says the following, "And having disarmed the powers and authorities, He made a public spectacle of them, triumphing over them by the cross." Thirdly, although the young man wasn't conscious at the time, what would have happened if he had only *acknowledged* the purpose of the antidote? He would have perished – died!'

This seemed to hit Tim and a cold shiver ran up his spine. He was aware of what had happened, even the severity of it, but it had not been spoken about in such terms before.

'*Acknowledgement* wouldn't have been good enough,' said Mark. 'In order for the young man to survive, he had to *accept* and *receive* the antidote. This describes perfectly the human walk. We have been bitten by the serpent, Satan – because of Adam's sin – and the poison of sin is in our lives, running through our very veins. It's impossible for us on our own to overcome it. No matter what we do or how we try, sin will eventually kill us. We need *God's* antidote to overcome this destructiveness, and the blood of Jesus Christ is that very antidote. Acknowledgement of the blood of Jesus as the antidote which overcomes sin is not sufficient, we need it flowing through our very veins in order for it to work – we must *accept* it.'

Something began to stir Tim's spirit and bring to life this application. He was able to put the two together, and the pieces started fitting into place. Tim livened. Was this what had been amiss to him? He had heard it spoken before, but the parallel, the practical example of that which had taken place in his own life, seemed to give him the ability to understand how it all worked. Tim marvelled, and his heart beat faster. He felt a little rattled though, not because it did not make sense, but because it was becoming real to him, and he mused. Was it just emotionalism? Considering the way Mark was presenting it, he could not lay that blame at his door. Was it the fact that he was in a church? He could not deny the influence, but then what about the times they had had discussions or the very real incident at the administration office? That was no church environment nor was there even a hint of anything related. There had only been that scripture verse, which itself had impacted upon him so powerfully, leaving him with an internal conflict between its proclamation and his perspective. He could not deny it. Was it truly an answer to his desire, that if God was real, He would show him what was missing? Tim shifted uneasily, for he believed it was, and if this was the case, he could neither run nor hide. There was no excuse he could make, yet internally there was no excuse that he wanted to make. It was clear to him, he understood the connection, the missing link so to speak. It was the blood of Jesus Christ and its direct application in the life of man. He could not refute it!

'John 3:1–7 says the following,' continued Mark, having flipped the pages in his Bible to the next reading, '"Now there was a man of the Pharisees named Nicodemus, a member of the Jewish ruling council. He came to Jesus at night and said, 'Rabbi, we know you are a teacher who has come from God. For no one could perform the miraculous signs you are doing if God were not with him.' In reply Jesus declared, 'I tell you the truth, no one can see the kingdom of God unless he is born again [born from above].' 'How can a man be born when he is old?' Nicodemus asked. 'Surely he cannot enter a second time into his mother's womb to be born!' Jesus answered, 'I tell you the truth, no one can enter the Kingdom of God unless he is born of water and the Spirit. Flesh gives birth to flesh, but the Spirit gives birth to spirit. You should not be surprised at my saying, "You must be born again."'

Mark stopped and looked up, having emphasised the last portion of the reading.

'What does Jesus mean,' asked Mark questioningly, 'when He says flesh gives birth to flesh, but the Spirit gives birth to spirit – You must be born again? John 1:12,13 tells us the following, "Yet to all who received Him [that is Jesus] to those who believed in His name, He gave the right [or power] to become children of God – children born not of natural decent, nor of human decision or a husband's will, but born of God." This clarifies what Jesus was saying to Nicodemus. He divides the natural birth from the spiritual birth – the natural birth into this world from the spiritual birth into God's kingdom. Salvation is a spiritual matter, and although it will have a direct outworking in our physical lives, it cannot be obtained through or by our physical lives. As we read, "children born not of natural decent, nor of human decision or a husband's will, but born of God", and "the Spirit gives birth to spirit."

Remember the free gift that Paul talks about in Ephesians 2:8,9 where he says, "For it is by grace you have been saved, through faith – and this not from yourselves, it is the gift of God – not by works, so that no-one can boast." It is God who has provided salvation for us, through the Lord Jesus Christ. Jesus says in Matthew 7:7,8,' continued Mark in a quiet monotone, directing his gaze first at Tim and then across the congregation, '"Ask and it will be given to you; seek and you will find; knock and the door will be opened to you. For everyone who asks receives; he who seeks finds; and to him who knocks, the door will be opened."'

Tim sat up a little more, and his eyes grew wider as his mind began to deliberate on past events while Mark continued his sermon. He started to recall in fast transcription the various aspects and discussions that he had had over the last quarter of a year, and the words that had been spoken that evening seemed to connect the whole lot together in one harmonious descriptive depiction. Tim shifted uneasily in the pew but did not distract Andrew sitting next to him. He looked diagonally to his right and across the way at about head height, one of the beautifully decorated stained glass windows with the picture of a man kneeling before a cross, his backpack beside him, seemed to light up. Tim sharpened his gaze and considered it for a moment, the voice of Mark drifting past his ears and not registering. Tim's big eyes narrowed as he contemplated all that he was looking at and the connection that had so vividly presented itself to him in a complete illustration. After a fraction of time had become history in the events of the world, Tim snapped from it, again directing his attention to the pulpit. He listened closely as Mark continued, the true Light of life having been clearly revealed!

Chapter 42

The decision

'**I**F you hear the voice of God's Spirit speaking to you tonight,' said Mark, not changing his quiet monotone and not trying to work up emotionalism, 'calling you to repent of your sins and accept Jesus Christ as your Lord and Saviour, do not turn Him away. Scripture says, "Today, if you hear His voice, do not harden your hearts as you did in the rebellion." [96] Open the door of your heart, ask Jesus to come into your life through the Holy Spirit and to wash you clean. God's Word is true. If you will open, He will enter, for He is ever faithful. Remember, the handle is always on the inside.'

Mark paused for a second as if gathering his thoughts.

'But preacher!' said Mark, continuing on. 'If God is speaking to me, how will I ask Him into my heart? How will I accept Him? Romans 10:9,10 says, "That if you confess with your mouth, 'Jesus is Lord', and believe in your heart that God raised Him from the dead, you will be saved. For it is with your heart that you believe and are justified [that is made just as if you had never sinned] and it is with your mouth that you confess and are saved [that is reconciled to God and spared eternal damnation, hell]." God requires us not only to believe it but also to confess it. But take note, this confession is not just a once-off declaration, it's a way of life – it is the confession or declaration in the daily life lived and the daily words spoken as an outward working of what is believed in the heart.'

Tim again seemed a little rattled as the realisation of this took hold. The words that July had spoken to him at Munchkins Theme Park – *"Jesus is the answer, but He's also the problem. The counter remark generally often made is that Jesus is the easy way out and that He's for those who 'need a support'. However, Jesus is the answer because we need a Saviour, not because we need a crutch. Furthermore, the moment you become a Christian you accept the ways of God and the teaching of the Bible, which is likely to conflict in certain areas of your life. If you don't accept this, then don't become a Christian, because all you'll become is a hypocrite, for Jesus says in John 14:15, 'If you love me, you will obey what I command.' You now introduce a standard that you never had to try and hold to before or principles that you never had to live by before. This isn't punishment, it's because God knows what's right and what He wants in us. You will now have friends that may not like your perspectives and viewpoints. In fact, peer pressure, the thought of 'what will my friends say, or what will my family say?' is probably somewhere at the top of the list as to why people don't take the step, not because it's a cop-out. You'll have to start asking yourself certain questions and will have to question some of your activities, something which you never had to do before. As I said, you will have friends who no longer appreciate your stance or viewpoint. There'll be those who will be offended by the fact that you no longer want to hang out and indulge with them in certain activities. They will put pressure on you at first to continue to join in, and if you hold out they will then look with disdain upon you. This doesn't mean that it will be like this, of course, but depending on the person's life that was lived up until then, it could be like this. You see, Romans 12:2 tells us not to conform any longer to the pattern of this world, but to be transformed by the renewing of our minds. Ephesians 4:23,24 also tells us to be made new in the attitude of our minds, and to put on the new self, created to be like God in true righteousness and holiness. You would ask yourself if getting drunk on New Year's Eve with your friends, and bearing the effects of intoxication the following day is something God is happy with, even though it may be a tradition with some. You would ask yourself – and God – about your attitudes, behaviours, character disposition, etc. if you were serious, and where they were shown up poorly in the light of Scripture it would be a task to change them, something you wouldn't have considered doing before. Remember, churches are not the standard, the Word of God is. If you didn't do this and, sadly, many Christians don't, you would be like the third point in the parable Jesus gave, as recorded in Luke 8, about the sower. It tells us that the seed that fell among thorns stands for those who hear, but as they go on their way they are choked by life's worries, riches and pleasures, and they do not mature. Before one becomes a Christian, self-indulgence and self-focus are normally what rules and reigns; in other words – what I want, and what I want to do, but they have no place in God's kingdom. I do not mean that Christians should become inwardly focused, but Christianity is a journey of being prepared to listen, being humble and teachable, and growing in the ways of God, which sometimes can be difficult to do. This would be like the fourth point in the sower parable, which tells us that the seed on good soil stands for those with a noble and good heart, who hear the Word, retain it and by persevering produce a crop. This doesn't mean that life has to be dull, but it needs to fit in with God's ways. The Christian walk is no cakewalk!"* – all crossed his mind in a flash.

'There's no such thing as a "sinner's prayer",' said Mark as he looked across the expanse of the church, 'for Scripture tells us that whoever calls on the name of the LORD shall be saved.[97] And king David says, "For thou, Lord, art good, and ready to forgive; and plenteous in mercy unto all them that call upon thee."[98] Therefore, call on Him! Humble yourself before the Cross of Christ, for the Word of God tells us, "God opposes the proud but gives grace to the humble."[99] What it requires is true repentance, a renouncement and turning away from one's sins and an embracing of the Lord Jesus Christ as Lord and Saviour, for Jesus himself said, "Not everyone who says to me, 'Lord, Lord,' will enter the kingdom of heaven, but only he who does the will of my Father who is in heaven."'[100]

Tim felt the conviction, for he understood that to embrace Christ would require embracing Christianity's principles, decrees and commands, all of which would be centred around God and His Word, otherwise it would be, as July had mentioned, useless hypocrisy and nothing less. He had been brought to the pinnacle of decision, there was no more deliberation, no more stalling, no more arguments, for it was now all before him. It was as crystal clear as the water that flowed down the stream alongside the Smoking Gorge trail, and that gentle voice that had previously warned him was now encouraging him to drink its living water.

Could he rebel in the face of it? Easily, for pride and arrogance knows no bounds, but to whose detriment if not to his own? If this gospel was true, would not the words of Peter, "what shall the end be of them that obey not the gospel of God?", [101] which Andrew had read to him the day before, also be true? Furthermore, had God not honoured his request and answered him in such a powerful way? Would he not prove himself to be insincere and a liar should he deny it? How could he deny such a providential work that used the very circumstance of his own life to reveal to him that which he could not see? Should he spurn such a mercy and grace now? How many chances would he be given in the future, if any? Tim trembled.

There was one thing greater however. Not only did he now see that man needed a saviour and Jesus as the Saviour, he personally desired it. If God was such a great God to provide atonement for him, and He was prepared to unfold the working of His grace before him where he could not previously understand it, there was something about Him that stirred his heart. He wanted a part of Him and wanted to get to know Him.

There was one last issue that now revealed itself powerfully and two aspects that he had to overcome. He would have to make what he previously considered as a leap of faith! Yet, it was not a leap of blind faith but a step of faith – truth could be understood as he had concluded in the car on the way back from Munchkins Theme Park. Now he understood a step of faith, for he would not be making it without understanding but in faith believing that it was real and true. He had a further hurdle to overcome: would he humble himself? He could see no other way of accepting Jesus other than through humility! Scripture revealed it, and Mark had mentioned it. Tim contemplated it all.

'As a help or guidance,' said Mark, Tim once again listening to the message, 'this confession or prayer or call to God can go as follows: Dear God in Heaven. Thank you for sending Jesus to die on the cross for my sins. Thank you Jesus that you came. I know dear God that I am a sinner. I believe that Jesus Christ died for my sins, that He was buried and that He was raised on the third day. I ask you, Jesus, to come into my heart through your Holy Spirit, to be my Lord and Saviour, to forgive me for my sins and to cleanse me from all sin and unrighteousness. I ask you to keep me, to grow me and to help me from this day forward to walk as one worthy of being called a child of God. In Jesus' name I pray, Amen.'

Tim, having closed his eyes when Mark began the prayer, opened them and again glanced at the stained glass window that had a short while ago drawn his attention. He looked at it for a moment not thinking much and then took a double take, his gaze sharpening as he fixed on it.

'Something's amiss,' thought Tim as he continued to look at it, not quite figuring out what it was. His eyes suddenly grew large as he realised that there was now no backpack lying next to the man kneeling at the foot of the cross, just like the instance of Christian in John Bunyan's book, *Pilgrim's Progress*!

'Dear people,' said Mark, turning Tim's attention back again, 'as an assurance of the saving grace of God through Jesus Christ, I leave you with two final scriptures, one you have already heard. The first is John 1:12,13, "Yet to all who received Him, to those who believed in His name, He gave the right to become children of God – children born not of natural decent, nor of human decision or a husband's will, but born of God." The second is 1 John 5:11–13, "And this is the testimony: God has given us eternal life, and this life is in His Son. He who has the Son has life, he who does not have the Son of God does not have life. I write these things to you who believe in the name of the Son of God [Jesus] so that you may know that you have eternal life.'" Mark stopped, looked down and folded his notes – his sermon had ended.

The very verse that had presented such a conflict in Tim's life, which had started a journey, not on the Smoking Gorge trail but in his own walk, had suddenly become real to him. He could not only see it and understand it but could feel its very presence. The conflicting battle had been hard, but the word of the Lord was true, and in his life it had become the true victor. God had answered him in a way that he could never have comprehended. He had taken him on the only path that would explain to him what true salvation really meant, the need for Jesus and the gift of true life.

Tim sat astounded but thankful for God's patient mercy, for which he knew he was an underserving recipient and therefore grateful all the more. His heart pounded at the comprehension of it and at the revelation that God had opened up to him, knowing also that there was much more to be learned.

Tim grieved at all his sins but rejoiced that he had been forgiven. He grieved over the years for which he had so vehemently stood against God but rejoiced that through the Holy Spirit, Jesus now stood with him.

Not to Andrew's surprise, Tim did not want to stay after the service but wanted to go to Roccocoa's for coffee and a chocolate chip muffin. What did surprise him though was that Tim asked him to invite June and July to come along as he wanted to tell them all something. The twins agreed to go, and once they had obtained consent from their parents, Andrew promising to see that they were not late getting home, they headed for the bistro in the annex of Sunny Valley Mall.

Once they all had received their order and were sipping coffee or munching on a muffin, Tim, to their surprise, told them the step he had taken and the decision made. The other three stopped and listened intently as Tim carefully explained to them how the whole aspect had fitted together for him. July grinned but also lightly blushed when Tim told how her words had flashed through his mind, making real the fact that such a step was not a joke or to be lightly taken – understanding the possibility of what lay before him.

In the end, they chatted quietly and enjoyed the time together. Andrew saw to it that the young ladies were back home well within curfew, dropped off Tim and headed home.

After washing and preparing for the night, Tim climbed into bed, pulling the bedcovers up over himself. He closed his eyes, and the stained glass window immediately appeared in his mind's eye. Tim considered some of the issues once more and as he began to fall asleep, unsure of what the future held, thought, 'Foolishness to many and a stumbling block to others, but true life really is in the Son and really does begin at the foot of the Cross!' [102]

Up Next

WHAT lies ahead for Tim now that he has accepted Jesus Christ as his Saviour? Will he make it through and be victorious or fall away and be a victim? Will Gloria, his mother, be receptive to him, and what transpires in her life?

Join Tim, Gloria and the others once again, as they face the sometimes pressing journey of life, with its confrontations, battles, and challenges. Be sure not to miss the next in the series:
BOOK 2,
Law & Grace: Divine Intervention

Enjoyed this book?

WHILE I hope you found this book enjoyable, I also hope that you found it insightful, thought provoking and even challenging.

If you would like to receive the occasional correspondence that gets sent out, you can do so by signing up at:
www.thehumblesaint.com/subscribe

For information on available titles, please visit:
www.thehumblesaint.com

Publisher contact:
www.thehumblesaint.com/contact/duke-of-valmary

Author contact:
www.thehumblesaint.com/contact/judson-mccawl

About

GOD, through the saving grace of Jesus Christ, has almost always been a part of my life. My mother sat quietly with me one day at her bedroom window in the warmth provided by the sun and explained with the aid of an illustrated book the salvation that we can receive through Jesus Christ. My young mind comprehended what was being told, and at the tender age of two and half, I asked Jesus into my heart through His Holy Spirit, praying without my mother's directive in the Name of the Father, and of the Son, and of the Holy Spirit.

The principle of Law and Grace was also taught to me by my mother as a foundational teaching, and the concept of placing it in a descriptive way through book form first presented itself to me late one night as I was about to go to bed.

Having never been an avid reader, let alone a writer, I climbed into bed thinking that it would be grand to be able to put pen to paper and create a practical, complete and detailed story around the Law and Grace principle but mentioned to the Lord my prior struggles at school just to manage the required word count for English exam essays. I've been one to admire the skill and ability of writers, particularly fiction. The art of creating a story and descriptively presenting it in the various scenes has captured my interest and respect. Numerous times I have asked the question, how do they manage to do it? Nevertheless, the thought came to mind that I should at least try – who knows!

Suddenly, as I contemplated some of the potential scenes, what I would term a flood of descriptive writ loomed large and clear in my mind. I was quite taken aback and although tired and ready for sleep, I opened my eyes and climbed out of bed. I headed to my work desk in the room next door and promptly jotted down on a notepad some of the words and sentences to describe the scenes that had flashed through my thoughts.

Although it was all taken cautiously, knowing that a few words does not produce a book, these notes were steadily worked on.

Little did I comprehend at the time that the specific work I set out to complete would be achieved and further blossom into a series. The four works produced thus far are for me nothing less than miraculous, for which I give the Lord thanks.

References

1. AR Williams, 1992. Long-age isotope dating short on credibility. CEN Tech. J. 6(1):2–5.

2. AA Snelling, 1998. The cause of anomalous potassium-argon 'ages' for recent andesite flows at Mt. Ngauruhoe, New Zealand, and the implications for potassium-argon 'dating'. Proc. 4th ICC, pp. 503–525.

3. Footprints in the Ash, J Morris and S A Austin, 2nd Printing 2005, p. 67, Master Books.

4. *Buried birth*, Creation 19(3):38–39, July 1997; https://creation.com/buried-birth, as at 10 July 2020.

5. Footprints in the Ash, J Morris and S A Austin, 2nd Printing 2005, p. 75, Master Books.

6. A Gansser, Geology of the Himalayas, Wiley Intersciences, London, 1964, p. 289. Creation answers book – chapter 12 p. 177-179.

7. What You Aren't Being Told About Astronomy, volume 1, Creation Astronomy Media, 2009. www.creationastronomy.com

8. Science News, 23 March, 2002.

9. Famularo, Silvio, *Where have all the people gone?*, Creation 31(2):18–19, March 2009; http://creation.com/human-population-growth, as at 10 July 2020.

10. *Focus, December 2004, p. 49.*

11. *Batten, Don, Plant geneticist: 'Darwinian evolution is impossible', Creation 30(4):45–47, September 2008; https://creation.com/geneticist-evolution-impossible, as at 10 July 2020.*

12. *Larry Witham, Where Darwin Meets the Bible, p. 23, Oxford University Press, 2002.*

13. *Horgan J., 1995. Profile: Fred Hoyle. Scientific American 272(3):24-25.*

14. *1 Peter 3:7*

15. *Christianity in Korea, Wikipedia, https://en.wikipedia.org/wiki/Christianity_in_Korea, as at 18 May 2020.*

16. *James 1:25*

17. *Psalm 107:10,11*

18. *Daniel 5:13–31*

19. *Jonah 1:1; 3:5–4:1,11*

20. *Nahum 1:2b,5b,6,7b,8,14*

21. *Jonah 4:11*

22. *Jonah 2:8,9b*

23. *Matthew 11:20–24 (KJV)*

24. *Proverbs 16:18*

25. *1 Thessalonians 5:9*

26. *Revelation 14:9–11 (KJV)*

27. *John 3:36*

28. David Pawson, YouTube: David Pawson – Official, published on January 12, 2015, Unlocking the Old Testament Part 4 – Genesis 3 (Genesis Part 3: Creatures and Evolution) https://www.youtube.com/watch?v=5DsSO1pM-fE, as at 24 May 2020.

29. Isaiah 44:24

30. Mark 10:6

31. Hebrews 11:7a

32. Richard Dawkins, The root of all evil? (TV diatribe) – Broadcast on Channel 4; 16 January 2006.

33. J Trefil, The Dark Side of the Universe (New York: Macmillan Publishing Company, 1988), p. 3 and 55. See also W Gitt, What about the big bang? Creation magazine 20 (3), p. 42 – 44, June – August 1998.

34. J Rankin, Protogalaxy Formation from Inhomogeneities in Cosmological Models, Ph.D. thesis, Adelaide University, May/June 1977.

35. Industry Tap (web news), Volume 69, newsletter, 03 January 2014.

36. H Noji, et al. – Direct Observation of the Rotation of F1-ATPase, Nature 386(6622) p. 299-302; 1997. Comment by S Block, Real Engines of Creation, same issue, p. 217-219. J Sarfati, Design in Living Organisms: Motors, Journal of Creation 12(1), p. 3-5; 1998.

37. C Darwin, Origin of Species.

38. Paul Davis, Australian Centre for Astrobiology, Sydney, New Scientist 179(2404) p.32; 2003.

39. Andrew H Knoll, PBS Nova interview, *How Did Life Begin? - 1 July 2004.*

40. Batten, Don, *15 questions for evolutionists,* point 1, *https://creation.com/15-questions-for-evolutionists,* as at 10 July 2020.

41. Batten, Don, *15 questions for evolutionists,* point 2, *https://creation.com/15-questions-for-evolutionists,* as at 10 July 2020.

42. Batten, Don, *15 questions for evolutionists,* point 3, *https://creation.com/15-questions-for-evolutionists,* as at 10 July 2020.

43. Franklin M Harold (Prof. Emeritus Biochemistry, Colorado State University, USA), *The way of the cell: molecules, organisms and the order of life,* Oxford University Press, New York, p. 205; 2001.

44. *Scientific America* 81-82.

45. D Batten and L Ev, *Weasel, a flexible program for investigating deterministic computer 'demonstrations' of evolution; Journal of Creation* 16(2): p. 84-88; 2002.

46. *Climbing Mt Improbable, Stumbling over the impossible; Journal of Creation* 12(1): p. 29-34; 1998. W Gitt and C Wieland, *Weasel words; Creation* 20(4): p. 20-21; September to November 1998. R Truman, *Dawkins's weasel revisited; Journal of Creation* 12(3): p. 358-361; 1998.

47. Sidney Fox, editor, *The Origins of Prebiological Systems* 299: p. 310. T Dobzhansky, *Synthesis of Nucleosides and Polynucleotides with Metaphosphate Esters (New York, NY: Academic Press, 1965).*

48. *R Dawkins, The Blind Watchmaker, W.W. Norton & Company, New York, USA, p. 1, 1986.*

49. *R Dawkins, Now, 3 December 2004, PBS Network, 'Battle over evolution' – Bill Moyers interview with Richard Dawkins.*

50. *SJ Gould and N Eldredge, Punctuated equilibrium comes of age, Nature 366: p. 223–224, 1993.*

51. *Matthew 28:19*

52. *Matthew 28:20*

53. *Genesis 2:2,3*

54. *Genesis 5:24*

55. *Genesis 9:8–17*

56. *Genesis 41:2,4*

57. *Exodus 24:15,16*

58. *Exodus 31:15*

59. *Leviticus 8:33*

60. *Leviticus 8:11*

61. *Leviticus 25:3,4*

62. *Leviticus 25:8,9*

63. *Deuteronomy 15:1*

64. *Joshua 6:3,4; 12–16*

65. *1 Kings 18:41–44*

66. *2 Kings 4:35*

67. *2 Kings 5:14*

68. *Job 42:7,8*

69. *Daniel 4:23,32; 9:24*

70. *Matthew 23:13–32*

71. Works: John 2:1–10; 4:46–53; 5:1–9; 6:1-13; 6:16–21; 9:1–11; 11:38–44

72. Words: John 6:35; 8:12; 10:7; 10:11; 11:25; 14:6; 15:1

73. Witnesses: John 1:14; 1:34; 1:49; 6:69; 8:58; 11:27; 20:28

74. Revelation 1:20

75. Revelation 6:1

76. Revelation 8:6

77. Revelation 15:1; 16:1

78. Revelation 11:2,3; 12:6

79. Ivan Panin, *The writings of Ivan Panin*, The Book Society of Canada, 1972.

80. Ivan Panin, *The writings of Ivan Panin*, The Book Society of Canada, p. 565–572, 1972.

81. Ivan Panin, *The writings of Ivan Panin*, The Book Society of Canada, p. 565–572, 1972.

82. Ivan Panin, *The writings of Ivan Panin*, The Book Society of Canada, p. 565–572, 1972.

83. Sarfati, Jonathan, *Should we trust the Bible?*, Creation 33(1):32–36, January 2011; https://creation.com/trust-the-bible, as at 10 July 2020.

84. Berean Publishers, The odds of eight Messianic prophecies coming true, www.bereanpublishers.com/the-odds-of-eight-messianic-prophecies-coming-true/, as at 10 July 2020.

85. A general internet search, *How many electrons are there in the universe?*, See also the article at www.bereanpublishers.com/the-odds-of-eight-messianic-prophecies-coming-true/, it contains further information and illustration related to this point.

86. *Dr C Wilson, radio interview by the Institute for Creation Research, radio transcript no. 0279–1004.*

87. *Leviticus 17:11*

88. *The Temple Institute, www.templeinstitute.org, as at 18 April 2018.*

89. *John 16:8*

90. *1 Peter 4:17–18 (KJV)*

91. *2 Peter 2:4-10 (KJV)*

92. *2 Peter 3:7 (KJV)*

93. *2 Corinthians 5:10,11a (KJV)*

94. *Hebrews 12:29 (KJV)*

95. *Luke 20:18 (KJV)*

96. *Hebrews 3:15*

97. *Romans 10:13*

98. *Psalm 86:5 (KJV)*

99. *James 4:6*

100. *Matthew 7:21*

101. *1 Peter 4:17 (KJV)*

102. *Taken from 1 Corinthians 1:22–24 and 1 John 5:12.*